TRA JP   £5-00   33/24

Gift Aid Non fiction
£

0 031140 052635

KU-114-041

TITLED TRAINS OF GREAT BRITAIN

TITLED TRAINS
OF
GREAT BRITAIN

BY
Cecil J. Allen
M.Inst.T., A.I.Loco.E.

LONDON:

Ian Allan Ltd

FIRST PUBLISHED   .   .   .   1946
SECOND EDITION   .   .   .   1947
THIRD EDITION   .   .   .   1953

Printed by McCorquodale & Co., Ltd., London S.E.1.

Foreword
TO THE THIRD EDITION

IT has been a pleasure to me to write this book. Many of the trains which figure in it, equally with their staffs, have become old friends to me, as a result of continuous travelling extending by now to over 44 years and to roughly 2,000,000 miles. There are few, indeed, of these trains with which I have not been closely acquainted; my only regret is that various others, in which much of my life has been spent, were barred from inclusion by the mere accident of their not having received any distinctive title. Some of the latter have been squeezed in, however, on the ground that they possessed unofficial titles by which they were widely known. Some of the descriptions are of trains which have ceased to run, or that no longer carry their titles, but these are included in order that the record may be as complete as possible.

Nothing ever remains static so far as railway train services are concerned. During the Second World War four trains only retained their distinctive titles—the " Flying Scotsman," the " Cornish Riviera Express," the " Aberdonian " and the " Night Scotsman." When the first edition of this book appeared, in 1946, many of the names had been restored, and the past and the present required descriptions of 70 trains; on publication of the second edition, in 1947, the number had grown to 79; and in the present 1953 edition 108 trains are described, though 36 of these trains no longer run, or have not resumed their titles since the war.

The wholesale revision that has been necessary for the third edition also has brought home to me very forcibly the constant state of flux of railway timetables. The schedules of some trains seem to ebb and flow like the tide, shorter in summer and longer in winter, with " recovery margins " put in and taken out, or easing of times due to the carrying out of engineering works which require restrictions of speed. This last has been the case particularly since the Second World War, and as a result the progress towards restoring pre-war speeds has been lamentably slow. The overall times of some " titled trains," indeed, already have receded from the fastest since the war, and as yet very few trains indeed are running once again at full pre-war speed.

The original intention in compiling this book was to include a complete timetable of the running of each express, but this raised such formidable complications, in the matter of summer and winter working, the times of the various sections of trains that divide *en route*, and so on, that the plan had to be abandoned. It has been necessary, therefore, to include in the text many figures concerning times, distances and speeds, in order that these important details of train working may be covered adequately. Notes on the gradients of the principal routes are included, so that the relative difficulties of each route may be properly understood. Titled trains are now run on so extensive a scale in Great Britain that practically every main line in the country is described in this way.

More than a mere title is needed to give a train a reputation ; comfort is essential and, equally, speed and punctuality, and during the last year or two Great Britain has been falling far behind France and certain other European countries, not to mention the United States of America, in the two respects last-mentioned. There are confident forecasts that the Coronation year 1953 is to see some revival of British prestige in these matters, and in presenting the third edition of " Titled Trains of Great Britain," I share in the hope that before very long we may once again be able to take justifiable pride, on every count, in the express passenger train services of these islands.

CECIL J. ALLEN.

Index

OF TRAINS BY REGIONS OF
BRITISH RAILWAYS

1—The "Aberdeen-Penzance Express"

IN 1921, two years before the railway grouping took place, the Great Central, North Eastern and North British Railways, in conjunction with the Great Western Railway, conceived the idea of establishing a through service between Aberdeen and Penzance, over a total distance of 785 miles. Existing trains were to be used from Aberdeen to York, and from Swindon to Penzance; the link between them was to be a new express from York to Swindon by way of Sheffield, Nottingham, Leicester and Banbury. In the reverse direction the G.W.R. required to run a special connection from Westbury to Swindon, off an up express to London, and the Swindon—York express connected with one of the night expresses from King's Cross to Aberdeen. Through passengers were allowed to make sleeping car reservations, and berths were reserved for them, either in the Paddington to Penzance sleepers into which they could change at Swindon going west, or in the King's Cross to Aberdeen sleepers which were available to them from York on the northbound journey.

On the day trains, restaurant cars were available from Aberdeen to York and from Penzance to Westbury; for the evening meals refreshment service was provided in the L.N.E.R. train which ran between York and Swindon. At first this was an ordinary restaurant car; then for a number of years the service was provided by a curious pair of articulated " twin " vehicles that had first been built to serve teas on the 4 p.m. express from King's Cross to York. One of the two coach-bodies of each set consisted of a brake compartment, kitchen, and small open third-class compartment with tables; the other housed four third-class and two first-class compartments and a *coupé*, in which tables were laid as required. It was not until a year or so before the Second World War that two composite buffet-restaurant cars of the latest L.N.E.R. type, beautifully equipped, were built specially for and installed on this service.

Actually, " Aberdeen—Penzance Service " would be a better heading for this chapter than " Aberdeen—Penzance Express," for during most of the history of these facilities, a single through composite coach, North British and Great Western stock alternately at first, and later L.N.E.R. and G.W.R., constituted the whole of the " through express." In summer the through portion expanded to two or more coaches, which came from both Glasgow and Aberdeen; but in winter the through working was cut down at both ends, and was between Edinburgh and Plymouth only.

On the southbound run, in the summer of 1939, the through coach left Aberdeen at 10.20 a.m., and on arrival at Edinburgh was transferred to the rear of the 2.5 p.m. express to London, which brought it into York at 6.8 p.m.; the Glasgow coach had arrived 15 minutes earlier. The Swindon train was booked to leave York at 6.22 p.m., and with stops at Sheffield, Nottingham, Leicester and

Rugby, was brought into Banbury and handed over to the G.W.R. at 10.7 p.m. Leaving Banbury 8 minutes later, the train continued *via* Oxford and the west curve at Didcot to Swindon, arriving at 11.32 p.m. Here the 9.50 p.m. sleeping car express from Paddington was due at 11.48 p.m., and, taking over the through coaches, deposited them at Penzance at 7.25 a.m., 21 hours, 5 minutes after leaving Aberdeen.

In the reverse direction, the through coach in winter was worked out of Penzance on the tail of the 11.10 a.m. London express, and reached Westbury at 5.3 p.m. From here it ran on a short special train at 5.20 p.m. through Trowbridge and Chippenham to Swindon, for attachment to the 6.20 p.m. from Swindon to York. Bristolians could make a smart connection with this train by means of a slip coach off the 5.15 p.m. express from Bristol, detached as the latter hurried through Swindon at 6.2 p.m. on its way to Paddington. The York train was due into Banbury at 7.35 p.m., and going out again with L.N.E.R. locomotive power 7 minutes later, reached York at 11.33 p.m.

Here the passengers by the Penzance—Aberdeen service, in recent years, were not as well treated as those in the reverse direction. For they missed the " Aberdonian " by 8 minutes, and the through coach from Penzance went forward on a following train at 11.50 p.m. In winter this was due into Edinburgh at 4 a.m., and as the " Aberdonian " did not leave till 4.15, with luck they could still catch it and be in Aberdeen by 7.30 a.m., in 20 hours, 20 minutes from Penzance. This meant changing, as in winter the through coach stopped short in Edinburgh.

In summer it turned west and went to Glasgow instead ; what is more, it did not even begin its journey at Penzance, for the congestion in that small station made it necessary to start the train for the north at St. Erth, $5\frac{3}{4}$ miles short of Penzance. Many people who were unaware of the reason must have wondered what could be the importance of this remote Cornish village sufficient to justify a through service from " St. Erth to Glasgow."

Between Swindon and York the formation of this train in winter finally consisted of a four-coach corridor set, restaurant car, and the one through coach ; in summer it was expanded as necessary, and going south there were the through coaches from both Aberdeen and Glasgow to Penzance. But the service made so important a link that to the passenger portion there were added a number of parcels vans, and at times the formation between Sheffield and Swindon was quite substantial. The fastest bookings on this section of the journey were over the 23·4 miles between Nottingham and Leicester, allowed 25 minutes each way.

Even during most of the Second World War, though no through coaches were run over the entire distance, it was still possible to maintain a through service between York and Swindon, but not with the same connections. To-day, leaving York at 6.28 p.m., it does not wend its weary way into Swindon until 2.5 the following morning, too late to connect with any of the G.W.R. night trains to the west, except the 2.53 a.m. to Swansea. Going north there is a 7.15 p.m. from Swindon, but this runs no further than Sheffield, reached at 12.32 a.m.

2—The "Aberdonian" and the "Highlandman"

Lineal descendant of the East Coast flyer which in 1895 raced the West Coast train to be the first from London to reach Aberdeen, the "Aberdonian" since that day has fallen sadly from grace in the matter of speed, though what it had lost up to the outbreak of the Second World War it had far more than gained in comfort. With comfort came vastly increased weight, and the weight in part provided the reason for the deceleration. Apart from that, however, slower running at night is justifiable; for the moderately-timed express causes far less interference with the dense night freight traffic than a very fast train, and after all, few night passengers want to arrive at their destinations in the "small hours."

The 1895 "Race" began with the modest announcement that from July 1st the West Coast Companies—London & North Western and Caledonian—would bring their 8 p.m. express from Euston into Aberdeen at 7.40 a.m., 15 minutes earlier than before, and only 5 minutes behind the corresponding train from King's Cross of the East Coast Companies—Great Northern, North Eastern and North British. Seven weeks later, the West Coast schedule had been cut by 2¼ hours, and the East Coast by 1 hour, 55 minutes, but the racing trains, which had been running well ahead of time, continued to do so.

On the East Coast side the record achievement was that of the night of August 21st–22nd, when the King's Cross train rolled into Aberdeen at 4.40 a.m., having covered the entire 523·7 miles, stops included, in 520 minutes. The train, weighing 105 tons, had been worked over the 105·5 miles from King's Cross to Grantham by a G.N.R. Stirling 8-ft. single in 101 minutes; another engine of the same type continued over the 82·7 miles to York in 76 minutes; there the North Eastern took charge, and ran the 80·6 miles to Newcastle in 78 minutes, with a 4–4–0 of the then N.E.R. class "M"; following this run a sister engine covered the 124·5 miles from Newcastle to Edinburgh in 114½ minutes.

In view of the difficulties of grading and curvature north of Edinburgh, it was a fine feat for the North British 4–4–0's to take the train first over the 59·2 miles to Dundee in 60 minutes, and then from Dundee to Aberdeen, 71·3 miles, in 77 minutes. The actual running times thus added up to no more than 506½ minutes, and had the East Coast been as free from scruples as the West Coast about leaving intermediate stops before time, the final outcome of the race might have been different. As it was, the rivals "won" on the following night with their amazing time of 8 hours, 32 minutes (512 minutes for 540 miles), including three stops, and by common consent the "Race" was then at an end.

But the night Highland "sleeper" from King's Cross still continued for years as the fastest train on the service. Up to the time of the First World War, while the "Flying Scotsman," bound by agreement, still pottered from London to Edinburgh in 8¼ hours, the 8.15 or 8 p.m. from King's Cross (the times varied in different years) took from 7 hours, 45 to 50 minutes. After the war, in 1923, the first year of the L.N.E.R., the working time from King's Cross to Edinburgh had crept back to 7¾ hours, and Aberdeen was reached in 11 hours, 5 minutes, but by 1924 the decline in speed had begun again.

In 1939 the "Aberdonian" was making a much more stately pilgrimage to the North. Its starting time had been advanced to 7.30 p.m., and it had acquired, on the rear, a composite restaurant car, which provided sustenance for its passengers as far as York. The timetable allowed 124 minutes to Grantham, and 96 minutes on to York, reached at 11.15 p.m. ; here the dining car was detached. Leaving York 10 minutes later, the express was allowed 101 minutes to Newcastle, and spending 8 minutes there, the longest non-stop run of the journey—124·5 miles to Edinburgh—was begun at 1.14 a.m. and completed at 3.50 a.m. At Edinburgh Waverley the train was split up ; and sleeping cars and through coaches for Fort William, Perth and Inverness were detached.

The Fort William section was scheduled to wait 40 minutes, till 4.30 a.m., and then to be worked across to Glasgow in exactly one hour, for attachment to the 5.50 a.m. from Queen Street through the wild West Highlands to Fort William and Mallaig. The comfort of passengers on this long and mountainous run was assured by a restaurant car from Glasgow, and Fort William, 562½ miles from King's Cross, was reached at 9.54 a.m. Meantime, the Perth and Inverness section had been taken out of Edinburgh at 4.20 a.m., and worked non-stop over the 47¾ miles of extremely difficult grades to Perth, arriving at 5.28 a.m., to wait the arrival of the "Royal Highlander" from Euston. After 57 minutes at Perth, the combined train was away at 6.25 a.m., and the Inverness "sleepers" reached that city at 9.50 a.m.—almost a "dead-heat" with the Fort William vehicles, and over an almost identical distance, actually 4 miles less in 4 minutes less running time.

Long before this the "Aberdonian" proper, which had left Edinburgh at 4.15 a.m., and made calls at Dundee, Arbroath, Montrose and Stonehaven, had come to rest in the Granite City. Scheduled time of arrival was 7.30 a.m., precisely 12 hours from London, 55 minutes more than in 1923, and 3 hours, 20 minutes slower than the best racing time in 1895 ! But by 1939, as previously mentioned, the "Aberdonian" had become an extremely heavy train. Fort William was content with a composite sleeping car and a composite brake ; Inverness usually required a first-class car, a third-class car and a composite brake ; to Aberdeen there were first- and third-class cars (the former an articulated twin), a composite and a third-class brake ; and various vans distributed about the train, with the dining car, made the customary formation at least 500 tons in weight from London.

In summer the train ran nightly in two sections, and often in three. At 7.25 p.m. the " Highlandman " left King's Cross, with the Fort William and Inverness sections, and an additional sleeping car portion for Nairn (detached from the Inverness cars at Aviemore); while the " Aberdonian," at 7.40 p.m., was the main Aberdeen train, with an additional section for Elgin and Lossiemouth, taken forward over the old Great North of Scotland line from Aberdeen and, very likely, by a 4–6–0 locomotive of the old Great Eastern Railway. South of Aberdeen, Pacific haulage was invariable between London and Edinburgh, but between Edinburgh and Aberdeen there was generally provided one of the fine Class " P2 " 2–8–2 locomotives of the " Cock o' the North " type, specially designed by the late Sir Nigel Gresley for this difficult route, and now unhappily converted to Pacifics also.

In the southbound direction the departure of the " Aberdonian " from Aberdeen, complete with dining cars to Edinburgh, had by 1939 become standardised at 7.35 p.m., and the run to London took 10 minutes under the 12 hours. With the same stops as in the reverse direction, Edinburgh was reached at 10.55 p.m. Long before the start from Aberdeen, the portion from Fort William was under way, at 4.7 p.m., and as this collected additional sleeping cars before leaving Glasgow at 10 p.m., the southbound Inverness cars were worked to King's Cross on a preceding express from Edinburgh. South of Edinburgh, the " Aberdonian " made the same stops as the northbound train to York, but then exchanged the Grantham stop for halts at Doncaster and Peterborough. It was due in London at 7.25 a.m.

This important service continued throughout the Second World War, but between King's Cross, Edinburgh and Aberdeen only, with a connection to Fort William. Leaving King's Cross at 7 p.m., the " Aberdonian "—one of the only four British trains to retain its title throughout the war—was allowed $13\frac{1}{2}$ hours to complete its run to Aberdeen, and, leaving there at 6 p.m., 13 hours, 35 minutes up to London.

In the general postwar speed-up, the northbound "Aberdonian " has settled down to a 7 p.m. departure, with restaurant car as far as York, and the pre-war 12-hour schedule now is beaten by 10 minutes in summer, and 7 minutes in winter. Throughout the journey it is relieved in summer by an express at 7.15 p.m. from London, which conveys the restored Fort William section, but no longer is called the " Highlandman." Southbound the " Aberdonian " leaves Aberdeen at 7.10 p.m., and is into London at 7.15 a.m.

3—The "Atlantic Coast Express"

Though for many years past, back into London & South Western days, an express had left Waterloo for the West of England at about 11 a.m., it was not until 1927 that the Southern Railway introduced the title of "Atlantic Coast Express" for this service—the Southern "ACE," as it has sometimes been called. The "Atlantic Coast Express" is the most multi-portioned train in the country. Nine different sections are included in the formation.

The leading end of the train comprises the Ilfracombe portion, of two third-class brakes and a composite coach between, together with composite brakes for Torrington, Padstow, Bude and Plymouth. After these the restaurant cars—first-class and kitchen car with open third-class car—can be classed as a "portion," for they are detached at Exeter. Then follow composite brakes for Exmouth, Sidmouth, and for stations between Salisbury and Seaton, the last-mentioned detached at Salisbury. In the days of the keenest competition between the L.S.W.R. and the G.W.R. for the traffic to and from the West of England, the predecessor of the "Atlantic Coast Express" was regarded as being a Plymouth train, with a connection for Ilfracombe; but the opening of the G.W.R. Westbury route enabled the latter company to accelerate its Plymouth services to such a degree that the S.R. fell into the background as a route from London to Plymouth, and the Ilfracombe section of the train then assumed the major importance.

On its peacetime schedule, through nine months of the year the "Atlantic Coast Express" was booked to leave Waterloo at 11 a.m., and to make its first stop at Salisbury at 12.26 p.m.—83·8 miles in 86 minutes. Although the provision of water-troughs on this route has often been mooted, and years ago Dugald Drummond, then Locomotive Superintendent of the L.S.W.R., even went to the length of fitting some of his tenders with water-scoops, the troughs never materialised. For reasons of water alone, therefore, it has never been possible to run non-stop from Waterloo to Exeter, though the Salisbury stop is desirable for more reasons than locomotive requirements merely, as important connections are made here. Through locomotive running had been tried from Waterloo to Exeter, but a change of engine at Salisbury was preferred until the advent of the Bulleid Pacifics, with which in 1950 the through working became a regular practice.

West of Salisbury the locomotive running is some of the most exciting in Great Britain. Nowhere else in the country are such high speeds run relatively to the severity of the profile. The route is particularly well aligned and there is practically no limit to maximum speeds ; in consequence the drivers make the utmost use of the falling gradients, in order that the impetus so gained may help them on the succeeding ascents. In the westbound direction, speeds of over 80 m.p.h. are frequently attained at Gillingham,

Sherborne, Axminster, Honiton and at Broad Clyst (between Sidmouth Junction and Exeter). The stiffest task set the locomotives in this direction is the ascent of Seaton bank ; beginning just to the west of Axminster, this rises for 1½ miles at 1 in 100, then for 4½ miles at 1 in 80, and finally for ¾ mile at 1 in 132 through Honiton tunnel to the summit at the latter's western portal, 153½ miles from Waterloo.

At Salisbury, on the peacetime schedule of the " Atlantic Coast Express," the rear coach was detached and went forward with a stopping train that followed at 12.38 p.m. The main train left for the West at 12.31 p.m., and was booked to run the 75·8 miles to Sidmouth Junction in 83 minutes. Here the Sidmouth and Exmouth coaches came off the rear of the train ; a tank engine of the 0–4–4 type collected them and worked them to Tipton St. Johns, continuing from there to Sidmouth with the Sidmouth coach, due at 2.23 p.m., while another 0–4–4 tank worked the other coach through Budleigh Salterton to an arrival in Exmouth at 2.46 p.m. The express itself was booked to leave Sidmouth Junction at 1.58 p.m., and to run the 12·2 miles into Exeter Central in 14 minutes. Arriving at 2.12 p.m., the " Atlantic Coast Express " had come down from Waterloo in 3 hours, 12 minutes.

Here a general break-up of the train occurred. The restaurant cars were detached from the rear, and the remaining coaches were divided into two parts. A Mogul backed on to the Ilfracombe and Torrington sections, and left with these coaches at 2.18 p.m., reaching Barnstaple Junction 62 minutes later. Ten minutes before this, a Great Western Railway " slow " from Taunton had put in an appearance at Barnstaple Junction with the through Ilfracombe coach off the " Cornish Riviera Limited " ; this the " Atlantic Coast Express " added to its formation, while leaving the Torrington coach behind. From Barnstaple Junction, the Ilfracombe train then continued over some of the steepest main line gradients in Great Britain, climbing for 3¼ miles at 1 in 40 to Mortehoe, and finally dropping for 2¼ miles at 1 in 36 down into Ilfracombe. This popular coast resort, 226·5 miles from Waterloo, was reached at 4.6 p.m., eight minutes after the Torrington coach had arrived at its destination.

The three remaining portions of the " Atlantic Coast Express " left Exeter in company at 2.25 p.m. for Okehampton, usually with a three-coach corridor set added to the Waterloo-Plymouth coach. At Okehampton the Padstow and Bude coaches were detached for the journey over the North Cornwall line, and it was not until 5.36 p.m. that the former ran into Padstow, 259·7 miles from Waterloo, after completing the longest daily through journey on Southern metals. The Bude coach, parting company with the Padstow portion at Halwill, reached Bude at 4.54 p.m. At Meldon Junction, where the Plymouth and Padstow lines separate to the west of Okehampton, after passing over a high lattice steel viaduct, the train attained the greatest altitude reached on the Southern system, which is 950 ft. above sea level.

A striking feature of the working of the Plymouth portions of Southern trains from London is the way in which they almost box the compass in the course of their journeys. Through Exeter they run for a short distance over G.W.R. metals between St. David's station and Cowley Bridge junction, where trains from Waterloo are travelling due north; through North Road station at Plymouth, formerly joint G.W.R. and S.R. property, they are running east; before reaching Plymouth Friary they have turned due west again. Moreover, twice in succession, both at Exeter St. David's and Plymouth North Road, they meet the G.W.R. expresses from Paddington to Plymouth travelling in the opposite direction! Up to the war, the Plymouth coach of the down "Atlantic Coast Express" came to rest in Friary terminus, 234 miles from Waterloo, at 4.19 p.m.

In the height of the summer season, two daily down services were needed to carry the traffic, at 10.35 a.m. to Ilfracombe, Torrington, Bude, and Padstow, and at 11 a.m. to Sidmouth, Exmouth, and Plymouth. On Saturdays the two branched out into no fewer than *eight* complete restaurant car trains between 10.24 a.m. and 12.5 noon—at 10.24 and 10.35 a.m. to Ilfracombe, 10.40 a.m. to Padstow, 10.54 a.m. to Bude, 11 a.m. to Plymouth, 11.45 a.m. to Sidmouth and Exmouth, 12 noon to Exeter, and 12.5 p.m. to Salisbury and all stations from Axminster onwards. Similar arrangements were in force in the opposite direction.

The up winter working of the single "Atlantic Coast Express" involved departures from Padstow at 8.40 a.m., Bude at 9.40 a.m., and Plymouth Friary at 10.28 a.m., joined at Okehampton and leaving there for Exeter at 11.28 a.m. Exeter Central was reached at 12.12 p.m., 12 minutes ahead of the Ilfracombe and Torrington sections, which had started at 10.30 and 10.28 a.m. respectively. Departure from Exeter was at 12.30 p.m., and from Sidmouth Junction, where the Exmouth and Sidmouth coaches came on, at 12.54 p.m. From here over the difficult gradients to Salisbury the allowance was only 82 minutes for the 75·8 miles; and after stopping at Salisbury for 6 minutes, the express finished with an 87-minute run over the 83·8 miles to Waterloo, arriving at 3.49 p.m.

As to locomotive power, until the middle of the war period it had been customary for some time to use "Lord Nelson" 4-cylinder 4-6-0's between Waterloo and Salisbury, and "King Arthur" 4-6-0's between Salisbury and Exeter. The advent of the "Merchant Navy" streamlined Pacifics, however, has resulted in the taking over by these extremely capable locomotives of the Salisbury-Exeter workings almost in their entirety, and of most of the Waterloo-Salisbury workings also. There can be little question that the speeds run regularly by the 4-6-2's west of Salisbury were higher than those attained on any other British main line during the war, barely distinguishable from the speeds of peacetime. West of Exeter, Moguls have shouldered the major proportion of the workings, until the light "West Country" Pacifics arrived to take over these duties.

During the war period, in common with other S.R. West of England Expresses, the "Atlantic Coast Express" stopped additionally at Woking; and long after the war had ended and the stop had been cut out, the increased 103-minute timing from Waterloo to Salisbury remained. Not until 1949 did it come down to 93 minutes for the 83·7 miles, the up train being accelerated at the same time to make the run in ninety minutes. But overall times of both workings were slower than before the war, particularly those of the up express, which as compared with pre-war days, on the winter service, made additional stops at Axminster, Yeovil Junction, Sherborne and Templecombe, and reached Waterloo at 4.20 p.m. instead of 3.49 p.m. All the eight through portions from and to Waterloo once again had come into operation.

An interesting event in the history of the "Atlantic Coast Express" occurred in the summer of 1948, when, as part of the extensive locomotive exchange trials of that year, it was worked between Waterloo and Exeter successively by an Eastern Region streamlined "A4" Pacific, and by a "Duchess" Pacific and a rebuilt "Royal Scot" 4-6-0 of the London Midland Region.

In the summer of 1952 a revolutionary speed-up of the Southern "ACE" took place, not only bringing the train back to pre-war times, but to times even faster than those booked in 1939, including the first run at over 60 m.p.h. from start to stop to appear in the Southern Region timetable. The down train, leaving Waterloo at 11 a.m., is now booked over the 83·7 miles to Salisbury in 83 minutes; then, after 5 minutes for station working and taking water (usually exceeded) comes 80 minutes for the 75·9 miles of very hard gradients to Sidmouth Junction, and, after a 3-minute stop there, 14 minutes for the 12·2 miles to Exeter, reached at 2.6 p.m. (public time 2.5). This, incidentally, beats the two-stop 11 a.m. from Paddington by a clear half-hour! Arrivals are earlier than those before the war by 18 minutes to Bude (now 4.21 p.m.), 16 minutes to Padstow (now 5.21 p.m.), 6 minutes to Exeter (now 2.6 p.m.), and by smaller amounts to the other points served by through coaches.

Similarly in the reverse direction, all stops between Sidmouth Junction and Salisbury once again have been cut out, bringing the arrival at Waterloo forward to 3.40 instead of 4.18 p.m.; this includes an easy booking of 18 minutes from Exeter (12.30 p.m.) to Sidmouth Junction (12.48-12.50 p.m.); 79 minutes from there to Salisbury (2.9-2.15 p.m.), and 85 minutes thence to Waterloo. In this direction the load is made up to eleven vehicles at Exeter (no Exmouth and Sidmouth coaches being attached at Sidmouth Junction), and thirteen from Salisbury; going down the load is twelve (about 397 tons tare) from Waterloo, eleven (364 tons) from Salisbury, and nine (just under 300 tons) from Sidmouth

Junction. These brilliant timings are being continued through the 1952–1953 winter.

4—The "Blackpool and Fylde Coast Express"

Under the helpful stimulus of a well-known L.M.S.R. Vice-President who had a house near the popular resort of Blackpool, much has been done since the grouping of the railways to improve the service between Euston and the Fylde coast. One of the trains put on in consequence was a morning express from Blackpool (Central) to Euston, giving passengers who so desired about 4 hours in London, with a swift and comfortable service back in the evening. Eventually these trains received the name " Blackpool and Fylde Coast Express."

The up service was very fast. In the years before the outbreak of the Second World War it left Blackpool Central at 8.25 a.m. and called at the usual stations round the coast—Blackpool South, St. Anne's, Ansdell, and Lytham—from which it ran to Preston, reached at 9.8 a.m. After standing 5 minutes here, it made the run of 51 miles to Crewe in 59 minutes, and then followed a high speed break over the 158·1 miles from Crewe to Euston in 154 minutes, at 61·6 m.p.h. Euston was reached at 12.50 p.m. and the time from Blackpool was thus 4 hours, 25 minutes. No additional sections were run in this direction, and a formation of seven or eight bogies, including restaurant cars, usually sufficed.

Going down, the " Blackpool and Fylde Coast Express " had a heavier load and a more leisurely journey. Leaving Euston at 5.10 p.m., the engine had 165 minutes at its disposal on the non-stop run to Crewe, and 40 minutes for the 36 miles from there to Wigan, reached at 8.40 p.m. The stop here was to detach through coaches for Blackburn, Burnley, and Colne, taken on by a most unusual route through Chorley, which was, however, the original L.N.W.R. route from Euston to Blackburn ; Colne was reached at 10.21 p.m. All other through Colne services were routed *via* Manchester.

Meantime, the express from London, leaving Wigan at 8.44 p.m., was into Preston by 9.5 p.m., and here a second through section was detached, destined for Barrow-in-Furness ; making its way along the main line to Carnforth, and then round the coast, this portion was into Barrow by 10.45 p.m. The main train, leaving Preston at 9.10 p.m., made the usual coastal stops and reached Blackpool Central at 9.57 p.m. This was a through locomotive working between London and Blackpool, usually with a Class " 5XP " 4-6-0, and run alternately by London and Blackpool engines and men ; but whereas the Blackpool men obtained quite a pleasant turn-round time in London, their London colleagues were less fortunate, as

18

their Blackpool arrival was too late in the evening for them to sample many of the attractions of this gay resort !

By October, 1946, a recognisable post-war version of the " Blackpool and Fylde Coast Express " was once again in operation, with restaurant cars complete. The down train leaves Euston at 5.5 p.m. and reaches Blackpool Central at 10.24 p.m. ; coming up, the train gets away from Blackpool at 8 a.m., and is into Euston by 1.10 p.m.—a journey 45 minutes slower than before the war, though with a considerably heavier load. It is no longer a " titled train."

5—The "Blackpool Club Train"

Just as the South Coast has always been a popular place of residence for London business men who could afford the cost of a season ticket and the time for travelling to and from London daily, so the nearest part of the West Coast has attracted the business fraternity of Manchester and Salford. In this case, Blackpool, Lytham, St. Anne's and Southport have been the most favoured resorts, and the late Lancashire & Yorkshire Railway did its utmost to encourage and develop this traffic.

In the year 1895, before corridor trains had come into general use, a number of first-class season ticket holders in the Blackpool area, thinking that it would be pleasant to enjoy a wider range of each other's company *en route* than was possible in the compartment stock of that time, approached the L. & Y. management with a novel request. It was that, in return for a guarantee that a specified number of first-class season tickets would be taken out annually between Blackpool and Manchester at higher than the ordinary rate, they should be provided with saloon accommodation.

The request was agreed to, and two (later three) comfortable saloons, provided with an attendant and facilities for serving light refreshments, were marshalled in one of the morning expresses from Blackpool, and a return express from Manchester shortly after 5 p.m. Although in the course of time central corridor stock was introduced by the L. & Y. R. throughout the trains concerned, and later was replaced by L.M.S.R. standard vestibuled cars of the latest and most luxurious type, the club cars never lost their popularity, and continued to run up to the outbreak of the Second World War. By then, too, the club saloons had become two palatial L.M.S.R. vehicles specially adapted for the purpose. In later years, club saloons were attached to other evening Blackpool trains also.

Participation in the travelling club has always been subject to very strict rules, so that all undesirable travelling companions might be excluded, and the regular members had their own recognised seats. Even any undesired opening of windows *en route* was strictly forbidden ! In later years a third-class section of the club was established also, and had its own third-class reserved car adjacent to the two first-class saloons.

The " Blackpool Club Train "—an unofficial though fairly widely known title—left Manchester Victoria station at 5.14 p.m., and up to the outbreak of the Second World War was due to make its first stop at Lytham at 6.14 p.m. This time of 60 minutes required far harder running than the distance of 41·9 miles might suggest. The older and more level main line through Bolton was not followed, but like most of the non-stopping expresses, the " Club Train " followed the Liverpool line as far as Dobb's Brow Junction, and from there took the spur line through Hilton House to join the Bolton line at Horwich Fork Junction, near Chorley.

Thus it was necessary to climb the $2\frac{1}{4}$ miles at 1 in 72—99 from Pendleton up to Pendlebury, and to follow on over sharp undulations, with the complication of slacks over colliery workings, to Dobb's Brow. Here a reduction of speed made an unfortunate prelude to an even steeper climb of $2\frac{1}{2}$ miles, partly at 1 in 69, to Hilton House, with a shorter drop from there to Horwich Fork. Finally, there was a slack at Euxton Junction, where the main line from Euston to Carlisle was joined, and another, almost to a walking pace, through the great station at Preston.

After that the hard-worked locomotive had practically level track on through the junctions at Kirkham and Wesham and round the coastline to Lytham and Blackpool. The usual four stops were made between these two points, and the arrival at Blackpool Central, 52·3 miles from Manchester Victoria, was at 6.36 p.m. In the reverse direction departure from Blackpool Central was at 8.10 a.m., and after stopping at the coast stations, the " Club Train " left Lytham at 8.31 a.m., and ran non-stop to Salford, arriving at 9.36 a.m., and Manchester Victoria at 9.40 a.m. The Salford stop is generally made by Manchester-bound trains, in order to enable those with business in that part of the city to alight there.

As to locomotive power, the Lancashire & Yorkshire 7 ft. 3 in. inside cylinder " Atlantics " designed by Aspinall held sway for many years, to be followed from 1906 by the Hughes 4-cylinder 4-6-0's—a much more suitable type of engine, after its efficiency had been improved by superheating, for such heavy grade work. Some years after the grouping, standard L.M.S.R. types began to filter into these Lancashire & Yorkshire services ; first the Class " 5 " 4-6-0's appeared, and then the Class " 5XP " 3-cylinder 4-6-0's, which in later years have been the engines principally used. The load grew eventually to between 9 and 11 bogie vehicles, according to season, centre corridor stock throughout and more than two-thirds first-class.

Since the war this popular express, still made up of the same stock though without the club saloons, leaves Manchester Victoria at 5.16 p.m., and has had its timing to Lytham eased to 67 minutes. Stopping as previously at Ansdell, St. Anne's, Squires Gate and

Blackpool South, it is due in Blackpool Central at 6.46 p.m. On the inward journey it leaves Blackpool at 7.40 a.m., makes the same stops to Lytham and additional halts at Kirkham and Salford, and reaches Manchester at 9.14 a.m.

6—The "Bournemouth Belle"

Before the days of corridor trains, the London & South Western Railway used to include Pullman cars in the formation of its principal trains between Waterloo and Bournemouth. These "Pullman Drawing Room Cars," as they were called officially in the timetables, were for the use of first-class passengers only, who were required, of course, to pay the Pullman supplement in addition. They were attached to the 12.30, 2.0, 4.50 and 6.55 p.m. trains from Waterloo, and to four corresponding expresses in the up direction. The introduction of restaurant cars, however, brought to an end this limited use of Pullmans on L.S.W.R. metals, and they were not seen again on the Bournemouth service until the introduction of the "Bournemouth Belle" by the Southern Railway. For some time this ran on Sundays only, but from the beginning of 1936 it became a daily service. Originally it was non-stop to Bournemouth.

There was nothing revolutionary about the "Bournemouth Belle" timing, which was but slightly faster than the general standard for the Bournemouth service (other than the "Bournemouth Limited"). The down "Belle" was booked to leave Waterloo at 10.30 a.m., thus bridging the gap in the hourly morning Bournemouth departures between 9.30 and 11.30 a.m. It made its first stop at Southampton Central, 79·2 miles from Waterloo, in 87 minutes, at 11.57 a.m., and after standing there three minutes, was timed to cover the 28·8 miles on to Bournemouth Central in 36 minutes, arriving at 12.36 p.m. A wait of three minutes sufficed here, and the short run on to Bournemouth West was completed at 12.47 p.m.

In the up direction, departure from Bournemouth West was at 4.35 p.m., and after a stop of two minutes, the "Belle" left Bournemouth Central at 4.45 p.m. From here to Southampton Central the time allowed was 33 minutes, and the up "Belle" then had the fastest start to stop timing of the day from Southampton Central to Waterloo, 79·2 miles in 85 minutes, thus making a two-hour run from Bournemouth Central, including the Southampton stop. Actually, however, the working timetable showed an arrival at Waterloo a minute later than the public time, at 6.46 p.m.

The normal formation of the "Bournemouth Belle" varied from 7 to 10 Pullmans, according to the season of the year. Two of these were first-class cars ; the two end ones were third-class brake cars and the remainder were thirds. A number of the cars were twelve-wheelers, and the others were eight-wheel vehicles ; the tare weight of the train was from 270 to 390 tons, and the working time-table limited the maximum load to 400 tons.

For the haulage of the " Belle," Nine Elms shed invariably turned out a " Lord Nelson " class 4-cylinder 4-6-0 locomotive, which made the round trip from Waterloo to Bournemouth West and back without change, so covering 222·8 miles in the day. The " Lord Nelsons " did well on this train, and as it had no connections or through portions to or from other destinations, good time was kept. The train was withdrawn on the outbreak of the Second World War. But it returned in all its glory on October 7th, 1946, now with a " Merchant Navy " Pacific at the head, and with ten Pullmans in the formation daily. Moreover, the fast pre-war timings were restored, of 2 hours, 5 minutes down and 2 hours up, between Waterloo and Bournemouth Central, both including the stop at Southampton Central. Unhappily, notwithstanding the present use of " Merchant Navy " Pacifics, the timings have now been eased to 2 hours, 10 minutes down and 2 hours, 5 minutes up, though it must be admitted that the load now frequently rises to twelve Pullmans.

7—The "Bournemouth Limited" and the "Royal Wessex"

Back in London & South Western days, in 1899, the first non-stop train was established between London and Bournemouth. It left Waterloo at 4.10 p.m., and at first was due in Bournemouth Central at 6.16 p.m., but in 1911 the time was cut to the even two hours. A corresponding service left Bournemouth for Waterloo in the morning. These were the forerunners of the " Bournemouth Limited," a title which was conferred on the train on its revival in July, 1929. In this reappearance, corridor stock, with restaurant cars, replaced the compartment stock of earlier days.

The non-stop run of 107·9 miles between Waterloo and Bournemouth Central is one of the longest regular breaks that has been made in Britain without the aid of track water-troughs. Such runs as these, and even the breaks of 88·1 miles between Salisbury and Exeter, 83·7 miles between Waterloo and Salisbury, and 79·2 miles between Waterloo and Southampton, were the justification for the eight-wheel tenders, with 4,500 gallons capacity, which the L.S.W.R. attached to all its larger express locomotives. Even with this provision, water supply could be a considerable problem at times to drivers on the London–Bournemouth run.

Between Waterloo and Bournemouth there are no very severe gradients, but the locomotives have to face some lengthy banks which, though of moderate inclination, can be very trying when loads are heavy. Out of Waterloo the work is mainly " against the collar " for the first 50 miles ; there is the long pull up to milepost 31 between Brookwood and Farnborough, though this is no steeper than 1 in 300 at any point, and then the line rises at 1 in 249 for five miles past Basingstoke to milepost 51, where the Southampton and Salisbury lines diverge. But the worst task is in the up direction, where trains have to negotiate an incline that averages 1 in 252 for 16½ miles continuously past Winchester to the summit at Litchfield tunnel. The only really severe slack is at Northam Junction, Southampton, where the line to Southampton Central diverges on a very sharp curve from the old line to Southampton Docks ; more moderate slacks are enforced round the curve between Redbridge and Totton, and through Christchurch station, which is at the foot of steep gradients in both directions.

The Drummond 4-cylinder 4-6-0's with 6 ft. 7 in. driving wheels, L.S.W.R. Nos. 443—447 and 458—462, which later, from their wide splashers, became widely known as the " Paddlebox " class, were introduced chiefly for use on the Waterloo—Bournemouth service, and took their share on the non-stops. Then followed the more efficient " King Arthurs," but the last stage in the pre-war history of the " Bournemouth Limited " was unique, for with the introduction of the " Schools " there came a reversion from the 4-6-0 to the 4-4-0 wheel arrangement. As the timetable allowance had now contracted to 116 minutes for the down and 118 minutes for the up journey, the task set the " Schools " was one of the most exacting entrusted to any 4-4-0 locomotive class in recent times.

In the years immediately preceding the Second World War, the normal formation of the " Bournemouth Limited " was one of 11 bogies, weighing empty about 360 tons ; the working book limit was 365 tons. In the summer and at week-ends the limit might be exceeded by a twelfth vehicle, in which event the " Schools " 4-4-0 was faced with a gross load of fully 415 tons, and work of a most exceptional description was then required. I have records, however, which show that *King's Wimbledon* has worked a 10-coach train of 345 gross tons over the 107·9 miles from Bournemouth Central to Waterloo in a net time of 108 minutes ; while *Malvern* has brought a 12-coach load of 415 tons up in 114½ minutes net—a wonderful performance.

On the down journey the " Bournemouth Limited " left Waterloo at 4.30 p.m., passed Southampton Central in 83 minutes, and was due in Bournemouth Central at 6.26 p.m. Here the Weymouth and Swanage coaches, in the front of the train, were detached, and headed usually by an *ex*-L.S.W.R. 4-4-0 locomotive, continued at 6.31 p.m. to Poole and Wareham, where the Swanage coaches came off. The Weymouth portion had a working arrival at Wareham at 6.51½ p.m., and a departure at 6.54 p.m. for Dorchester and Weymouth, reached at 7.24 p.m., in 2 hours, 54 minutes for the 142·8 miles from Waterloo. Meantime the Swanage coaches had reached that Purbeck resort 3 minutes earlier, and the main section of the " Limited," including the restaurant cars, restarting from Bournemouth Central at 6.35 p.m., and with the " Schools " 4–4–0 at the head, was into West by 6.43 p.m.

In the morning, the earliest start for users of the up " Bournemouth Limited " was from Weymouth at 7.42 a.m., for a journey of 2 hours, 56 minutes to Waterloo. In the Weymouth—Bournemouth stretch one very fast booking was over the distance of exactly 15 miles from Dorchester to Wareham in 16 minutes (begun at 7.57½ and finished at 8.13½ !) from start to stop, but this is mainly downhill. Stopping after that at Poole, the train from Weymouth found the Bournemouth West section, which had started at 8.20 a.m., awaiting it at Central, and ran through and backed on to it at 8.35 a.m. The combined train started for London at 8.40 a.m., and reached Waterloo at 10.38 a.m. The " Bournemouth Limited " was withdrawn on the outbreak of war, and since then there has been no daily non-stop running between Waterloo and Bournemouth.

From October 1st, 1945, however, an express from Weymouth at 7.38 a.m. (since altered to 7.34 a.m.) and Bournemouth Central at 8.40 a.m. to Waterloo was reinstated, and in 1951, in honour of the Festival of Britain, it received the title " Royal Wessex." With additional stops at Southampton and Winchester, the " Royal Wessex " is into Waterloo 12 minutes later than in 1939, at 10.50 a.m., and in consideration of its much heavier loading, the effort required of the " Pacifics " to-day is greater than with the " Schools " before the war. In the reverse direction the name is borne by the 4.35 p.m. train, which makes the same stops (and Brockenhurst in addition) reaching Bournemouth Central at 6.55 p.m., West at 7.13 p.m., and Weymouth at 7.55 p.m.—26 minutes slower than the pre-war " Bournemouth Limited."

8—The "Brighton Belle"

About the beginning of the century, the popularity of Pullman accommodation on the London, Brighton & South Coast Railway suggested that something in the nature of a " Pullman Excursion " between London and Brighton on Sundays would be a successful venture. So it proved ; and in 1899 the " Brighton Sunday Pullman Limited " came into all-the-year-round service. First-class cars only were used, flanked at each end by six-wheel brakes provided specially with clerestory roofs to match the Pullman stock. Departure from Victoria was at 11 a.m., and 60 minutes were allowed for the 51-mile run.

Billinton's 4–4–0 locomotives had come into use, and it was

one of these, No. 70, *Holyrood*, that was used on the occasion of a special test run on July 26th, 1903. On this journey, the schedule was cut to 48 minutes, 41 seconds and a maximum speed of 90 m.p.h. was reached at Haywards Heath. Coming back in the evening, *Holyrood* made a start-to-stop time of 50 minutes, 21 seconds. But these runs, remarkable as they were in relation to the modest dimensions of the locomotive used, were not followed by any regular acceleration of the express.

The success of the Sunday " Pullman Limited " prompted the idea that it might be expanded to a daily service, and by November, 1908, this materialised. A train of seven new and luxurious 12-wheel cars was specially built, and received the attractive name of " Southern Belle." So that it might be put to adequate use, shortly after its introduction the service was doubled ; the " Southern Belle " went out of Victoria at 11 a.m., and returned from Brighton at 12.20 p.m., so being back in London at 1.20 p.m. ; then it made a second trip to the coast at 3.10 p.m., and a final journey to Victoria at 5.45 p.m. from Brighton—a total of 204 miles each day, covered in exactly four hours. For the weekday services, which like the Sunday services were still first-class only, four cars often sufficed, but the number was increased at week-ends and on Sundays, when three trips in each direction were made. By now the Marsh Atlantics had appeared on the L.B. & S.C.R., and these frequently hauled the train, or the highly efficient " I3 " 4-4-2 superheater tanks, interspersed at times with 4-4-0 tender engines.

For some years third-class coaches were run with the Pullmans on the midday workings ; but after the formation of the Southern Railway it was decided that the " Southern Belle " should include third-class Pullmans with the first-class cars in the formation of the train. This change entailed a considerable increase in weight, and shortly before electrification it was not unusual, at summer week-ends, for the " Belle " to total as many as eleven or even twelve Pullmans, with a gross weight of fully 400 tons. Such a load provided quite a tough locomotive task, but in addition to the big Brighton 4-6-4 tanks, grouping had introduced more powerful locomotives to the Brighton line, particularly the 4-6-0 " King Arthurs," so that the 60-minute schedule could still be observed. By now, also, as another " Belle " had come into service on the Southern Railway, the " Southern Belle " had had its name changed to the rather less euphonious " Brighton Belle."

The steam-hauled " Southern Belle " made its last run on December 31st, 1932. On the following day its place was taken by a brand-new electric train, which was distinguished by incorporating the only motor-driven Pullman cars in the world. The " Brighton Belle " electric stock was in units of five cars, usually run in pairs, and thus making a ten-car all-Pullman train. Every day the " Brighton Belle " now covered 306 miles by making three journeys in each direction, at 11 a.m., 3 p.m., and 7 p.m. from Victoria, and at 1.25 p.m., 5.25 p.m., and 9.25 p.m. from Brighton, but on Sundays the 3 p.m. down and 1.25 p.m. up workings were replaced by ordinary corridor sets with Pullmans included, instead of the all-Pullman train.

The " Brighton Belle " was withdrawn on the outbreak of the Second World War ; the five-car all-Pullman sets reappeared in October, 1946, attached to standard S.R. corridor sets, but the all-Pullman workings are now again in operation. The present timings are 11 a.m., 3 p.m., and 7 p.m. from Victoria, and 1.25 p.m., 5.25 p.m., and 8.25 p.m. from Brighton on weekdays ; on Sundays the 3 p.m. down and 1.25 p.m. up runs are omitted.

9—The "Bristolian" and the "Merchant Venturer"

To mark the centenary of the opening in 1835 of the Great Western main line between Paddington and Bristol, it was decided by the G.W.R. management to put on a new express which would link the two cities in a shorter time than ever previously. There had been hopes that a schedule of 90 minutes might have been tried, but eventually, in order that excessively high speeds might not be necessary, a booking of 105 minutes in each direction was brought into operation, 15 minutes less than the previous best.

This required a slightly higher average speed on the down journey than on the up, for the down and the up trains took different routes. Brunel's original main line, 118·3 miles in length from Paddington to Temple Meads Station, Bristol, was used in the west-bound direction, and the end-to-end average was thus 67·6 m.p.h. ; but on the up journey the train left Temple Meads by way of Stapleton Road, climbed the 1 in 75 of Ashley Hill bank (2¼ miles long), and from Filton Junction used the Badminton cut-off, which was opened in 1901, rejoining the older main line at Wootton Bassett. This reduced the distance to 117·6 miles, and the overall speed to 67·2 m.p.h. But because of the Ashley Hill bank, the slowing through Filton, and the long 1 in 300 climb to Badminton, the up journey was probably the harder of the two.

A seven-coach train sufficed for normal " Bristolian " needs. This formation included two third-class brakes, three composites, one third, and in the centre one of the latest buffet cars, with a counter along its full length, and pedestal seats for passengers taking refreshments. The coaches were of the latest wide type, with recessed end doors, and the weight of the seven-coach formation was 221 tons empty, or 235 tons with the normal passenger complement. In the first months of the " Bristolian's " running, a " King " class 4–6–0 was thought to be necessary, but it was soon found that the speed was well within the capacity of a " Castle," and the working was turned over to the highly competent link of engines and crews at Old Oak Common shed that were responsible also for the working of the " Cheltenham Flyer."

Departure from Paddington was at 10 a.m., and Bristol was reached at 11.45 a.m. In the reverse direction, the " Bristolian " left Temple Meads at 4.30 p.m., and was due in London at 6.15 p.m. This was probably the only express on Great Western metals which served two stations only—the starting point and the destination— without any intermediate stop. The down " Bristolian " also could claim to have the most level main line in Britain on which to maintain its high speed.

When Brunel engineered his original line between Paddington and Bristol, by using the Thames Valley as far as Didcot, and curving across the flat country between there and Wootton Bassett, he contrived to keep his maximum steepness of gradient down to 1 in 754, and for the major part of the distance to work to nothing steeper than 1 in 1320. West of Wootton Bassett he dropped down Dauntsey bank with 1½ miles at 1 in 100 ; and from Corsham he cut through to the Avon valley by means of the Box tunnel, with 1¾ miles down at 1 in 100 and ¾ mile at 1 in 120; but both these gradients are in favour of down trains, so that the down " Bristolian " had no hindrance to speed whatever, other than the severe service slack through Bath. It was booked to pass Swindon, 77·3 miles, in 66½ minutes. The fastest part of the journey was between Slough and Chippenham, a distance of 75·5 miles for which the timetable allowed only 61 minutes ; this entailed an average speed of 74·3 m.p.h.

On the up journey, after negotiating the gradients and slacks of the Badminton route to which reference has been made earlier, the train was allowed 62 minutes from passing Swindon to Paddington, which called for roughly the same speeds as those of the " Cheltenham Flyer." Coming up, the fastest stretch was from Badminton to Southall, 91 miles allowed only 71 minutes for an average of all but 77 m.p.h. There was no time to spare on this run ! The " Bristolian " was withdrawn on the outbreak of war, and up to the winter of 1952–1953 no faster timing than 2 hours, 10 minutes between Paddington and Bristol had appeared in the Western Region timetable.

But two other trains since have assumed the title of " Bristolian," as part of the Festival of Britain celebrations of 1951. They are the 9.5 a.m. down, calling at Reading and Bath, and the 4.15 p.m. from Bristol, which calls at Bath and slips a coach at Reading. Both take 2 hours 20 minutes for the journey, and even allowing for the fact that, with eleven-coach formations of new standard stock, they are much heavier than the pre-war " Bristolian," the 35 minutes difference in timing represents a sad decline in speed.

Another title chosen to commemorate the Festival of Britain was one associated intimately with the port of Bristol—the " Merchant Venturer." It has been applied to the 11.15 a.m. from Paddington to Bristol and Weston-super-Mare, and the 4.35 p.m. return train. As far back as 1902, the mid-morning express

27

from Paddington led the country in speed by being accelerated to cover the 118·3 miles to Bristol in the even two hours, at 59·2 m.p.h.; Bath was served by slip coaches. After the First World War this timing in due course was reinstated; eventually the Bath slip was replaced by a stop, and without any increase in journey time, which made it necessary to cover the 106·9 miles from Paddington to Bath in 102 minutes, at 62·9 m.p.h. start to stop.

The pre-war 11.15 a.m. departure remains, but like the "Bristolian," the present "Merchant Venturer" is far inferior in speed to its predecessor, for it takes 113 minutes to get to Bath and 2 hours 17 minutes to Bristol; Weston-super-Mare is reached at 2.6 p.m. At first the up "Merchant Venturer" had a painfully leisurely journey, for with a start from Weston at 4.35 p.m., and stops at Yatton, Bristol, Bath, Chippenham, Swindon and Reading, it was not due in Paddington till 8.15 p.m. But in the summer of 1952 the position was slightly improved by cutting out the Swindon stop, and substituting a slip coach for the stop at Reading, so that the London arrival now is at 8 p.m., in 2 hours 35 minutes from Bristol.

10—The "Cambrian Coast Express" and the "Inter-City"

In the summer of 1910 the Great Western Railway brought to completion the last of four important cut-off routes by which the worst circuits made by the original main lines from Paddington were eliminated. This was the main line from Paddington to the North. The original route, *via* Didcot and Oxford, following the Thames valley, was almost perfect in its absence of gradients as far as Leamington Spa; but a distance of 129¼ miles from Paddington to Birmingham hampered the G.W.R. considerably in competing with the then London & North Western Railway for the traffic from London to Birmingham and beyond. It was planned, therefore, to make a much more direct route from London to Banbury, and in the task the Great Western found an unexpected ally.

The Great Central Railway in 1899 had opened its London Extension into Marylebone terminus, to which access was obtained by using the then Metropolitan line from Quainton Road Junction, north of Aylesbury, to Harrow; from Harrow into Marylebone the G.C.R. built its own independent tracks. But the Great Central soon found itself hampered both by the extremely heavy gradients and the dense occupation of the Metropolitan line; the latter affected chiefly the express passenger services, whereas the former severely limited the freight train loads. Consequently the Great Western and Great Central companies combined to build a new joint line, the former to shorten its distance and the latter to ease its gradients to the North.

The project involved the building of no less than 59 route miles of new line. No existing route was used other than that of the G.W.R. single line branch from Maidenhead to Oxford *via* Thame ; the course of this was followed roughly from High Wycombe to Princes Risborough, but actually complete reconstruction and realignment with doubling of the track were needed to adapt the earlier branch for high speed passenger work, so that to all intents and purposes this 8 miles formed part of the new construction.

Of the whole line the portion actually joint—later, of course, between the Great Western and London & North Eastern Railways—was the $32\frac{3}{4}$ miles from Northolt Junction through High Wycombe and Princes Risborough to Ashendon Junction. Connecting with this the G.C.R. built a spur $6\frac{1}{2}$ miles long from Neasden to Northolt, with the down line making a burrowing junction at Northolt, and another line 6 miles long from Ashendon to their existing main line at Grendon Underwood Junction, 9 miles north of Aylesbury. The new Great Western connections were from Old Oak Common West Junction, 3 miles out of Paddington, to Northolt (7 miles), with a spur from West Ealing to Greenford, and from Ashendon for $18\frac{1}{4}$ miles through Bicester to Aynho Junction, 5 miles south of Banbury. There was a fly-over for the up G.W.R. Bicester line at Ashendon, and for the down line at Aynho.

Until the opening of the Wycombe and Bicester route to Birmingham and the North in July, 1910, the G.W.R. had never ventured a less time than 2 hours, 17 minutes for their $129\frac{1}{4}$ miles between Paddington and Birmingham, and no more than four trains made the journey in 2 hours, 20 minutes or less. But with the distance cut to $110\frac{1}{2}$ miles, the G.W.R. immediately put into operation a series of two-hour trains in each direction, equalling the current London & North Western times, and over a considerably more difficult route. Considerable use was made of slip coaches, in order to avoid as many intermediate stops as possible ; at different periods Princes Risborough, Bicester, Banbury, Leamington and Knowle were all served by various "slips" going north, the last-mentioned in order to set down residents in the southern suburbs of Birmingham.

The principal destination of northbound trains from Paddington was Birkenhead, though some of the Birmingham two-hour trains stopped short at Shrewsbury, and portions of them were detached at Wolverhampton. But the Bicester cut-off has also been of considerable value to the Welsh coast resorts on Cardigan Bay, and in particular to Aberystwyth, reached by way of Shrewsbury, the then G.W. & L.N.W.R. joint line to Buttington, and what was the Cambrian Railway from there onwards through Welshpool and Machynlleth. From the beginning of 1923 the Cambrian became the property of the Great Western, and development of this seaside traffic soon began.

But before that date, in July, 1921, the precursor of the
" Cambrian Coast Express " had been put into operation, as a
restaurant car express from Paddington at 9.50 a.m. for Aberystwyth,
Barmouth, and Pwllheli, on every weekday during the summer
season. By 1922 the start had been altered to 10.15 a.m., and the
train was travelling by way of Ealing, to pick up passengers at Ealing
Broadway, and rejoining the Birmingham main line at Greenford.
In 1923, when the G.W.R. was fighting the L.M.S.R. strongly for
the traffic between London, Shrewsbury, Chester, and Birkenhead,
the 10.20 a.m. from Paddington, as it was now, had become a
Birkenhead express, non-stop to Birmingham in two hours, with an
Aberystwyth portion detached at Snow Hill. The year 1924 saw
the introduction of systematic departure times from Paddington,
and the starting time was changed to 10.10 a.m., thus splitting up
the interval between the 9.10 and 11.10 a.m. Birkenhead departures.
During these years departure of the up train from Aberystwyth had
been at or about 12 noon.

The first appearance of the name " Cambrian Coast Express "
seems to have been in 1927, from which time this became the official
title of the train ; but by now the express, still leaving Paddington at
10.10 a.m. during the summer months, had become a Friday and
Saturday working only. In the last summer before the outbreak of
war the starting time from London had moved back to the 10.20 a.m.
of 1923, while the working was restricted to Saturdays only. The
87·3 miles to Leamington were run in the fast time of 90½ minutes,
and after a stop of 3 minutes there, 26½ minutes were allowed for the
23·3 miles on to Birmingham, where the arrival at Snow Hill was at
12.20 p.m. The usual 19 minutes for the difficult 12·4 miles to
Wolverhampton brought the " Cambrian Coast Express " into that
town at 12.44 p.m.

Here the " Castle " 4–6–0, which had brought the train from
London, was exchanged for motive power more suited to the light
track and bridges of the Cambrian line—either one or two " Duke "
4–4–0 locomotives, or, latterly, one of the " Manor " 5 ft. 8 in. 4–6–0
engines, which were now permitted to run over the route. This
arrangement was necessary, as the train avoided Shrewsbury, and
used the Abbey Foregate curve in order to make a non-stop run
from Wolverhampton to Welshpool, covering the 49·7 miles in
71½ minutes. The remaining stops were at Machynlleth, Dovey
Junction, and Borth, and Aberystwyth was reached at 3.55 p.m.
The up train now left the popular Welsh resort at 10 a.m., made the
same stops as on the down journey, with a " conditional " halt in
addition at Newtown, and reached Wolverhampton, for the change
of engine, at 1.28 p.m. After 7 minutes there, and a 19-minute run
to Birmingham, the " Cambrian Coast Express " was ready to take
its place at 2 p.m. as one of the hourly departures for Paddington,
calling at Leamington from 2.25 to 2.28 p.m., and due in London at
4 p.m. The up run thus took 25 minutes longer than the down.
The total journey was one of 234¾ miles.

There is little need to stress the difficulty of the running west of Welshpool. Much of the route is single track, and the gradients are very trying, especially on the climb to Talerddig summit, between Moat Lane and Machynlleth, where the line is 693 ft. above sea level. From the Aberystwyth direction the ascent begins 3 miles from Machynlleth, and is unbroken for 10½ miles, finishing with 3¼ miles at 1 in 52 from Llanbrynmair to the top. From the east the difficulty is not so great, and is confined to short stretches at 1 in 71 and 1 in 80. There are also 6½ miles of 1 in 75 ups-and-downs between Borth and Aberystwyth. The locomotive or locomotives hauling the " Cambrian Coast Express " over the 111¾ miles between Wolverhampton and Aberystwyth thus had quite a tough task before them.

Some of the most brilliant locomotive work on the entire Great Western system has been done on the Birmingham two-hour trains. When the service began in 1910 the most powerful locomotives available were 2-cylinder " Saint " and 4-cylinder " Star " class 4-6-0's ; from 1923 onwards the " Castles " began to give much-needed relief, and it was not long after the introduction in 1927 of the " Kings " that these, the most powerful express passenger class on the G.W.R., were drafted to the Birmingham route. From then on a number of these engines have been stationed at Wolverhampton for this purpose, and have shared the trains with " Kings " stationed at Old Oak Common, and with occasional " Castles."

As compared with the L.M.S.R., which had little or no difficulty other than the start out of Euston, G.W.R. drivers *en route* to Birmingham had to reduce speed at Old Oak Common West Junction, High Wycombe, and Leamington, and less severely at Ashendon and Aynho Junctions, and to master some long climbs, such as 7 miles at 1 in 175–264 from Denham ; 5 miles at 1 in 179 to 1 in 164 past West Wycombe ; 5½ miles at 1 in 200 past Bicester ; and, worst of all, a bank which includes 3¼ miles averaging 1 in 110 past Warwick up to Hatton.

There are correspondingly arduous grades on the up journey, all to be covered at the high average speeds required by the two-hour schedules. Except for Hatton bank, most of the long inclines were surmounted regularly by the two-hour trains at speeds of over 50 m.p.h., even with trains up to 400 tons ; and maximum speeds of 80 to 90 m.p.h. were common north of Princes Risborough and approaching Leamington on the down journey, and near Warwick, Bicester and Denham coming up.

In the first summer after the war there was a revival of the Saturday " Cambrian Coast Express " working, though without any distinctive name, and again on Saturdays only. The train left Paddington at 10.10 a.m., and made the only non-stop run of the day to Birmingham, with an allowance of 2¼ hours ; with the same stops as before the war, and also Newtown in each direction, Aberystwyth was reached at 4.35 p.m. In the reverse direction, leaving Aberystwyth at 9.30 a.m., the express called additionally at Leamington Spa, and reached Paddington at 4.10 p.m. By 1950 the down train was starting at 10.50 a.m., and reaching Aberystwyth at 5.15 p.m., but the up times remained unchanged. Restaurant cars are run no longer.

At long last, in October, 1950, a daily " titled train " made its appearance on the Paddington–Birmingham main line. Since the war the 9.10 a.m. down Birkenhead express has become so popular that a regular relief train has been run from Paddington at 9 a.m., except on Saturdays, for Birmingham and Wolverhampton. This is the one train of the day that can afford to miss Leamington, as the 9.10 a.m. down carries the Leamington traffic ; but, like the 9.10 a.m., the 9 a.m. halts at High Wycombe to pick up passengers. It is the latter which now has been titled the " Inter-City " ; it is due in Snow Hill, Birmingham, at 11.10 a.m.—this 130 minutes is the nearest yet reached to the pre-war two hours—and in Wolverhampton at 11.35 a.m. The stock, title included, returns from Wolverhampton at 4.25 p.m. and Birmingham at 4.50 p.m. ; in this direction stops are made at both Leamington and High Wycombe, and the " Inter-City " is back in Paddington at 7.5 p.m.

11—"Cambridge Buffet Expresses"

In May, 1932, a remarkable experiment was inaugurated by the L.N.E.R. It was realised that additional traffic might be created between London and Cambridge if there were a better train service ; but the route principally used, to and from Liverpool Street, was so congested and difficult at the London end as to provide a serious difficulty. It was therefore decided that an attempt should be made to popularise the slightly longer route between Cambridge and King's Cross ; and for this purpose five new expresses were put on in each direction.

Each one included third class corridor coaches with armrests dividing the seats into three—a novelty at that time—and an open car with buffet counter at one end and seating for those taking meals. Intermediate stops were made in each direction at Welwyn Garden City and Letchworth—hence the words " Garden Cities " in the titles of these trains—and at Hitchin. At first the times were fixed at 82 minutes down and 77 minutes up, but the following year saw these curtailed to 75 and 72 minutes respectively.

Success was immediate. So much so, indeed, that in a very short time the original three-coach formations had doubled in length and at times the loads grew to nine or ten vehicles, in which event the locomotive work required became exceedingly difficult. Light-hearted Cambridge undergraduates soon found a much shorter soubriquet for the service than the official mouthful, " Garden Cities

[C. G. Pearson

On rival metals—The down " Atlantic Coast Express," Southern Region, in the Western Region St. Davids Station, Exeter, with S.R. " Battle of Britain " Class Pacific No. 34060 *25 Squadron*

[R. D. Swift

Diesel-hauled—The up Sunday " Bournemouth Belle," Southern Region, at full speed near Farnborough, behind No. 10201

THIS PAGE :
Above : The "Brighton Belle" Pullman near Haywards Heath, S.R.
[*D. C. Duncan*]

Right : Gas Turbine Loco. No. 18100 approaches Twerton Tunnel, west of Bath, with the up "Bristolian," W.R.
[*G. F. Heiron*]

FACING PAGE :
Above : The "Coronation Scot" streamliner, headed by L.M.S. Pacific No. 46222 *Queen Mary*, at speed among the Westmorland Hills
[*M. W. Earley*]

Below : One of the "Cambridge Buffet Expresses," E.R., near Hatfield behind Class "B1" 4-6-0 No. 61333
[*E. D. Bruton*]

[C. Lawson Kerr

On the Aberdeenshire cliffs—The southbound " Aberdonian," hauled by Peppercorn Class
" A2 " Pacific No. 60531 *Bahram*, climbs past Cove Bay

[R. E. Vincen

Before the 1952 acceleration—E.R. Class " B1 " 4–6–0 No. 61042 heads the down " Broadsman "
north of Shenfield

and Cambridge Buffet Expresses " ; it was, *tout court,* the " Beer Trains." By 1939 the King's Cross departures had stabilised at 9.35 a.m., 12.40, 2.10, 8.10 and 11.40 p.m., with slight alterations on Saturdays. Coming up, the trains left Cambridge at 9.25 a.m., 12.30, 3.30, 5.25 and 10.10 p.m.

Going down, the engines had to face the climb out of King's Cross, and then the 8 miles at 1 in 200 up to Potter's Bar, and to stop at Welwyn Garden City, 20·3 miles in 25 minutes. Next, the 11·6 miles on to Hitchin, with a start on a 1 in 200 up grade, had to be completed in 14 minutes. For the short run of 2·6 miles from Hitchin to Letchworth the allowance was 5½ minutes ; and the final 23·4 miles from Letchworth into Cambridge were allowed 28 minutes, including the slack round the curve at Shepreth Branch Junction. Two of the trains were allowed 2 minutes extra—all too little—for an additional stop at Royston.

Coming up, the junction slack last-mentioned, and the 7-mile climb from Meldreth to Ashwell (5 miles at between 1 in 100 and 1 in 183), made it hard going to reach Letchworth in 28½ minutes ; from there to Hitchin was allowed 5 minutes. Hardest of all the point-to-point bookings in this direction, probably, was 14 minutes for the 11·6 miles from Hitchin to Welwyn Garden City, for it began with 3½ miles up at 1 in 200. Then the last stage was a lightning run from Welwyn Garden City into King's Cross, allowed 22 minutes only for the 20·3 miles, on which speed often rose well above the 80 m.p.h. mark down from Potter's Bar to Wood Green. In this direction also two trains had 2 minutes extra for a stop at Royston.

A great variety of engines was used on tnese trains, including Great Northern " C1 " Class Atlantics and an occasional " C6 " from the Great Central line ; Great Eastern " B12 " and " Sandring-ham " (" B17 ") 4–6–0's ; Great Eastern " Claud Hamilton " 4–4–0's, and other classes at times. With the heavier loads the running on these expresses, which ceased to operate with the out-break of war, was some of the most brilliant ever seen on L.N.E.R. metals.

Four of these trains each way are now back in the timetable, with the simpler title " Cambridge Buffet Expresses." In line with the systematic departure scheme of the E.R., since October, 1950, they leave King's Cross at 9.5 a.m., 12.5 noon, 2.5 and 8.5 p.m. and return at 9.10 a.m., 12.10, 3.10 and 6.10 p.m. Several of the trains make additional stops, and the overall times have been eased out to between 80 and 93 minutes. Class " B1 " 4–6–0's now supply most of the motive power, though Class " B17 " 4–6–0's also take a considerable share. As the maximum speed between King's Cross and Hatfield is now restricted to 60 m.p.h., and there are also restrictions between Hitchin and Cambridge, reversion to **the** pre-war times would not be possible in the present conditions.

12—The "Capitals Limited"

Little needs to be written about the "Capitals Limited," introduced with the summer time-table of 1949, for it is nothing more than the non-stop "Flying Scotsman" of previous years. Indeed, at both London and Edinburgh, where supplies of the new carriage headboards were waiting, the actual "Flying Scotsman" trains were transformed into the "Capitals Limited" overnight by the simple expedient of changing one set of headboards for the other. The reason for the change of name was that from time immemorial the "Flying Scotsman" has left both King's Cross and Edinburgh Waverley at 10 a.m., whereas it was more convenient to run the non-stop, which in effect is a relief train, at an earlier departure time than this.

In the summer of 1949, the northbound "Capitals Limited" left King's Cross at 9.30 a.m., and was booked into Edinburgh at 5.30 p.m.; southbound the times were 15 minutes later. This 8-hour timing was exactly 60 minutes longer than that of the non-stop "Scotsman" in 1939, though some of 1949 increase was due to the slow running needed over the temporary bridges between Berwick and Dunbar, following the disastrous wash-outs of the previous summer. The "Capitals Limited" carried through coaches between London and Aberdeen, in the northbound direction taken on from Edinburgh Waverley by a special additional summer train at 5.45 p.m., and reaching Aberdeen at 9.20 p.m.; while the start from Aberdeen to the south was at the uncomfortably early hour of 5.55 a.m., in order to reach Edinburgh in good time (9.28 a.m.) for attachment to the southbound "Capitals Limited." For the first time since the war these schedules brought London and Aberdeen within less than 12 hours of each other—actually 11 hours, 50 minutes each way.

The "Capitals Limited" (and winter "Flying Scotsman") set of cars, apart from all-Pullman trains, is the heaviest in the country in relation to the number of vehicles composing it. The 13 cars have a tare weight of 473 tons. Of this, no less than 158 tons is monopolised by the enormously heavy kitchen car, the buffet car, and the two open restaurant cars. These and other amenities entail a rigid limitation of seating in the rest of the train, from which first class passengers are the worst sufferers; on the up journey, owing to the provision of a ladies retiring room, the only full length first has no more the five compartments, there are three more in the Aberdeen portion—48 seats all told—and passengers are required to occupy seats in the three end bays of the first-class restaurant, bringing the total up to 66. In the summer this accommodation at times has been inadequate, and disappointed passengers who could not obtain seats have had to use the "Flying Scotsman" instead, losing half-an-hour in the process. For the reasons given, the "Capitals Limited" has been in the most literal way a *limited* train.

By the summer of 1950 the "Capitals Limited" was into

Edinburgh by 5.10 p.m., in 7 hours, 40 minutes from King's Cross, and the up train was reaching King's Cross at 5.30 p.m., in 7¾ hours. The Aberdeen connection also had been speeded-up to an overall time of 11 hours, 35 hours from and to London. The 1951 summer saw a further cut to 7 hours, 20 minutes both ways, and by 1952 the times were further reduced to 7 hours, 6 minutes northbound (with the King's Cross start altered to 9.35 a.m.) and to 7 hours, 7 minutes southbound—very nearly back to the pre-war 7 hours. But the reduction in time was accompanied by increasing restrictions in the load to 12 vehicles in 1951, and no more than 11 (400 tons maximum) in 1952. Again it was the first-class end of the train that suffered, for the first-class restaurant accommodation was pared ruthlessly to 18 seats in a combined restaurant and kitchen car, and the total first-class compartment seating in the train from 66 to 42 places. The London-Aberdeen times by this service in 1952 were 11 hours 1 minute northbound and 11 hours 2 minutes southbound.

13—The "Cheltenham Spa Express"

It was as a very ordinary train that the " Cheltenham Spa Express " began its course. After the First World War an afternoon service was put on from Cheltenham and Gloucester to Paddington, due shortly after 5 p.m. But in 1923 the Great Western Railway, which had been steadily speeding up its long-distance services, decided to lay claim to the blue riband of railway speed in Great Britain, held until then by the North Eastern Railway—and later the London and North Eastern—with its 43-minute run over the 44·1 miles from Darlington to York. The almost perfectly level and well-aligned stretch from Swindon to Paddington was ideal for the purpose and the Cheltenham train was selected to make the new record. Its timing over the 77·3 miles from Swindon was cut to 75 minutes, and now required a start-to-stop average of 61·8 m.p.h.

The first step had thus been taken to turn the " Cheltenham Spa Express " into the " Cheltenham Flyer "—the nickname by which this train was always known in later years, though it never came into official use. Railway speeds all over the world were advancing rapidly, and the 75-minute schedule was not destined to remain in force for long. Six years later, in July 1929, the timing was cut to 70 minutes, and the booked speed rose to 66·2 m.p.h. ; at the time this was the fastest regular railway run in the world. Then the supremacy was challenged from an unexpected quarter. In 1931 the Canadian Pacific and Canadian National Railways were fighting for the traffic between Montreal and Toronto, and the competition grew so vigorous that the C.P.R. cut the time of its fastest service to 108 minutes for the 124 miles from Montreal West to Smith's Falls, which called for an average of 68·9 m.p.h. from start to stop. In September, 1931, therefore, the G.W.R. accelerated the " Cheltenham Flyer " to a 67-minute run from Swindon, so bringing the average speed up to 69·2 m.p.h. Finally, in order to reduce the schedule to a round figure, there came, in September, 1932, the cut to 65 minutes, and the raising of the start-to-stop average to 71·4 m.p.h.

After this final acceleration, the " Cheltenham Flyer " was still the fastest train in the world. But from then onwards, the march in world railway speed became so extraordinarily rapid that the " Cheltenham Flyer," though still running on its 71·4 m.p.h. schedule, by 1939 had to be content with a place well below the one-hundredth among the world's fastest runs, largely, of course, owing to the introduction of diesel-electric streamline trains in Germany and the United States. In Great Britain the " Cheltenham Flyer's " speed was just beaten by the 71·9 m.p.h. of the L.N.E.R. " Coronation " streamliner between London and York.

The best recorded journey of the " Cheltenham Flyer " was made on June 6th, 1932, when the 77·3 miles from Swindon to Paddington were covered in 56 minutes, 47 seconds, at an average of 81·7 m.p.h.—the fastest start-to-stop speed, so far as is known, that has ever been achieved in Great Britain. For 70 miles on end, between mileposts 72 and 2, an average rate of 87·5 m.p.h. was maintained, though this feat was beaten by the 70 miles covered at 91·8 m.p.h. on September 27th, 1935, by the L.N.E.R. " Silver Jubilee " streamliner. On this G.W.R. run the engine was No.5006, *Tregenna Castle*, a 4-cylinder 4-6-0 " Castle " of the class which has always been responsible for working the train ; the load was one of six bogie vehicles, weighing 186 tons empty, and 195 tons gross.

It was only between Swindon and Paddington that the "Cheltenham Flyer " developed any turn of speed, and over this section the schedule demanded a sustained 80 m.p.h., or something closely approaching that figure, for most of the distance. The main train, which latterly consisted usually of a six-coach set, was made up of third-class brake, corridor composite, restaurant car, corridor composite, third class, and third-class brake. Leaving St. James station at Cheltenham Spa at 2.40 p.m., and calling at Malvern Road, it ran down to Gloucester, 7½ miles, in 13 minutes. Here reversal was necessary ; the engine for the run to London was attached to what had been the rear of the train, and at the other end a through composite brake coach which left Hereford at 1.15 p.m., and had come across to Gloucester *via* Ross, calling at all stations. Previously, for some years, the main train avoided Gloucester, running direct from Engine Shed Junction to Gloucester South Junction, where the Hereford coach was attached.

Departure from Gloucester was at 2.58 p.m., and between there and Swindon stops were made at Stroud and Kemble ; also on this length the " Castle " had to tackle the stiff climb up 4 miles at

1 in 60–90 from Brimscombe to the summit at the east end of Sapperton tunnel. The 44¼ miles from Cheltenham to Swindon thus took 71 minutes, by contrast with the high speed from Swindon onwards. Swindon was left at 3.55 p.m. and Paddington was reached at 5 p.m. This train has not reappeared since the war, and the quickest run in the public timetables to-day from Swindon to Paddington takes 90 minutes.

There was no corresponding down service. The stock of the main train, including the engine, went down from Paddington daily at 10.45 a.m., but this was a semi-fast train of no distinctive speed.

On the day of the record run referred to earlier, arrangements were made for an extremely fast run in the opposite direction on the 5 p.m. down " Cheltenham Spa Express," which normally was non-stop to Kemble ; on this trip, " Castle " class 4–6–0 No. 5005, *Manorbier Castle*, with a load of 205 tons, worked the train to a special stop at Swindon in one second over the hour. The 5.15 p.m. non-stop two-hour express from Bristol to Paddington was then stopped specially at Swindon to pick up those who had been recording the test journeys, and brought them back to Paddington in 66½ minutes. Between 3.48 and 7.12 p.m., these recorders made *three* journeys over this 77.3 miles of line, so covering 232 miles in 3 hours, 24 minutes, and in an actual running time of 3 minutes over 3 hours.

14—The "City Limited"

It is a tradition that the " City Limited " will always run, notwithstanding fog, strike, war, or Act of God, and for over a century this famous train and its predecessors have kept the tradition in being. So much so, indeed, that during the Second World War, almost alone among British express trains, the " City Limited " maintained its 60-minute schedule from London Bridge to Brighton, even though a considerable part of London Bridge terminus disappeared in the *blitz*, and the track at the London end of the journey suffered greatly from bomb damage. In the up direction the only alteration has been a trifling addition of two minutes to cover an intermediate stop at Haywards Heath, later reduced to a single minute. Also the Pullman cars were withdrawn about the middle of the war period.

The first forerunner of the " City Limited " came into operation on September 21st, 1841, leaving Brighton for London Bridge at 8.30 a.m., and returning at 4.45 p.m. In the up direction the time allowed was 1¾ hours, and in the down two hours ; the only advertised stop was Croydon, though additional stops may have been needed to take water. By the beginning of 1850, the time had come down to 75 minutes, and the London Bridge departure had been altered to the time-honoured 5 p.m. The 8.45 a.m. departure from Brighton had come into force in 1844.

In 1862, with the opening of Victoria, West End portions were added to both trains, but by 1865 the 5 p.m. down was running from London Bridge only, and a year later was slipping a portion for Tunbridge Wells at Three Bridges. In the following decade the slip portion was for Eastbourne, and was detached at Haywards Heath, while the up train was slipping its Victoria portion at East Croydon, instead of stopping there. The up express also had come down to a 70-minute run to London Bridge. It was in the summer of 1912 that the 5 p.m. down first became a 60-minute train, and after the interlude of the First World War, when the schedule went back to 75 minutes, and 82 minutes in the reverse direction, the 60-minute timing was restored in February, 1921. The up express, now for London Bridge only, was cut to 62 minutes at the same date, and to the even hour from July, 1928.

At the beginning of the present century, the up " City Limited " was one of the heaviest trains in the country, notwithstanding the fact that it carried first-class passengers only. From 1901 onwards, the London Bridge portion consisted of six-wheeled brakes at each end, six bogie firsts, and three eight-wheel Pullmans in the centre, with a Victoria " slip " composed of six-wheel brake, two bogie firsts and a twelve-wheel Pullman. On Mondays each section contained an additional bogie first, and the entire train then comprised 17 vehicles (67 axles) weighing 348 tons empty and at least 370 tons with passengers and luggage ; it is no small tribute to the small London, Brighton & South Coast engines of the period that such a load could be worked single-headed.

New stock 9 ft. wide, introduced in 1907, made it possible to cut the London Bridge formation to nine bogies, weighing 217 tons ; in the reverse direction, with the Victoria portion, the load was twelve bogies weighing 304 tons. In the entire train, which was still first-class only, there were four Pullmans as before. This was the first L.B. & S.C.R. train to be steam-heated throughout. It was not until 1919, when the up Victoria portion began to run as a separate train, that third-class passengers were admitted on weekdays to the " City Limited," but the predominance of first-class passengers made it necessary, when electric haulage was introduced in 1933, to build special sets of coaches for the working, owing to the unusually large proportion of first-class accommodation required. In 1924 standard Southern Railway corridor stock replaced the previous compartment stock in a train of eleven bogies, one only of which was now a Pullman car. The total weight was about 360 tons.

From Stroudley days many special locomotive classes that were built at Brighton were designed in the first instance to work the "City Limited," such as the first Stroudley 0-4-2 express engines *Richmond* and *Cornwall* in 1878 and 1879, the " Gladstone " 0-4-2's in the early 1880's, and the Billinton 4-4-0's *Siemens*, *Sirdar* and *Empress* in 1899. Then came the turn of the Marsh Atlantics, and of the Lawson Billinton 4–6–2 and 4–6–4 tanks. The final run of the " City Limited " with steam power, made on Friday, December 30th, 1932, was by 4–6–4 tank No. 332, which, with a gross load of 385 tons, ran the 50·9 miles in 57¾ minutes.

For the electric working, as previously mentioned, special six-car sets were built. Each comprises two centre-corridor third-class motor brakes, three side-corridor firsts, and a composite Pullman. The entire twelve-coach train seats 276 first and 240 third-class passengers, and weighs 526 tons empty, and about 565 tons with all seats occupied and a small amount of luggage. In the last years before the Second World War the down " City Limited," though nominally a 60-minute train, was scheduled in the working timetables to reach Brighton at 5.56 p.m., and so to maintain an overall average of 54·2 m.p.h. On the outbreak of war the Brighton arrival reverted to 6 p.m. The up " City Limited " now leaves Brighton at 8.43 a.m., calls at Haywards Heath from 8.58½ to 8.59½ a.m. and reaches London Bridge at 9.44 a.m., but it is no longer a named train.

15—The "Comet"

It was doubtless the up working of this express that suggested as distinctive a name as the " Comet," for the down train carrying the same name did not lay quite the same claim to speed. For a good many years there had been a fast evening service from Manchester to Euston, which passed through various changes ; at one time it left Manchester as late as 6.15 p.m., and for some time through Manchester coaches were attached at Crewe to the rear of the up " Midday Scot." Finally, however, Manchester had its up direct evening express once again, with a journey time cut to 3¼ hours, similar to that of the up " Mancunian " and the down " Lancastrian."

When the " Comet " first received its name, in 1932, it left London Road Station at 5.40 p.m., but this was altered later to 5.45 p.m., with an arrival in Euston at 9 p.m. The train travelled by the Styal line, passed Crewe without stopping, and made its only intermediate halt at Stafford, from 6.49 to 6.52 p.m. (54·9 miles in 64 minutes). From here the 133·6 miles to Euston had to be done in 128 minutes, at an average speed of 62·6 m.p.h., and this was one of the fastest scheduled runs on the L.M.S.R. The train was very popular, and always ran filled to capacity ; on Fridays a relieving express left Manchester at 5.40 p.m., and ran non-stop to Euston, arriving at 8.57 p.m.

A " Royal Scot " 4–6–0 was used invariably on the " Comet " workings, both up and down, and in either case the working of the train was a severe test of locomotive capacity. The up train consisted of a set of six coaches—first-class brake, open first, third and kitchen car (a 12-wheeler), open third, third and third brake—to which was attached, in front, the set of cars which had worked down the same day on the 8.30 a.m. from London—third brake, third restaurant car, kitchen car, and first restaurant car—making a minimum of eleven vehicles, and a minimum tare weight of about 340 tons. Extra vehicles were frequently attached, and if the load was thirteen bogies or more, the 4–6–0 was allowed a pilot, usually a 4–4–0 three-cylinder compound.

In the down direction the " Comet " left Euston at 11.50 a.m., and was the lineal descendant of the 12.10 p.m. express from Euston to Liverpool and Manchester that ran up to the First World War. The down " Comet " ran non-stop over the 158·1 miles from Euston to Crewe, for which 165 minutes were allowed (57·5 m.p.h.) ; a stop of three minutes was allowed at Crewe for division of the train, after which the " Comet " was booked to cover the 24·9 miles to Stockport in 29 minutes. At Stockport a three-minute stop sufficed, and the final 5·9 miles into London Road took 10 minutes, for an arrival at 3.20 p.m.

The down " Comet " left London with the six-coach set of cars, including 12-wheel restaurant car, to which reference has already been made, and this formed the complete train from Crewe onwards. To Crewe there was attached on rear a seven-coach set for Liverpool —third brake, third, third, third restaurant, kitchen, first restaurant, and first brake—with a through composite brake for Birkenhead as the rearmost vehicle. This made a minimum load of fourteen bogies, and a substantial tare load of about 430 tons for the " Royal Scot " to work to Crewe at 57·5 m.p.h.

To Liverpool, departure from Crewe was at 2.42 p.m., and after a non-stop run Liverpool Lime Street was reached at 3.25 p.m. The Birkenhead coach was attached to a train made up at Crewe, and leaving at 2.43 p.m. ; with intermediate stops at Chester, Hooton, and Rock Ferry, this reached Birkenhead Woodside Station at 3.40 p.m., and gave the Birkenhead passengers the fastest service of the day between London and that Merseyside town.

With post-war conditions the " Comet " reappeared, leaving Manchester at 5.50 p.m., stopping at Stockport and Crewe in place of Stafford, but not due in Euston till 9.36 p.m.—a journey of just over 3¾ hours as compared with the pre-war 3¼ hours. By the 1952 winter the Euston arrival had advanced to 9.25 p.m. The stock used goes down on the 9.45 a.m. from Euston to Manchester (instead of the pre-war 11.50 a.m.), and the former has therefore assumed the name " Comet " in the present service. It is non-stop form Euston to Stoke and after that makes the usual calls at Maccles-field and Stockport, reaching London Road at 1.40 p.m., except on Saturdays. On that day the unhappy train, after getting down the main line at its usual speed as far as Colwich, is compelled to hang about for half-an-hour between Colwich and Stoke, because of the difficulty of finding a path through the Saturday workmen's traffic of the Potteries, so not reaching Manchester until 2.12 p.m.—a very far from " Comet "-like proceeding !

16—The "Cornishman"

Among well-known titled trains of the past, the " Cornishman " of the G.W.R., though this title was never official enough to appear in timetables or other railway literature of the period, certainly was of sufficient note to deserve a place. It began its career in the days when the main line from Paddington to Penzance was still being operated on Brunel's 7 ft. gauge, and on May 20th, 1892, had the distinction of being the last broad gauge express to leave London for stations in Cornwall before the final change of gauge from 7 ft. to 4 ft. 8½ in. was made.

When the " Cornishman " came into operation in the summer of 1890, it was the fastest train between London and the West of England, and one of the fastest in the country. Leaving Paddington at 10.15 a.m., it reached Bristol at 12.45 p.m., Exeter at 2.20 p.m., Plymouth at 3.50 p.m., and Penzance at 6.57 p.m. ; but, contrary to present practice, the up run was faster, and with departure from Penzance at 11.15 a.m. and arrival in Paddington at 7.50 p.m., the overall time was reduced to 8 hours, 35 minutes. This, of course, was *via* Bristol, and a total distance of 325¼ miles, as compared with the present 305 miles *via* Westbury. A popular feature of this express was that it deigned to carry third-class passengers, at a time when not a few important trains were still first and second only.

In those days the agreement between the G.W.R. and the company controlling the hotel and refreshment rooms at Swindon station made it compulsory to stop every express at Swindon for at least 10 minutes to give passengers time to obtain refreshments. It was not until 1895 that the railway, by paying the large sum of £100,000, obtained release from their engagement, and until 1895, therefore, the " Cornishman " stopped at Swindon in both directions. The time allowed for the 77·3 miles from Paddington to Swindon was 87 minutes, calling for an average speed of 53·3 m.p.h. from start to stop over this length.

By 1895 the G.W.R., now on the standard 4 ft. 8½ in. gauge throughout from Paddington to Penzance, had laid down water-troughs near Goring and at Keynsham, between Bath and Bristol, so that with the abolition of the Swindon stop from October 1st, 1895, the " Cornishman " was able to make the first regular non-stop runs between Paddington and Bristol. Departure from London was altered from 10.15 to 10.30 a.m., and the time allowed for the 118·3 miles was cut to 135 minutes, calling for an average speed of 52·6 m.p.h. By a further cut of 15 minutes in 1903 the down " Cornishman " became the first train on record to put Bristol within 2 hours of Paddington daily ; the average of 59·2 m.p.h. start-to-stop still kept this express in the front rank of British high speed trains.

Well before this date a division into two parts of the " Cornishman " in each direction, during the height of the summer season, had earned a new record for the train. A relief section for Newquay, timed to leave Paddington at 10.25 a.m., was booked to run the 193·6 miles from Paddington to Exeter without a stop, from July 20th, 1896. The running times as far as Bath were unchanged ; the train avoided Temple Meads station at Bristol by the relief line, and was due in Exeter at 2.10 p.m., in 3¾ hours from London. Average speed for the run was thus 51·6 m.p.h., but the load was five bogie vehicles only. The 10.25 a.m. from Paddington reached Plymouth at 3.37 p.m., and stood there 5 minutes ; the next stop was at Par at 4.45 p.m., and arrival in Newquay was at 5.47 p.m. In the reverse direction, leaving Newquay at 11.5 a.m., calling at all stations up to Par and after that at Liskeard, Devonport, Plymouth, Exeter and Bristol, the up express was due in Paddington at 6.48 p.m.

By an easy margin the run between Paddington and Exeter at that time was the longest in the world without intermediate stop. From 1899 non-stop running in the up direction became regular throughout the year, and from 1902 in the down direction also ; then, from July 1st, 1904, came the complete eclipse of the " Cornishman " by the new " Cornish Riviera Limited " express, with its daily runs of 245·6 miles in each direction between Paddington and North Road station at Plymouth. Even when the distance became reduced to 225·5 miles with the opening of the Westbury cut-off in 1906, the " Limited " retained the non-stop " blue riband " for a good many years.

In the summer of 1952 the name " Cornishman " was revived, but this time officially, and applied to an entirely different service— that running daily between Wolverhampton, Birmingham, Plymouth and Penzance by way of Stratford-on-Avon and Cheltenham. In the earlier years of Great Western history, G.W.R. communication between the Midlands and the West of England had to be made circuitously by Oxford and the west curve at Didcot on to the Bristol main line. Then, in 1908, the G.W.R. opened a new and costly direct route which enabled this company to compete much more effectively than before with the Midland Birmingham-Bristol route through Cheltenham. The new Great Western line took off from the London main line at Tyseley, 3 miles south of Birmingham (Snow Hill), cut in a south-westerly direction through Stratford-on-Avon to the northern fringes of the Cotswolds, connecting with the Oxford-Worcester main line at Honeybourne, and then continuing through Broadway to a new station at Cheltenham called Malvern Road.

The new line then used the joint Midland-Great Western line from Cheltenham to Gloucester, but left it just short of

Gloucester to join the G.W.R. Gloucester-London line, so by-passing Gloucester to the east. At Standish Junction the trains of the Great Western Birmingham-Bristol service crossed over to the parallel Midland line, and, with the aid of running powers, made use of the latter as far south as Yate. There they branched off, to run up a short spur to the Swindon-South Wales main line of the G.W.R., which they followed to Stoke Gifford, there branching eastwards down through Filton and Stapleton Road into Temple Meads station at Bristol.

At first, several through services in each direction daily were established, but in the course of years their number diminished, until by 1939 only one through service continued to run throughout the year, at 10.40 a.m. from Wolverhampton and 11.20 a.m. from Birmingham, reaching Bristol at 1.35 p.m., Plymouth at 4.52 p.m., and Penzance at 7.45 p.m. It returned from Penzance at 10.45 a.m., Plymouth at 1.40 p.m., and Bristol at 4.45 p.m., reaching Birmingham at 7 p.m. and Wolverhampton at 7.30 p.m.

This train was suspended during the Second World War, but subsequently reappeared, running in much the same times until the summer of 1952, when its timing was altered completely, and it received the title of " Cornishman." The new " Cornishman " leaves Wolverhampton at 9.15 a.m., and Birmingham (Snow Hill) at 9.50 a.m. Calling after that at Stratford-on-Avon and Chel-tenham (Malvern Road), it now diverts from the previous Gloucester by-pass to stop in the one-time Midland station, before resuming its journey to Bristol, which is reached at 12.28 p.m. Restarting 7 minutes later, it serves Taunton by means of a slip-coach, and runs into Exeter at 2.8 p.m. Incidentally, the stop here explains why it is no longer necessary to stop the " Cornish Riviera Express " at Exeter to give a good after-lunch service to Plymouth and Penzance. The next stop is Plymouth (3.30–3.35 p.m.), and after calls at principal stations in Cornwall, Penzance is reached at 5.55 p.m.

The return journey is begun from Penzance at 10.30 a.m.; stops are made at St. Erth, Truro, St. Austell and Par (not at Bodmin Road or Liskeard in this direction), and Plymouth is left at 12.58 p.m. The Exeter stop is at 2.19-2.22 p.m. and that at Bristol at 3.56-4.2 p.m., and with the same stops beyond as on the reverse run, Birmingham is reached at 6.38 p.m. and Wolverhampton at 7.28 p.m. Refreshment facilities are available for the entire journey, and through coaches, detached and attached at Exeter, are run between Wolverhampton, Torquay and Kingswear. The present westbound run is 20 minutes faster than before the war.

17—The "Cornish Riviera Express"

It was in July, 1904, that the forerunner of the "Cornish Riviera Express" first made its appearance in the Great Western Railway timetables. Leaving Paddington at 10.10 a.m., the new express, for the first time in G.W.R. history, was booked to run daily to Plymouth without a stop; and as the Westbury route had not then come into use, it had to travel *via* Bath and the Pylle Hill avoiding line at Bristol, to avoid the small and congested Temple Meads station of those days. The Paddington-Plymouth run was therefore one of 245·7 miles, and by a considerable margin was the longest regular non-stop run in the world at that time.

A variety of engines was used; normally a "City" class 4–4–0 appeared at the head of the train, but the locomotive might be one of the three French compound Atlantics; the first G.W.R. 4–6–0's, and the 4–4–2's that were built for the purpose of direct comparison with the French engines, were also becoming available. The original "Limited," at that time unnamed, was a train of seven vehicles—six clerestory-roofed eight-wheelers of the old G.W.R. type, one of which ran through to Falmouth and the remainder to Penzance, with a new 68-ft. elliptical-roofed dining car. The total load was about 200 tons.

July, 1906, saw the bringing into use of the shorter Westbury route, which cut the distance between Paddington and North Road, Plymouth, from 245·7 to 225·7 miles. The non-stop run to Plymouth was reintroduced, but from that date the train came into operation permanently, summer and winter alike. From Paddington the start was altered to the time-honoured hour of 10.30 a.m., which has continued unaltered for nearly forty years. Arrival at Plymouth was fixed at 2.37 p.m., and at Penzance, including stops at the principal stations in Cornwall, at 5.5 p.m.

By now the Great Western Railway was bringing into use its 70-ft. coaching stock—the longest and most capacious corridor eight-wheelers that have ever been seen in Great Britain—and the "Cornish Riviera Limited," as the train had become, was formed of these. Another new departure was the inclusion of slip portions for stations intermediate between Paddington and Plymouth; coaches were slipped at Westbury, Taunton, and Exeter, and the "Limited" thus created another new record by detaching three successive sections before the first stop was reached. Of these the innermost, or Exeter, slip carried the usual slip tail-lamps (red and white side by side); the Taunton slip showed a similar pair of lamps arranged vertically; and the outermost, or Westbury, slip had a special tail lamp indication, consisting of a triangle of lamps, two red and one white.

The effect of this slipping was nicely to proportion the load to the increasing severity of the gradients, as the train worked its way westwards. It would be difficult to find a single run anywhere else in the country with so great a variety of gradients within its length;

from Paddington to Reading the course is virtually level ; from there to Taunton the inclinations on the westbound journey are no more than moderate. But beyond Taunton there is first the 3-mile climb at 1 in 80–90–127 through the Blackdown Hills to Whiteball summit ; and then, after Newton Abbot, there are the formidable ascents to Dainton summit, and from Totnes up to Brent, the former including a short strip as steep as 1 in 36, and the latter 1¼ miles at an average of 1 in 68, and 1½ miles averaging 1 in 50.

Space does not permit a detailed description of the way in which the load of the " Limited " had developed to the standard prevailing immediately before the Second World War. By that time the traffic to Exeter, and the desirability of picking up passengers at Exeter for Cornwall, had resulted in the substitution of a stop at Exeter for the previous slip, leaving only the Westbury and Taunton slip portions, though these had expanded to two coaches each. In all, the " Limited " now consisted of no fewer than eight through portions daily, except in the height of the summer; these were the main train, with the restaurant cars, for Penzance ; a through coach for St. Ives, detached at St. Erth ; one for Falmouth, detached at Truro ; one for Newquay, detached at Par ; one for Kingsbridge, detached at Exeter and worked forward by a stopping train ; the Taunton slip, consisting of through coaches for both Ilfracombe and Minehead ; and the two Weymouth coaches slipped at Westbury. At times of week-end pressure, an additional coach might be included for Plymouth, making a ninth portion.

Many different types of stock appeared in succession on the " Cornish Riviera Limited " in the intervening years. The original 70-ft. coaches, with recessed end doors only, were succeeded by flush-sided 70-ft. cars with side doors, then by 60-ft. vehicles, and, finally, by some new and luxurious stock, introduced shortly before the war, again of maximum width and with recessed end doors. The original composite restaurant car and kitchen also had given place to an independent kitchen and first-class car coupled to a third-class open car, of very modern design. Again, the " Star " class 4-cylinder 4-6-0's had been succeeded, first by the " Castles " in 1923, and then by the more powerful " Kings " in 1926.

By 1939 the winter weight of the down " Limited " had increased to a normal minimum of fourteen bogie vehicles out of Paddington, weighing 468 tons empty and nearly 500 tons with a normal complement of passengers and luggage, and its haulage had become one of the most exacting locomotive tasks in the country. New cut-off routes had been built to avoid both Westbury and Frome, so cutting out the service speed restrictions through both stations (incidentally, the Westbury cut-off now made it necessary to detach the Weymouth slip portion at Heywood Road junction, and to work it over the mile from there into Westbury with a shunting engine), and slightly reducing the Paddington-Exeter distance to 173·5 miles, but this was scheduled in the working time-table to be covered in 169 minutes start-to-stop, so involving an average speed of 61·6 m.p.h. throughout. For the 52 miles from Exeter to Plymouth 72 minutes were allowed, and at North Road station, where engines were changed, the booked arrival was 2.35 p.m. Stopping after that at Par, Truro, Gwinear Road, and St. Erth, the "Limited" reached Penzance at 5 p.m. Through Cornwall the train was usually worked by a "Castle" class 4–6–0, as this is the heaviest type permitted to work over Saltash bridge. Since then the high pressure "Counties" and the "Britannia" class Pacifics have become available.

During the currency of the summer timetable, the "Limited" reverted to a nominal non-stop run between Paddington and Plymouth, covering the distance in 4 hours, 2 minutes, and reached Penzance at 4.55 p.m. In the working timetable, however, a stop was shown at Newton Abbot from 1.43 to 1.47 p.m. to take an assisting engine between there and Plymouth. The summer formation consisted only of sections for Penzance, St. Ives, Falmouth, Newquay, and Weymouth ; the other through portions of the normal winter load were run on additional trains which operated during the summer season only. The summer load of the "Limited" was normally twelve to fifteen bogies to Westbury and two less from there.

For most of its history the "Cornish Riviera Limited" has been an easier working in the up direction than in the down ; the schedule has not been quite so fast, and the absence of Ilfracombe, Minehead and Weymouth portions to some degree has lightened the load. On its peacetime schedule, for many years past the departure from Penzance has been at 10 a.m., and from North Road, Plymouth, at 12.30 p.m. ; in the summer the train has run non-stop from here to Paddington, with an allowance of 4¼ hours, but during the remaining nine months a stop at Exeter has been included, and the train has been booked to run up from there in 2 hours, 55 minutes, arriving at 4.45 p.m.

One of the most remarkable happenings in the history of this famous train occurred for a week in May, 1925, when on the Monday, Wednesday and Friday in the down direction and the Tuesday, Thursday and Saturday in the up, it was worked by the L.N.E.R. Class "A1" Pacific No. 4474, *Victor Wild*, turn-and-turn-about with the G.W.R. 4–6–0 No. 4074, *Caldicot Castle*. In this exchange trial, which was not without its effect on later L.N.E.R. locomotive design, the "Castle" made slightly the better times, and did so on a lower fuel consumption.

When the Second World War broke out, the 10.30 a.m. down at first was altered to travel *via* Bath and Bristol, combining the work of the previous 10 a.m., 10.30 a.m., 11.15 a.m., and 12 noon trains, but it was soon found impossible to accommodate all these passengers in a single service. So a combined "Cornish Riviera" and "Torbay" service reappeared at 10.30 a.m., and soon the "Torbay" was split off as a separate train at 10.40 a.m., leaving the 10.30 a.m. as a recognisable wartime edition of its peacetime self, non-stop between Paddington and Exeter, even to the extent of being one of the very few trains in the country still to carry its name on the carriage headboards. Use of the Westbury route was resumed.

There were no through portions other than the main train from Paddington to Penzance, but as many additional coaches for Plymouth were run on the rear as required. The allowance to Exeter was 3½ hours (a slowing of 41 minutes); Plymouth was reached at 3.25 p.m., and Penzance at 6.25 p.m. In the up direction departure from Penzance was at 9.30 a.m., from Plymouth 12.30 p.m., and from Exeter 1.55 p.m., and Paddington was reached at 5.30 p.m. A cut of 15 minutes each way between Paddington and Exeter was made from October 1st, 1945. The allowance over the 173·5 miles from Paddington to Exeter came down to 195 minutes (53·4 m.p.h.), and Penzance was reached 35 minutes earlier, at 5.50 p.m., in 7 hours, 20 minutes from London. Restaurant cars, of an entirely new internal design, reappeared on the last day of 1945.

The summer of 1946 saw a further improvement, with a non-stop run in each direction between Paddington and Plymouth (4¼ hours down and 4 hours, 40 minutes up), and the London—Penzance time cut to 6 hours, 55 minutes down and 7¼ hours up. With the winter timetables of 1950-51, the Westbury slip portion was restored to the train.

The summer timetables of 1952 showed another substantial speed-up of the " Cornish Riviera Limited," with 4¼ hours now allowed in both directions for the 225·5 miles between Paddington and Plymouth, and no stop other than that required for attaching and detaching the assisting locomotive at Newton Abbot. In the 1952-1953 winter timetables, the Exeter stop was not reinstated ; the present time of 6 hours 40 minutes from London to Penzance is only 10 minutes slower than that of pre-war winters, while the Penzance-London time of 6¾ hours (the arrival in Paddington is now 4.30 p.m.) is right back to the pre-war figure. But the train is lighter in weight, for none of the old through portions are carried, other than the Weymouth slip on the down journey. This service is now known officially as the " Cornish Riviera Express," but to the staff it is, and probably always will be, simply " The Limited."

18—The " Coronation "

Experience with the " Silver Jubilee " having proved that the British public both wanted high speed and was prepared to pay for it, the L.N.E.R. management decided in 1936 to add to its streamline trains. The second L.N.E.R. streamliner thus to come into service, in July, 1937, was the " Coronation," so named in honour of the coronation in that year of King George VI and Queen Elizabeth.

The " Silver Jubilee " had shown that time could be maintained without difficulty on a 4-hour schedule over the 268·4 miles between King's Cross and Newcastle, and a further 2 hours over the 124·5 miles between Newcastle and Edinburgh would put the Scottish capital within 6 hours of London. Such a time had not been dreamed of since the " Race to Aberdeen " in 1895, when the quickest time from King's Cross to Edinburgh Waverley came down to 6 hours, 19 minutes.

But that was with a train weighing 105 tons only ; and when the new " Coronation " appeared, in all its glory, it was found that the weight of the nine coaches complete was no less than 312 tons, or 42 per cent. more than the original " Silver Jubilee " seven-car train. It was over 26 per cent. heavier than the " Jubilee " as rebuilt with eight cars. This difference was destined to influence the locomotive performance considerably, and the " Coronation " was always a very much harder locomotive working than its predecessor, especially as the " Coronation " locomotive was required to work through between London and Edinburgh.

The new " Coronation " set consisted of nine cars, of very striking appearance both outside and inside. The exterior had an enamelled motor-car body finish in two shades of blue, with light blue upper panels, and a dark shade, known as " Garter blue," for the lower panels. The set of nine cars consisted of four articulated " twins," with a tail car that was unique in British coach-building practice.

The rear end, of " beaver tail " design, reversed the wedge front of the streamlined locomotive, and was designed to reduce the air resistance caused by the suction of a normal square coach-end on the back of a train travelling at high speed. Further, this rear coach was designed as an observation car—the first of its kind since the building of the Pullman observation car, *Maid of Morven*, for the Glasgow-Oban service—and so was equipped with loose armchairs, and was available to passengers of both classes on payment of a small fee of 1s., for one hour's stay.

The rest of the train, from south to north, consisted of third-class brake, third and kitchen, two firsts, third, third and kitchen, third and third brake. Two kitchens were provided in order that passengers might be served without moving from their seats, as in Pullman practice. For the first time in Great Britain, air conditioning, electrically operated, was provided throughout the train, changing the air in each coach automatically every three minutes.

This made it possible to provide each coach with double windows, permanently closed, and with the help of acoustic blankets, something as nearly approaching silent travel as could ever be hoped for, together with an equable temperature and complete absence of draughts, was actually achieved. Even the cutlery was provided with flat handles, so that the quietness might not be disturbed by rattling when the tables were laid ! Each first-class seat was

[*B. E. Morrison*

A Western Region Mogul, No. 6361, heads the "Cambrian Coast Express" through Wellington, Salop. The engine is working from Abberystwyth to Wolverton, and the train is of L.M.R. stock

[*P. J. Lynch*

Setting out on its 393-mile run from Kings Cross to Edinburgh—the "Capitals Limited," drawn by the record-braking Class "A4" Pacific No. 60022 *Mallard*

[C. R. L. Coles

Above : Taking water at Bushey—L.M.R. " Royal Scot " Class 4–6–0 No. 46120 *Royal Inniskilling Fusilier* heads the " Comet " northwards to Manchester

Below : With passengers who have just crossed from the Hook—E.R. Class " B1 " 4–6–0 No. 61130 climbs out of Colchester with the " Day Continental "

[C. W. Footer

[*J. D. Mills*

y the " Cornish Riviera Express " to the West. *Above :* W.R. " King " Class 4–6–0 No. 6027 *ing Richard I* heads the down train up Dainton Bank, and (*below*) Standard Class " 7MT " 4–6–2 No. 70019 *Lightning* finishes the westbound journey round Mounts Bay into Penzance

[*B. A. Butt*

[*F. O. J. Otway, H. C. Casserley*

The " Devon Belle " negotiates the mountainous ascent from Braunton to Mortehoe behind
S.R. " West Country " Class 4–6–2 No. 34015 *Exmouth*, with banking assistance. *Inset :*
One of the two " Devon Belle " Pullman Observation cars

[*H. Gordon Tidey*

Northbound with the " Devonian "—W.R. " Castle " Class 4–6–0 No. 4077 *Chepstow
Castle* on the sea wall near Dawlish, South Devon

arranged in an alcove, and had a swivelling chair and a table tapering outwards towards the window, so permitting the traveller to turn his chair towards the window, and enjoy the view to better advantage. The decorations, in aluminium and colour throughout the train, were very original, and the vista along the central aisle, through the succession of partition openings framed in their aluminium architraves, was most attractive.

A long-felt need was met by starting the down " Coronation " from King's Cross at 4 o'clock in the afternoon, so permitting a business man to have almost the entire day in London, and yet to be in Edinburgh by 10 p.m. In order not to interfere with the existing 4 p.m. down Leeds express, the timetable authorities arranged for the two trains to start simultaneously, the " Coronation " from No. 5 platform, and the Leeds train from No. 10 ; the latter took the slow road, and followed the " Coronation " on the main line from No. 5 box at the north end of Finsbury Park.

From King's Cross to York the " Coronation " was booked to cover the 188·2 miles in 157 minutes, and the start to stop average speed of 71·9 m.p.h. so entailed made this the fastest regular scheduled run in the British Empire. The train passed Peterborough, 76·4 miles, in 64 minutes ; Grantham, 105·5 miles, in 88 minutes ; and Doncaster, 156 miles, in 128½ minutes. York was thus reached at 6.37 p.m. ; and here a stop of 3 minutes was made.

At first the run of 204·7 miles from York to Edinburgh was made non-stop, but as the up " Coronation " called at Newcastle, it was soon realised that, even allowing for the " Silver Jubilee " 1½ hours later, the Newcastle traffic on the down journey was too important to be overlooked. It was therefore arranged that the down " Coronation " should make two stops, at both York and Newcastle, within the compass of its 6-hour allowance, and from then on the 80·2 miles from York to Newcastle were run in 77 minutes, and the Tyneside city was reached at 7.57 p.m. Leaving Newcastle at 8 p.m., the " Coronation " had two hours left for the final 124·5 miles.

In the up direction, departure from Edinburgh was fixed half an hour later than in the down, at 4.30 p.m. This brought the " Coronation " into Newcastle at 6.30 p.m., and it left at 6.33 p.m. on a non-stop journey of 268·4 miles to King's Cross, reached at 10.30 p.m. Newcastle was therefore in the enviable position of having two streamline trains in each direction to and from London, down at 4 and 5.30 p.m. in 3 hours, 57 minutes and 4 hours respectively, and up at 6.33 p.m. and 10 a.m.

The " Coronation " soon became as popular as the " Silver Jubilee " and began to run daily filled to capacity. For the through journey between London and Edinburgh the supplementary fare charged was 6s. first-class and 4s. third-class. In the winter, as most of the journey was made after dark, it was decided to detach the observation car, and this had the effect of reducing the weight behind the locomotive to 278 tons, which was particularly advantageous when weather conditions were at their worst. The full 312-ton load, which with passengers and luggage made about 330 tons with all seats occupied, ultimately was run during the height of the summer season only.

Unlike the " Silver Jubilee " and the " West Riding Limited," the " Coronation "required two complete trains for the maintenance of daily service, and a fifth set of streamline cars was built to be used as a substitute for any of the regular streamline sets when they went into the works for overhaul. On the outbreak of war all the streamliners were withdrawn and the five trains were stored in remote places, where they would be unlikely to suffer damage, to wait for the return of peace. Since then the sets of cars have been split up, and used for ordinary passenger purposes.

Five streamlined " A4 " Pacifics were specially allocated to the " Coronation " service—Nos. 4488, *Union of South Africa*; 4489, *Dominion of Canada*; 4490, *Empire of India*; 4491, *Commonwealth of Australia*; and 4492, *Dominion of New Zealand*. Other engines of the same class took their turns in the working, however, when occasion required.

19—The "Coronation Scot"

Since the days of West Coast and East Coast competition, which reached its culmination in the " Race to Edinburgh " of 1888, and the still more exciting " Race to Aberdeen " in 1895, the railways up the two sides of the country have worked in a certain measure of harmony, and have declared to one another in advance any plans that they might be making for improvements of their service. When the L.N.E.R., in the autumn of 1936, announced its intention of celebrating the Coronation year by introducing in the summer of 1937 a streamline high-speed train between London and Edinburgh, it seemed highly probable that the L.M.S.R. would follow suit.

Probability changed to certainty in November, 1936, when the L.M.S.R. staged an unprecedented test journey from Euston to Glasgow and back. On November 7th, the non-streamlined Pacific No. 6201, *Princess Elizabeth* (no streamlined 4-6-2's had been built to that date), was attached to a train of seven coaches, and worked non-stop over the 401·4 miles from Euston to Glasgow Central in 5 hours, 53½ minutes. On the following day, in rain and high wind, the same locomotive, with one coach more, ran from Glasgow to Euston, again non-stop, in the astonishing time of 5 hours, 44¼ minutes, so completing the entire run at an average speed of precisely 70 m.p.h. It has to be remembered that this remarkable feat of locomotive endurance included lifting the train in succession to the summits at Beattock and Shap, respectively 1,015 and 915 ft. above the sea, with a drop intermediately to sea level north of Carlisle.

The feasibility of high-speed schedules having been demonstrated in this striking way, it was, perhaps, a little disappointing when the booking of the " Coronation Scot " was fixed at 6½ hours in each direction, inclusive of a two-minute stop at Carlisle ; even if a 6-hour overall time, like that of the L.N.E.R. " Coronation " over a distance 8·7 miles less, were cutting it fine, one of 6¼ hours might well have been tried, especially now that the first streamlined Pacifics were available. A later afternoon departure had also been confidently expected, but it was held that this would cause too much interference with the night freight trains, and the start from both terminals was therefore fixed at 1.30 p.m.

Before the " Coronation Scot " began its regular running, a test trip took place on June 29th, 1937, from Euston to Crewe and back. On the down journey, the point-to-point bookings of the new schedule were worked to as far as Stafford, but the engine, *Coronation*, was then opened out, and at the foot of the 1 in 177 past Madeley reached 114 m.p.h. On the return journey, the 270-ton train was worked from Crewe to Euston, 158·1 miles, in the record time of 119 minutes, at an average speed of 79·7 m.p.h. from start to stop, reaching 100 m.p.h. at Castlethorpe. The fact that 25 minutes were gained on the " Coronation Scot " schedule from Crewe once again demonstrated how ample a margin of time the new train would have on its booking in day-to-day running.

The original " Coronation Scot " train consisted of nine bogie vehicles weighing 297 tons. Actually it was not a streamlined train but consisted of standard stock adapted for the purpose, and painted blue, with horizontal white lines which continued the white lines carried by the streamlined blue locomotive and tender. On the northbound journey, from the engine backwards, the train consisted of corridor third-class brake, open third-class, kitchen car, two open thirds, kitchen car, open first, corridor first, and corridor first brake.

In 1939 the first vehicles of a new and more luxurious " Coronation Scot " train were built, including a first-class buffet lounge of novel design ; externally, instead of the original blue, the new coaches were painted standard L.M.S.R. red, with horizontal gold lines, and most of the streamlined Pacifics were painted to match. The new vehicles were sent to New York for exhibition at the New York World's Fair in 1939, with the locomotive *Coronation* ; the latter returned to this country during the war, but in view of the risks of sea transport, the coaches were loaned by the L.M.S.R. to the United States, to serve as a rest train for officers until after the war, when they also returned to England.

The " Coronation Scot " was booked to leave Euston, as previously mentioned, at 1.30 p.m., displacing the " Midday Scot " which for more than ten years previously had made a 1.30 p.m. departure. The former was booked to pass Rugby at 2.46 p.m., and Crewe at 3.54 p.m., reaching Carlisle at 6.13 p.m. The 299·1 miles had thus to be covered in 283 minutes, at an average speed of 63·4 m.p.h. Departure from Carlisle was at 6.15 p.m., and the remaining 102·3 miles over Beattock Summit to Glasgow had to be run in 105 minutes, with an arrival at 8 p.m.

In the reverse direction the " Coronation Scot " left Glasgow Central at 1.30 p.m., called at Carlisle from 3.15 to 3.17 p.m., and was due in Euston at 8 p.m. The two trains were booked to pass each other at Preston ; the northbound train was due through this Lancashire city at 4.44 p.m., and the southbound at 4.45 p.m. A seat charge of 2s. 6d. was required of both first-class and third-class passengers.

The locomotive was invariably one of the streamlined Pacifics, which worked through between Euston and Glasgow in both directions, with a change of crew at Carlisle. On one or two occasions an extra coach was run in the train for some special purpose, but normally the nine-coach formation was strictly adhered to. In signalling the " Coronation Scot " a special " Is line clear ? " bell signal was used : this was 4–4–4, or four beats repeated three times. This train has not been reinstated since the war.

20—The "Devon Belle"

On June 16th, 1947, the Southern Railway, as it then still was, broke some entirely new ground by instituting an all-Pullman service between London and Devonshire. Pullman cars had been seen previously in the county of cream and cider, during the short-lived reign of the Great Western " Torquay Pullman " in 1929, but never west of Basingstoke on the Southern line. The main objective of the new train—the " Devon Belle "—was Ilfracombe, but it was decided to add a through portion for Plymouth also. At first six cars for Ilfracombe and four for Plymouth were thought to be adequate, but it soon became apparent, especially at the height of the season, that the Ilfracombe section was nothing like capacious enough, and the " Devon Belle " frequently has been increased to a total of fourteen cars. This is a train of 545 tons tare, or 575 tons with passengers and luggage—a tremendous load to work over the heavy gradients west of Salisbury, especially up the long 1 in 80 from Seaton Junction to Honiton Tunnel, but one for which the " Merchant Navy " Pacifics have proved themselves thoroughly adequate.

It was hoped, when the advent of the new train was announced, that the schedule would be something which would enable the Bulleid Pacifics to display their real powers, and it was an acute disappointment to discover that the new train was to amble down from Waterloo to Salisbury in almost exactly the same time as the " Atlantic Coast

Express " (actually 102 minutes), while the up train would have the same allowance (96 minutes) as the up " Atlantic Coast Express." As it was not intended to pick up or set down passengers at Salisbury, it was decided not to obstruct the platforms by changing engines there—a non-stop run of 159¾ miles from Waterloo to Sidmouth Junction was, of course, impossible, as the engine tenders could not carry anything like enough water for the purpose—but to do so at the next station, Wilton, instead. In all the history of the S.R. and its predecessors, no trains had ever previously run through Salisbury without stopping, apart from the Plymouth-Waterloo boat trains of 1903-1904, which ran non-stop from Templecombe to Waterloo, but these ran at intermittent intervals only ; the " Devon Belle " has been the first train ever to do so regularly.

The " Devon Belle " was booked to leave Waterloo at 12 noon, and to run the 86.3 miles to Wilton in 107 minutes, arriving at 1.47 p.m. After a six-minute halt, the " Belle " then had to cover the 73.3 miles to Sidmouth Junction in 83 minutes—a vastly harder proposition than the initial stage. After a stop from 3.16 to 3.20 p.m. at Sidmouth Junction (to connect with Sidmouth and Budleigh Salterton) a 16-minute run over the 12.2 miles brought the " Belle " into Exeter Central at 3.36 p.m. Here the train was split into its two sections. The Plymouth section left first, at 3.41 p.m., in charge of a " West Country " Pacific, and after going over the top of Dartmoor, and, stopping at St. David's, Okehampton and Devonport, it made its way into Plymouth North Road at 5.25 p.m. and Friary at 5.36 p.m. As for the Ilfracombe section, this got away from Exeter Central at 3.48 p.m., and after a stop at St. David's ran the 39.1 miles to Barnstaple Junction, largely single line, in 56 minutes. Every station was called at from there on—Barnstaple Town, Braunton, and Mortehoe—and banking assistance was essential up the 1 in 40 from Heddon Mill to Mortehoe. After the abrupt drop from Mortehoe into Ilfracombe, the popular Devon resort was reached at 5.33 p.m., in just over 5½ hours from Waterloo.

The up " Devon Belle " had the better timing of 5 hours, 20 minutes, partly because of following the Plymouth portion into Exeter, and thus having a shorter stop at Central. So, whereas the Plymouth and Ilfracombe times from Waterloo more or less tied, the Plymouth portion coming up made its exit from Friary station at 11.30 a.m., half-an-hour before the Ilfracombe departure at 12 noon. The Ilfracombe section, very likely with a " West Country " Pacific at the rear as well as one in front, had to start by tackling the steepest main line gradient in Great Britain, 2¼ miles at 1 in 36. The 1 in 37 from Exeter St. David's up to Central demanded a couple of ex-Brighton 0-6-2 tank bankers, and very likely a similar engine as pilot, if the full ten cars were in the Ilfracombe section. Leaving Exeter Central at 1.44 p.m., and Sidmouth Junction at 2.4 p.m., the " Devon Belle " ran the difficult 73.3 miles to Wilton in 89 minutes, and then, after a six-minute stop to change engines, from 3.33 to 3.39 p.m., the " Devon Belle " was into Waterloo by 5.20 p.m.

Two vehicles of a very original description in the " Devon Belle " formation are the observation cars. These were two third-class cars, Nos. 13 and 14, which were completely rebuilt in the Pullman shops for service on these trains. They were not the first observation cars in Great Britain, as they were long preceded by the first-class Pullman observation car *Maid of Morven*, run for years during the summer season, originally by the Caledonian Railway and later by the L.M.S.R., between Glasgow and Oban. The " Coronation " streamline trains of the L.N.E.R. between King's Cross and Edinburgh also had their beaver-tail observation cars ; and there have been more primitive vehicles of the same description in use elsewhere. But the " Devon Belle " cars were the first ever to run on Southern metals. Rather more than half of each car is given over to observation, with an almost unbroken range of windows along each side and across the back end. The seating is of an " occasional " type, in comfortable single armchairs and double settees that can be swung to any angle. The other end of the car is occupied by a refreshment buffet, with small kitchen and pantry.

Complicated car-turning and re-marshalling arrangements were necessary at both the London and Ilfracombe ends of the journey to ensure that the observation car was always on the rear of the train, with the observation end outward. As for the remainder of the " Devon Belle," there were two first-class cars in the Ilfra-combe portion, and one in the Plymouth portion ; the rest of the train was third class, except for the space taken up by kitchens and pantries, of which there were two, so that passengers might be served with meals and refreshments at their own seats throughout the length of the train. It should be added that the " Devon Belle " at first was run at week-ends only, but in the summer of 1949 it ran five days a week in each direction—Thursdays to Mondays inclusive in the down direction, and Fridays to Tuesdays in the up, Sundays, of course, included. The running of the "Devon Belle" has been confined to the currency of the summer time-table—from the end of May to the end of September inclusive.

The summer of 1950 saw a considerable change in the working, for the Plymouth section was withdrawn, and what had been the Plymouth cars were detached at Exeter Central on the down journey, and attached there on the up. The stop of the Ilfracombe section at Exeter was curtailed accordingly, and Ilfracombe was reached 6 minutes earlier than previously, at 5.27 p.m. No change was made in the up schedule, other than a slight adjustment of station times at Exeter. In 1952 it was decided at first to withdraw the "Devon Belle", owing to lack of patronage on other than Saturdays, but eventually it was reinstated, down on Fridays, Saturdays and Sundays, and up on Saturdays, Sundays and Mondays, during the summer season.

21—The "Devonian"

Strictly speaking, for more than half of each year " Devonian " was rather a misnomer for the train to which it was attached as a title. For the express proper ran over L.M.S.R. metals between Bradford and Bristol, and did not actually touch Devonshire. A set of three coaches, however, was handed over to the Great Western Railway at Temple Meads station, Bristol, and run through by that company to Torquay and Paignton, and it was this through coach working that gave the necessary " Devonian " flavour to the service.

The trains on which the through Bradford-Paignton coaches worked were of old standing, and had seen little change up to the time when the title " Devonian " was conferred in 1927. After that they participated in the general Midland Division accelerations of 1937, and became very fast over the Birmingham-Bristol section.

The southbound " Devonian " was due to leave Bradford at 10.25 a.m., to reverse in Leeds City station and leave at 10.52 a.m. on a 50-minute run to Sheffield. After 5 minutes there, the express made a non-stop run to Derby in 53 minutes. Here the train dropped a through coach from Bradford to Bournemouth and acquired a through Newcastle-Bristol coach which had come south on the 10.20 a.m. from York. For the 41·3 miles from Derby to Birmingham the allowance was 47 minutes, and a wait of 6 minutes was enjoined at the great Midland city.

Within the compass of 53 minutes allowed from Birmingham to Cheltenham, 45·5 miles, the " Devonian " had to climb to Barnt Green and make a service stop at Blackwell before descending the Lickey incline, after which it was travelling at over a mile a minute all the way to Cheltenham. The stops here and at the closely adjacent town of Gloucester, with the short run between, took up 16 minutes, and the concluding run on L.M.S.R. metals was over the 37 miles from Gloucester to Bristol in 44 minutes. For cross-country running of this description over a hard road, with numerous stops, the time of 4 hours, 40 minutes for the 206 miles from Leeds to Bristol was an excellent one ; it was the best of the day. The through Paignton coaches waited at Temple Meads from 3.32 to 3.50 p.m., and then left on a Great Western express of no special distinction, making numerous intermediate stops and reaching Torquay at 6.44 and Paignton at 6.51 p.m. The entire journey of 323 miles from Bradford to Paignton thus took 8 hours, 26 minutes, but the G.W.R. section lowered the average speed considerably.

Northbound, the through coaches of the " Devonian " left Paignton at 9.15 and Torquay at 9.22 a.m. for a similarly leisurely run to Bristol, reached at 12.13 p.m. From here the " Devonian," with its restaurant cars, was timed to start at 12.35 p.m. First came a 43-minute run to Gloucester, beginning with the tremendous pull up to Fishponds, 2 miles at between 1 in 69 and 1 in 90, so that high-speed travelling was necessary from Yate onwards to maintain this timing over a 37-mile run. After Cheltenham, too, this train was one of those booked to cover the 31·1 miles from Cheltenham to Bromsgrove in 31 minutes, start-to-stop, before attaching the " banker " required for assistance up the Lickey incline. Yet the 45·5 miles from Cheltenham to Birmingham were run in 54 minutes.

The rest of the journey needs little description ; there was an additional stop at Burton-on-Trent, and leaving Birmingham New Street at 2.37 p.m., the " Devonian " was in Derby at 3.25 p.m., Sheffield at 4.25 p.m., Leeds at 5.24 p.m., and Bradford at 5.54 p.m., 8 hours, 39 minutes after leaving Paignton. Between Leeds and Bristol the engines used were almost invariably of the " 5XP " 3-cylinder 4–6–0 type, though a Class " 5 " 4–6–0 might appear at times, and would prove quite an efficient substitute.

From May to September inclusive the entire train, including L.M.S.R. stock and restaurant cars, ran through between Bradford and Kingswear. On Saturdays it ran in several parts. The through service came to an end on the outbreak of the Second World War, but was restored in October, 1946, with a time of 8¾ hours from Bradford to Torquay and 8 hours, 57 minutes back. At present the train carries its name and runs through between Bradford and Kingswear in the summer only, with a much increased journey time of 9 hours, 48 minutes from Bradford to Torquay, and 9 hours, 37 minutes in the reverse direction. In the winter it is nameless and runs between Bradford and Bristol only, taking 6 hours, 8 minutes from Leeds to Bristol, as compared with the 4 hours, 40 minutes of 1937. There are restaurant cars once again between Bradford and Bristol and through to and from Kingswear during the summer season.

22–The "East Anglian" and the "Norfolkman"

In the Coronation year, 1937, when new streamline trains were being put on between London and Edinburgh, and London, Leeds and Bradford, the L.N.E.R. authorities thought the time opportune for extending somewhat similar facilities to East Anglia. It was therefore decided to build a new six-coach train with interior furnishing similar to that of the streamliners, and to instal it on the Liverpool Street-Norwich service. For the working of the train, two " B.17 " three-cylinder 4–6–0 engines, Nos. 2859 and 2870, were specially streamlined, and received the names *East Anglian* and *City of London* respectively.

But when the new schedules were made public, they proved, by comparison with the streamline achievements elsewhere, to be somewhat of an anti-climax. The down " East Anglian " was to start from Liverpool Street at 6.40 p.m., call at Ipswich from 8.0 to 8.4 p.m., and reach Norwich Thorpe at 8.55 p.m. This entailed average start to stop speeds of 51·5 and 54·5 m.p.h. respectively over the two stages. In the up direction, departure from Norwich was at 11.55 a.m., a stop was made at Ipswich from 12.46 to 12.50 p.m., and Liverpool Street was reached at 2.10 p.m.

A year later the schedule was reduced from 2¼ hours to 2 hours, 10 minutes, with 2 minutes cut from the Ipswich stop and 3 minutes from the Ipswich-Norwich timing ; the latter became one of 48 minutes for 46·3 miles, and required a start to stop average of 57·9 m.p.h.—the fastest ever known on Great Eastern metals. The " East Anglian " now left Norwich at 12 noon, and was back into Thorpe Station at 8.50 p.m. Nevertheless, in recollection of the fact that the 50-ton Great Eastern " Claud Hamilton " 4–4–0's used to get the " Norfolk Coast Express," made up to 12, 13 and even 14 bogies, through Ipswich in 83 minutes, and past Trowse, a mile outside Norwich, in 2 hours, 14 minutes, it was felt by many that with a streamlined 4–6–0 and a six-coach train a two-hour timing to and from Norwich might have been reasonably possible. Actually this ideal was not destined to be realised until 15 years after the " East Anglian " first came into service.

The formation of the "East Anglian," on the down journey, from the engine backwards, was third-class brake, first-class and kitchen, open first, open third, third and kitchen, and third brake ; the entire train was of centre corridor stock, and passengers were served with meals and refreshments without leaving their seats. The tare weight of the six cars was 219 tons, and the normal full weight 235 tons. As the speed hardly reached the recognised streamline level it was not thought advisable to make any supplementary charge for the use of the train, which was therefore open to ordinary ticket-holders without restriction.

At times there was some very lively running, especially north of Ipswich. Actual times were recorded of 44½ minutes from Norwich to Ipswich and 42 minutes in the reverse direction for the 46·3 miles, and between Ipswich and Liverpool Street there were net times as little as 72 minutes up and 70¼ minutes down, so demonstrating the feasibility of a two-hour schedule, despite the difficulties of the route. The " East Anglian," which was withdrawn on the outbreak of war, ran from Mondays to Fridays inclusive, but not on Saturdays.

The " East Anglian " was restored to the timetable on October 7th, 1946, at the old starting times of 6.40 p.m. down and 11.50 a.m. up (later 11.40 a.m.), and on a schedule of 2 hours, 20 minutes. Also, in October, 1948, the " East Anglian " was joined by a new express called the " Norfolkman," designed to give exactly the same facilities between Liverpool Street, Ipswich and Norwich down in the morning and up in the evening as the " East Anglian " gives in the reverse direction. The " Norfolkman " left Liverpool Street at 10 a.m., reaching Norwich Thorpe at 12.20 p.m. ; return was at 5 p.m. and Liverpool Street was reached at 7.20 p.m. In the summer service, the " Norfolkman " prolonged its journey to

Cromer, with a time of 3 hours, 22 minutes down and 3 hours, 20 minutes up, even though the latter included a wait of no less than 15 minutes at Norwich. Stops were made at Wroxham and North Walsham. Normally the " East Anglian " and the " Norfolkman " were loaded to eight bogie vehicles apiece, and were worked by " B1 " 4-6-0's between London and Norwich.

In the summer of 1951, with the arrival of the new " Britannia " class Pacific engines at Stratford and Norwich sheds, a complete recasting of the Great Eastern timetable took place. Uniformly with the other principal expresses, the down " Norfolkman " and " East Anglian " were altered to start at 30 minutes past the hour —9.30 a.m. in the former case and 6.30 p.m. in the latter—and had their London-Norwich times cut to 2 hours, 10 minutes each (76 minutes Liverpool Street to Ipswich and 51 minutes thence to Norwich). In the reverse direction, to conform to the 45-minute departures from Norwich, the up " East Anglian " was moved to 11.45 a.m., and the up " Norfolkman " to 5.45 p.m., with 51 minutes allowed to Ipswich, 77 minutes thence to Liverpool Street, and again an overall time of 2 hours, 10 minutes. These timings are laid down for a maximum of nine bogies, but on Fridays the " East Anglian " is expanded to twelve bogies, and allowed 11 minutes more, while on Saturdays the same happens to the " Norfolkman." The " Norfolkman " continues to run through to and from Cromer, taking 3 hours, 10 minutes each way.

23—The "Easterling" and the "Broadsman"

The summer of 1950 saw two more train titles added to those over the Colchester main line of one-time Great Eastern Railway, one over a route which has not previously carried any regular titled train. This is the East Suffolk line between Ipswich and Yarmouth, and the train concerned is named the " Easterling " ; it runs during the summer months only between Liverpool Street and the South Town station at Yarmouth. The other is the " Broadsman "—an all-the-year-round title conferred on a pair of expresses which have run for many years past—the 7.30 a.m. (since altered to 7.45 a.m.) from Norwich to Liverpool Street and the 3.40 p.m. (now 3.30 p.m.) from Liverpool Street to Cromer.

In the days before the First World War, as a contemporary of the " Norfolk Coast Express," the G.E.R. used to run, during the summer months, a non-stop express over the 121.7 miles between London and Yarmouth in 2¼ hours each way. This was a very creditable time for a 4-4-0 locomotive of the " Claud Hamilton " type. Not only did it include the steep gradients and speed restrictions between Liverpool Street and Ipswich, but even steeper gradients from there to Beccles, and, to make matters worse, slacks to walking pace over the swingbridges at Beccles and St. Olave's in order to pick up a pilotman before crossing each bridge, and to set him down on the far side. In later years the bridges were rebuilt, and the speed restrictions were eased, though they still remained severe. The down train left Liverpool Street at 9.50 a.m., and the return run was begun at 1.35 or 1.40 p.m. in different years. Non-corridor stock was used.

Between the wars non-stop running was revived between Liverpool Street and Yarmouth, and at one stage the up journey time came down to 147 minutes—the fastest on record—but by 1939 various rearrangements had been made. The non-stops to and from Yarmouth had become restaurant car trains, ran on Saturdays only, at 12.15 p.m. down and 1.50 p.m. up, and needed $2\frac{3}{4}$ hours for the run. Then came the interruption of the Second World War, and it was in the recovery period, in the summer of 1950, that a new restaurant car service appeared with the title of the " Easterling," serving both Yarmouth and Lowestoft. Leaving Liverpool Street at 11.3 a.m., the " Easterling " makes a non-stop run over the $109\frac{1}{4}$ miles to Beccles in the creditable time of 135 minutes ; after division, the Yarmouth and Lowestoft portions complete their journeys at 1.22 and 1.24 p.m. respectively. The return run is begun from both terminals at 7.10 p.m., and, leaving Beccles at 7.35 p.m., the " Easterling " is into Liverpool Street at 10 p.m., a non-stop time of 145 minutes.

The "Broadsman," when its title was first conferred, made a not very exciting journey from Cromer at 6.28 a.m. and Norwich at 7.30 a.m., to reach Liverpool Street at 10.16 a.m. ; returning at 3.40 p.m., the train reached Norwich at 6.16 p.m. and Cromer at 7.15 p.m. But in the summer of 1951 the " Broadsman " shared in the tremendous speed-up which followed the introduction of the " Britannia " class Pacifics between Liverpool Street and Norwich. The start of the Sheringham coaches was altered from 6.3 to 6.20 a.m., and of the main train from Cromer to 6.45 a.m. ; from Norwich the train got away at 7.45 a.m., to reach Liverpool Street 9 minutes earlier, at 10.7 a.m. This meant an acceleration of 26 minutes on the run. The down " Broadsman " joined the fleet of 130-minute expresses between London and Norwich, now leaving Liverpool Street at 3.30 p.m., and getting into Norwich by 5.40 p.m., Cromer by 6.40 p.m., and Sheringham by 7.6 p.m., a cut of 26 minutes in this direction also.

But in mid-September, 1952, a more startling acceleration of the " Broadsman " took place, introducing the first mile-a-minute timing on record in East Anglia. For the down train is now booked to reach Norwich in the even two hours from Liverpool Street, divided in the proportion of 73 minutes for the 68·7 miles to Ipswich, and 45 minutes only for the 46·3 miles from there to Norwich Thorpe. The up " Broadsman " also has been speeded up, and with stops at Diss, Stowmarket and Ipswich must make the 115-mile run in $2\frac{1}{4}$

hours, reaching Liverpool Street at 10 a.m. Both trains are limited to a maximum load of nine bogies, weighing about 300 tons tare. To those acquainted with past travel conditions in East Anglia, this daily run of the " Broadsman " is one of the most revolutionary railway happenings that could well be imagined.

24—The "Eastern Belle Pullman Limited"

During the period from the railway grouping in 1923 to the beginning of the Second World War, one or two trains of Pullman cars, first and third class, were assembled by the Pullman Car Company chiefly for use in connection with race meetings. On the L.N.E.R. these were run, when required, between Liverpool Street and Newmarket.

Later on, some wider uses for this stock suggested themselves and the first of these on L.N.E.R. metals was a Sunday all-Pullman train, between Liverpool Street and Clacton-on-Sea, down at 9.55 a.m., and up at 5.10 p.m., which made a 90-minute non-stop run in each direction over this 70-mile route ; it was called the " Clacton Belle." From this there developed the idea of the " Eastern Belle Pullman Limited," giving high-speed excursion facilities of a very luxurious kind on selected days to a variety of East Coast holiday resorts.

A kind of " sailing list " was published in advance, enabling holiday-makers to pick their own days for visiting the resorts of their choice. Passengers with ordinary tickets were admitted, provided that they paid the Pullman supplements, but the greatest attraction was the cheapness of the round-trip day tickets, with supplements included, which took the " Eastern Belle " patrons as far afield as Cromer, Sheringham, Yarmouth, Lowestoft or Skegness and back for no more than 11s. 3d. first class and 7s. 9d. third class. Cheap meals, served to passengers in their seats from the two kitchens in each train, were another attractive feature. A further novelty was the issue of season tickets covering a week of this varied travel.

Over all of the routes covered, the times of the " Eastern Belle " at least equalled those of the best ordinary trains, and to or from some of the resorts concerned, the Pullman train was faster than any regularly scheduled service. If travelling down the Colchester line from Liverpool Street (except to Clacton-on-Sea) departure was at 11 a.m. On the Cromer days the schedule of 2 hours, 55 minutes equalled that of the old G.E.R. " Norfolk Coast Express," though with stops both at Wroxham and North Walsham. On other days the run was to West Runton and Sheringham, reached at 2.5 p.m. To Yarmouth and Lowestoft, non-stop in either case, the time allowance was $2\frac{1}{2}$ hours, and to Felixstowe 2 hours.

Coming back, the arrival time at Liverpool Street was 10.35 p.m., and this meant leaving Sheringham at 7.20 p.m., or Cromer at 7.40 p.m., or Yarmouth or Lowestoft at 8.5 p.m. ; from Felixstowe there was an earlier timing, leaving at 7.35 p.m., and arriving at 9.35 p.m.

Other weekday runs were made to Frinton-on-Sea and Walton-on-the-Naze at 11.50 a.m., reaching Walton at 1.40 p.m., and to Clacton at the same time, with an overall journey of 100 minutes ; in the reverse direction, departure was from Walton at 7.50 p.m., or Clacton at 7.55 p.m., to reach Liverpool Street at 9.37 p.m. Alternative runs were made down the Cambridge line, starting at 11.5 a.m.   One of these was to Hunstanton, 112 miles from London, nominally non-stop over the 97 miles to King's Lynn, but actually, in the absence of water-troughs, requiring the engine to stop for water at Cambridge or Ely.   Hunstanton was reached at 1.57 p.m., and the return journey, begun at 6.55 p.m., brought the train into London at 9.35 p.m.

Another interesting departure at 11.5 a.m. was to Skegness. Until then this Lincolnshire coast resort, on what was once the Great Northern Railway, had always been a King's Cross preserve, and a service from Liverpool Street was a novelty.   The route was through Cambridge and Ely to March and Spalding, where the old G.N.R. line from Peterborough to Boston and Grimsby was joined. For the entire 144·4 miles the time allowance was 3½ hours, but the return journey was 20 minutes quicker ; departure was at 6.50 p.m., and arrival at Liverpool Street 10 p.m.

The journeys which required the " Eastern Belle Pullman Limited " to make non-stop runs of over 100 miles were Cromer or Sheringham (non-stop to Wroxham, 122·8 miles in 145 minutes, average 50·8 m.p.h.) ; Yarmouth, 121·7 miles in 150 minutes, 48·7 m.p.h. ; and Lowestoft, 117·7 miles in 150 minutes, 47·1 m.p.h. In view of the difficulties of each route the locomotive work needed was of a high order.   The engines used were generally either 3-cylinder 4–6–0's of the " B 17 " or " Sandringham " type, or the large reboilered ex-Great Eastern 4–6–0's of the " B 12 " class. The load was one of eight Pullmans, of both eight-wheel and twelve-wheel types, weighing in all about 320 tons.

25—The " Fenman "

It could hardly be said that the " star turn " of Eastern Region train services is found on the Cambridge main line out of Liverpool Street.   Since the halcyon days before the Second World War, when five-coach buffet car trains were making the run of 55¾ miles between Liverpool Street and Cambridge three times daily in 65 minutes each way—the fastest service ever offered—the train service over this line has steadily worsened. Today the fastest train on the service, the "Fenman," subject of this chapter, needs 80 minutes to make the non-stop run in the down direction, and 75 minutes for the return run to London.

There are, of course, extenuating circumstances. The 5–mile exit from Liverpool Street to Copper Mill Junction is the most tortuous and difficult used by any main line trains out of London. Between Hackney Downs and Clapton Junction it is double line only, and the Cambridge trains have to be dovetailed in with the dense Walthamstow and Chingford suburban service. In the last two decades, the Lea Valley has become highly industrialised, and this has made it necessary to superimpose on a double-track main line (with a fair length of goods loops) already carrying a very heavy freight traffic and a number of main line passenger trains, a busy outer suburban passenger service, with very frequent stops between Tottenham and Cheshunt. At rush hour periods, it is practically impossible to arrange a clear path for express passenger trains, and the whole line between Tottenham and Broxbourne Junction is in urgent need of doubling.

Possibly rather more speed use could be made of the section between Broxbourne and Cambridge, where the only serious obstacles are the severe speed restriction over Bishops Stortford station curve, and the modest climb (more long-drawn-out from the north side) up to Elsenham summit in both directions. The extraordinary layout of Cambridge station, with its one enormously long platform for both up and down main line trains, also is the reverse of helpful to down trains in making a punctual arrival at the university town.

The main portion of the "Fenman," with buffet car, begins its journey at Hunstanton each morning at 6.45 a.m., calling at all stations over the $15\frac{1}{4}$ miles to King's Lynn, reached at 7.21 a.m. In the terminal station here the train is reversed, and leaves for London at 7.30 a.m. With stops at Downham and Ely, it strolls across the flat Fenland to make its appearance in Cambridge at 8.31 a.m. Meantime a through portion has left Bury St. Edmunds at 7.57 a.m., making westwards through Newmarket to run into Cambridge 10 minutes later. The train is assembled in similarly unhurried fashion, and leaves for Liverpool Street at 8.48 a.m., arriving at 10.3 a.m., the journey of $112\frac{1}{4}$ miles from Hunstanton having taken no less than 3 hours, 18 minutes.

Similar leisurely progress characterises the return journey. Going north, the "Fenman" is the lineal descendant of the 4.30 p.m. from Liverpool Street to York, a Great Eastern express of days before the First World War which also was non-stop to Cambridge, but in 72 minutes rather than the present 80 minutes. To-day's "Fenman" reaches Cambridge at 5.50 p.m., and the Bury section is the first to leave, at 5.58 p.m. ; it reaches Bury St. Edmunds at 6.45 p.m. The Hunstanton train follows at 6.4 p.m., running into Ely at 6.24 p.m. (17 minutes later than the G.E.R.

4.30 p.m. fifty years earlier!), King's Lynn at 7.14 p.m., and Hunstanton at 7.55 p.m., having taken 3 hours, 25 minutes for an overall average of 33 miles per hour!

The locomotive is usually one of the ubiquitous "B1" 4–6–0's, but this may be replaced by a "B17" 4–6–0 of the "Sandringham" type, or an *ex*-Great Eastern "B12/3" 4–6–0, as a reminder of earlier and happier days. The name "Fenman" was conferred on these trains with the introduction of the 1949 summer time-tables.

26—The "Flying Scotsman"

Probably the distinction of being the first Anglo-Scottish express to receive a title belongs to the train which, without interruption from June, 1862, to the present day, has moved out of King's Cross terminus in London at 10 o'clock every weekday morning on its journey of 392¾ miles to Edinburgh Waverley. For a brief period during the First World War, in 1917 and 1918, the train left London at 9.30 a.m., but the 10 a.m. departure was soon restored, and there has been no such interruption in the Second World War period or since.

Precisely when the name "Flying Scotsman" came into use it is difficult to say; it has certainly been in vogue for well over half a century. But it was not until after the formation of the London & North Eastern Railway had brought into one company the three partners in the East Coast route—the Great Northern, North Eastern and North British lines—that the title was officially adopted, and began to be shown on the headboards of the carriages, and in timetables and other public announcements.

When it first appeared, the 10 a.m. from King's Cross was known as a "Special Scotch Express." As far as Retford it carried a through portion for Sheffield and Manchester; at York there was a halt from 2.25 to 2.55 p.m., to enable passengers to obtain lunch; and Edinburgh was reached at 8.30 p.m., in 10½ hours from London. The corresponding up train, however, took an hour longer. In January, 1871, the N.E.R. line was opened from Shaftholme Junction, north of Doncaster, to York through Selby (the previous route was through Knottingley and Church Fenton), and in 1872 the same company completed the direct Team Valley line from Durham to Newcastle; and with these and other aids to faster running the journey in both directions had come down to 9 hours by 1876.

In November, 1887, the decision was reached to admit third-class passengers to the "Flying Scotsman"; and this momentous announcement helped to precipitate the "Race to Edinburgh" of the following year. Schedule times were slashed by both the

East Coast and West Coast companies ; in the 17 days from July 27th to August 13th, the East Coast accelerated the " Flying Scotsman " from 9 to 7¾ hours, and on August 14th the famous train made its appearance in Edinburgh Waverley at 5.32 p.m., 13 minutes early, in 7 hours, 32 minutes from London. Matters then quietened down until the last day of the month, when this time was bettered with one of 7 hours, 26¾ minutes, notwithstanding 26½ minutes spent at York for lunch.

The final schedule of August, 1888, allowed 117 minutes for the 105·5 miles from King's Cross to Grantham, 88 minutes for the 82·7 miles on to York (reached in 3½ hours), and 20 minutes at York ; next came 93 minutes for the 80·6 miles on to Newcastle, reached by the old High Level Bridge, and, after reversal there, 137 minutes for the 124·5 miles from Newcastle to Edinburgh. Water-troughs were not yet in use, and the North Eastern 4-4-0 locomotives had to carry enough water in their tenders for this lengthy run. Between London and York, of course, the famous Stirling " 8-footers " of the Great Northern were used. Engines were changed at Grantham, York and Newcastle.

After the 1888 " Race " had collapsed by agreement between the competitors, the schedule of the " Flying Scotsman " settled down to 8½ hours each way and, apart from the 15 minute curtailment of the York " lunch " stop after the introduction of restaurant cars in 1900, it was destined to remain unchanged for many years. This was the result of an agreement reached between the East and West Coast companies, after the " Race to Aberdeen " in 1895, that the overall times of the day trains between London and both Edinburgh and Glasgow should not be cut below 8¼ hours.

It is astonishing that the " Flying Scotsman " should have had to wait 21 years from the introduction on the Great Northern Railway of the first British dining cars before being provided with cars of its own ; but the development, when it came, was one of great thoroughness. On August 1st, 1900, two new trains appeared on the 10 a.m. services from King's Cross and Edinburgh Waverley. Each consisted of eight 12-wheel cars, 65 ft. 6 in. long, with bow ends, Buckeye automatic couplers, Pullman vestibules, and clerestory roofs—a revolutionary advance on the stock previously in use. The trains weighed 265 tons, and seated 50 first-class and 211 third-class passengers. Locomotive power had increased to suit, for on the Great Northern the Stirling 4-2-2 engines had given place in turn to the Ivatt 4-4-0's, and then to the first of the Ivatt Atlantics. The North Eastern Railway in 1900 was just bringing into use the efficient " R " class 4-4-0's of Wilson Worsdell's design.

For reasons already given, the next stage of " Flying Scotsman" history was dull. Trains of new rolling stock appeared in 1914, including a set of three restaurant cars in which, for the first time, an entirely separate kitchen and pantry car was included. Three years later, in the middle of the First World War, the restaurant cars were withdrawn, and the " Flying Scotsman " was slowed

Left: During the short reign of the " Eastern Belle Pullman,"—L.N.E.R. Class " B12 " 4–6–0 No. 8509 hauling the down express in pre-electrification days near Shenfield

[*H. Gordon Tidey*

Below: The " Flying Scotsman " on its northbound course near Hatfield, headed by E.R. Class " A3 " Pacific No. 60039 *Sandwich*

[*E. D. Bruton*

Left : The Bury St. Edmunds portion of the down " Fenman " at the north end of the lengthy platform at Cambridge, headed by Class " D15 " 4–4–0 No. 62508 (since scrapped)

[*H. N. A. Shelton*

Centre Left : The Lowestoft portion of the down " Easterling " leaves Beccles behind a tender-first Class " J15 " 0–6–0
[*R. E. Vincent*

Above : Compound 4–4–0 No. 41125 pilots Standard Class " 5 " 4–6–0 No. 73005 out of Aberdeen with the " Granite City " for Glasgow
[*C. Lawson Kerr*

Lower Left : E.R. streamlined Class " B17 " 4–6–0 No. 61659 *East Anglian* (now de-streamlined). winds its namesake into Liverpool Street on the up run
[*R. E. Vincent*

Below : A humdrum duty for the one-time " Silver Jubilee " stock—Class " B1 " 4–6–0 No. 61403 approaches Elie with the down " Fife Coast Express "
[*W. J. V. Anderson*

Above : Curving round the Bickley-Petts
Wood Loop, Class " 7MT " 4–6–2 No.
70004 *William Shakespeare* heads the
down " Golden Arrow "

[*B. E. Morrison*

Inset right : S.R. Class " D " 4–4–0 No.
31549 approaches Canterbury East with the
Canterbury section of the 1951 " Kentish
Belle "

[*P. Ransome-Wallis*

Below : E.R. Class " A4 " Pacific No.
60033 *Andrew K. McCosh* eases the down
" Heart of Midlothian " into York

[*Leslie Overend*

ultimately to 9 hours, 50 minutes in each direction. But the end of the war saw a rapid return to normal, with restaurant cars early in 1919, and the old 8¼ hour schedule restored by 1923. Another pair of new trains came into service in 1924, and the " Flying Scotsman" for the first time acquired a set of three restaurant cars articulated on the Gresley system, and also equipped for cooking by electricity.

While the schedule time agreement between the East Coast and West Coast Companies continued in force, it was necessary for the rivals to find other outlets for their competitive energy. One form taken by this rivalry was non-stop running over great distances, which finally resulted, from May, 1928, in the " Flying Scotsman " being scheduled to make the longest non-stop run in the world, over the 392·9 miles between King's Cross and Edinburgh.

A new train was put into service, including a coach, marshalled next the restaurant cars, which contained a cocktail bar, a retiring room for ladies, and a hairdressing room with barber complete— all novelties in British practice, and designed to beguile, in various ways, the hours of this lengthy journey.

To make possible a change of crew *en route* without stopping the train, corridor tenders were built which could be vestibuled to the leading coach, and so provided a through passage from the train corridor on to the footplate. The ludicrous aspect of the new non-stop schedule, however, was that, despite the availability of the powerful Gresley Pacific locomotives which had been first introduced in 1922, the L.N.E. and L.M.S. train time agreement compelled the " Flying Scotsman " to spin out the full 8¼ hours on the journey, and so to maintain an average speed of no more than 47·6 m.p.h. The much heavier main train that followed the " non-stop " daily made all the usual stops and took exactly the same time !

At last, in 1932, when trains in all parts of the country were being speeded up, the minimum time agreement could be maintained no longer. In May of that year came the first acceleration of the " Flying Scotsman " that had taken place for 32 years ; 25 minutes were cut from the schedule in each direction, reducing the time to 7 hours, 50 minutes between King's Cross and Edinburgh. When the non-stop first portion, which has always operated during the summer only, began to run in July, a more enterprising cut of 45 minutes on the previous summer's schedule brought the overall time down to 7½ hours, and the speed up to 52·3 m.p.h.; in 1936 this became 7¼ hours, and in 1937 7 hours, with an average speed now raised to 56·1 m.p.h. Corresponding reductions were made in the winter schedule, until in 1938 and 1939, up to the outbreak of the Second World War, the " Flying Scotsman," with all the stops included, was running between London and Edinburgh in 7 hours, 20 minutes each way.

This winter schedule provided one of the hardest locomotive tasks in the country. For in 1938 yet another new pair of trains

E

had been introduced, and this time with electrically-driven air-conditioning plant on each coach, which increased the weight of the stock considerably. Going north, the formation from the engine was a brake third and composite coach for Glasgow; a composite with luggage compartment for Perth; three thirds, a buffet car, a triplet articulated restaurant car set and a first for Edinburgh; and a composite, third, and brake third for Aberdeen, fourteen vehicles in all, weighing no less than 504 tons. Occasionally one of the Edinburgh thirds might be cut out; but more often, especially at week-ends and in the up direction, the load would be added to, and the hard-worked locomotive might then have behind the tender 15 or 16 bogies of this heavy stock, with a total load behind the tender of fully 600 tons. The use of a full-length buffet car for light refreshments, in addition to the restaurant cars proper, was an innovation derived from American practice.

By some curious tradition, for many years past, the work demanded of the engines south of York, relatively to the gradients, had always been harder than north of that point. So it was with the "Flying Scotsman." From King's Cross northwards, the 10 a.m. was required to run the 105·5 miles to Grantham, notwithstanding the 1 in 105 start, the 8-mile pull at 1 in 200 to Potter's Bar, the severe slack through Peterborough and the lengthy grind at 1 in 200 and 1 in 178 to Stoke Summit, in 110 minutes. A stop of 2 minutes there was followed by a mile-a-minute sprint to York—82·7 miles in 83 minutes—and that city was reached at 1.15 p.m. After 4 minutes at York, there was a relatively easy allowance of 90 minutes for the 80·2 miles to Newcastle, almost dead level to Darlington, and with no severe handicaps beyond, other than the slowing through Durham. For the 67·0 miles from Newcastle to Berwick the train had 77 minutes, and for the 57·5 miles on to Edinburgh 67 minutes; neither of these lengths had any grades more severe, in the northbound direction, than those between London and Grantham.

Southbound, the "Flying Scotsman" had to tackle the formidable Cockburnspath bank, south of Dunbar—4 miles at 1 in 96 up—in the course of a 65-minute schedule to Berwick; from Berwick to Newcastle in 75 minutes was relatively easy, as also the 48 minutes allowed for the 36 miles from Newcastle to Darlington, where the only severe obstacle was the recovery up a short 1 in 101 gradient from the bad slack through Durham. But it was after leaving Darlington, at 1.18 p.m., that the hard work began, and it got progressively harder as the journey proceeded. The straight and level 44·1 miles from Darlington to York had to be run in 45 minutes (58·8 m.p.h.); the 82·7 miles from York to Grantham in 85½ minutes (58·4 m.p.h.); and then, to crown all, the engine was left 105½ minutes in which to run the 105½ miles on to King's Cross at exactly 60 m.p.h. With a load of 550 to 600 tons, the schedule of this train had no superior in the country for difficulty, and probably, indeed, no rival. Engines were changed in each direction at

Newcastle only. Such was the precision of timing that the stop at Grantham was booked to half-minutes—from 3.32½ to 3.34½ p.m. !

As to the sections of the northbound " Flying Scotsman," the Aberdeen portion, on the rear, was drawn back on arrival at Edinburgh, and attached to the 5.40 p.m. restaurant car express, calling at Kirkcaldy, Cupar, Leuchars Junction, Dundee, Broughty Ferry, Arbroath, Montrose and Stonehaven, and reaching Aberdeen at 9 p.m. In summer, however, when the non-stop service was being run between London and Edinburgh, a much faster service was arranged ; passengers then left Edinburgh at 5.15 p.m., and were in Aberdeen at 8.15 p.m., in 10¼ hours from London. The Glasgow coaches were taken off the front of the " Flying Scotsman," and transferred to the 5.43 p.m. restaurant car express, which brought them into Queen Street at 6.45 p.m., and the Perth coach was worked forward similarly by the 5.55 p.m. train, reaching Perth at 7.13 p.m. In the reverse direction, the first section to start was that from Aberdeen, in a breakfast car train at the early hour of 6.40 a.m. ; the Perth coach left at 8.25 a.m., and the Glasgow vehicles at 8.35 a.m., all being marshalled in order in the London train before departure from Waverley at 10 a.m.

During the Second World War there were numerous changes in the schedule of the " Flying Scotsman " ; the through service was confined to London-Edinburgh, and for most of the war period two trains in each direction ran daily. Preceded by a relief train at 9.40 a.m., the " Flying Scotsman " proper, at 10 a.m. from King's Cross, settled down to a call at Peterborough only (11.38–11.45 a.m.) between London and York, reached at 2.2 p.m. ; then, after a stop of 13 minutes, at Newcastle (3.55–4.5 p.m.) and Berwick (5.29–5.34 p.m.), with an arrival in Waverley at 6.55 p.m. Coming south, the train called at Berwick and Newcastle, and then at Darlington from 1.41 to 1.46 p.m., after which York was missed, and the next stop was at Grantham from 4.25 to 4.35 p.m. The up " Flying Scotsman " reached London at 6.45 p.m., in 8¾ hours.

From October 1st, 1945, however, there was a revolutionary speed-up. The down " Flying Scotsman," complete once again with its restaurant cars, but with stops unchanged, was accelerated by no less than 50 minutes, to reach Edinburgh at 6.5 p.m. The up express came down to an 8-hour schedule, arriving in London at 6 p.m., and the relief services in each direction received equally drastic treatment. In October, 1946, new timings came into force ; the old Grantham stop replaced that at Peterborough, and then followed a non-stop run to Newcastle, 162·9 miles ; with a third stop at Berwick, the " Scotsman " was due into Edinburgh at 6.10 p.m. Coming south the 8-hour schedule and the stops remained unaltered.

To make up for increased times, vast loads have been run. For a matter of years, during the earlier part of the war, the train was seldom made up of less than 20 bogie vehicles, with a loaded weight of 680 tons or more, but on many occasions this increased, in the up direction especially, to 21, 22, and even 23 bogies, which with packed complements of passengers and their luggage brought the total weight behind the engine tenders to little short of 800 tons. These trains were worked single-headed for the most part by the highly competent streamlined Pacifics of the " A4 " class. In the late stages of the war, however, with indifferent coal and lower than normal standards of maintenance it became necessary to lay down a limit of 18 bogies, bringing the gross load down to about 625 tons, and later 15 bogies became the maximum. To-day the train is further restricted to 13 bogies, with a tare weight of about 475 tons.

In the summer of 1949, as it became more convenient to run the non-stop service between London and Edinburgh as a relief to the " Flying Scotsman " proper, and as it was not desired to alter the time-honoured 10 a.m. start of the latter, a new train called the " Capitals Limited " took over the non-stop working. It is of interest to recall that during September, 1948, while the then non-stop " Flying Scotsman " was being diverted between Tweedmouth and Edinburgh by way of Kelso and Galashiels (because of the breaches in the main line north of Berwick), there were several occasions on which the journey of 408½ miles was actually made without stopping—the longest non-stop runs ever made in British history. The " Flying Scotsman " itself has settled down to a schedule with stops at Grantham and Newcastle only, involving non-stop runs in succession of 105·5, 162·9 and 124·5 miles. The 1952–53 winter timetable allows 7 hours, 50 minutes each way between King's Cross and Edinburgh, and that of the previous summer 12 minutes less.

The pre-war Glasgow section of the " Flying Scotsman " has now become a complete restaurant car train, which acts as a relief to the " Flying Scotsman." The former leaves Kings Cross at 10.5 a.m., and, calling at Peterborough, York, Darlington, Durham, Newcastle and Berwick, reaches Edinburgh at 6.26 p.m. and Glasgow at 7.53 p.m. In the southbound direction the corresponding train, with the same stops, leaves Glasgow at 8.35 a.m. and Edinburgh at 10.10 a.m., and is due in London at 6.27 p.m. The down Glasgow train carries the pre-war Aberdeen coaches of the " Flying Scotsman," but in the up direction these are once more attached on the rear of the " Flying Scotsman " itself from Edinburgh.

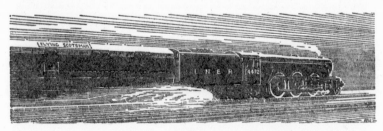

27—The "Golden Arrow"

For many years the South Eastern & Chatham Railway and its successor, the Southern Railway, had maintained a service to Paris leaving Victoria at 11 a.m., but the title " Golden Arrow " was not bestowed on the train until 1929, when, in the palmy pre-depression days, it was decided to inaugurate a service exclusively for first-class Pullman passengers between the two capitals. A special steamer, the *Canterbury*, was built to provide for the Channel crossing between Dover and Calais, and the trains of both sides—the " Golden Arrow " in England and the " Flèche d'Or " in France—were composed exclusively of Pullman cars, with the necessary vans added for luggage. An independent service of trains on both sides, with a separate steamer, provided for ordinary first and second-class passengers who desired to travel at a cheaper fare than the inclusive £5 rate for the " Golden Arrow " journey.

Leaving Victoria at 11 a.m., the " Golden Arrow " was due at Dover Marine station at 12.38 p.m. For transfer to the *Canterbury* the time allowed was 17 minutes, and for the crossing from Dover to Calais 75 minutes. On what was then the Northern Railway of France, the " Flèche d'Or " was waiting on the quayside, headed by one of the famous four-cylinder compound Nord Pacifics, and was booked to cover the 184 miles from Calais to Paris in 190 minutes, bringing passengers into the French capital at 5.35 p.m. On the English side, a train of ten Pullmans and two brakes was needed to accommodate the traffic.

As the first-class traffic began to fall off in the depression years, however, and with the increasing tendency of this class of passenger to save time by making use of air travel, before many years had passed it was found impossible any longer to justify a service confined to first-class passengers alone. Most of the hitherto exclusive *trains-de-luxe* on the Continent were beginning to admit second-class passengers, and second-class sleeping cars were appearing on the " Blue Train," the " Rome Express," and many other famous services. The " Golden Arrow " then followed suit ; on the English side the first-class Pullmans were supplemented by first and second class corridor coaches, and on the French side, where two trains were still necessary, a second-class Pullman joined the first-class cars, as well as the through sleepers for the " Blue Train " and other long-distance services. This change took place in May, 1931.

For many years the " Lord Nelson " four-cylinder 4-6-0's generally monopolised the " Golden Arrow " workings, though " King Arthurs " have taken their turn from time to time. The maximum load that the 4-6-0's of either type have been permitted to take over this difficult route has been 425 tons. Before the outbreak of the Second World War a train of four Pullmans, six corridor coaches, and two 6-wheel brakes normally sufficed for the " Golden Arrow," and as the tare weight of such a formation was about 375 tons, it could be expanded by two coaches, if necessary.

The route between Victoria and Dover is anything but easy from the locomotive point of view. The principal difficulty is concentrated in the 30½ miles between London and Tonbridge, with its lengthy ascents in both directions to Knockholt summit. The down journey begins with the 1 in 62 climb out of the terminus on to the Grosvenor Bridge, and subsequent adverse gradients include 1½ miles at 1 in 102 to Penge tunnel, and 2 miles at 1 in 95 to Bickley Junction, with slow running round the curve to Orpington. But the worst continuous climb is on the up run, where the " Golden Arrow," after reducing speed for the curve beyond Tonbridge, is faced with 4 miles up at 1 in 122, and 2 miles at 1 in 144, the latter through Sevenoaks tunnel. Over the well-aligned and fairly level stretch east of Tonbridge, however, high speeds are possible, and in normal conditions are frequently attained.

The down " Golden Arrow " had always left Victoria at 11 a.m., and latterly was booked to reach Dover Marine at 12.35 p.m., so covering the 78 miles in 95 minutes, at an average of 49·3 m.p.h. But the allowance of 41½ minutes for the 41·4 miles from Tonbridge to Folkestone Junction demanded a mile-a-minute average over this length.

Whereas the boat on the outward service worked from Dover to Calais, for some years up to the war the return service was routed *via* Boulogne-Folkestone, and the inward " Golden Arrow " therefore started from Folkestone Harbour. Alternative paths were provided in the working timetable, including one 10 minutes later, but if the boat was punctual, the normal scheduled departure was 3.44 p.m. The first stage of the journey was up the steepest gradient on the entire Southern Railway system, at 1 in 30 for ¾ mile, from the Harbour to the sidings at the Junction station, for which at least two and sometimes three 0–6–0 tanks were needed; the allowance for the 1·2 miles was 5 minutes.

At Folkestone Junction, the " Lord Nelson " 4–6–0 was waiting, and backed on to the opposite end of the train, leaving for London at 3.54 p.m. The start of the run was very fast, as the " Golden Arrow " was booked to pass Tonbridge, 41·4 miles, in 42½ minutes; of this distance the 35·9 miles from Sandling Junction to Tonbridge were allowed 33 minutes only, a scheduled average of 65·3 m.p.h. Then followed the stiff climb to Knockholt and the cautious running required through the London suburbs, so that 43½ minutes were conceded for the 30·6 miles from Tonbridge into Victoria, where the arrival was 5.20 p.m.

The " Golden Arrow " disappeared, of course, with the outbreak of war, but was reinstated on April 15th, 1946, leaving Victoria at 10 a.m., and with 100 minutes (later accelerated to 95 minutes and in 1952 to 92 minutes) allowed to Dover Marine. The formation is now ten Pullmans and two vans, and the locomotive, usually a " Merchant Navy " Pacific, carries large gilt arrows on its sides and on the smokebox door. In the 1952–1953 winter timetable a radical alteration was made in the outward journey, for the " Golden Arrow," for the first time in its history, was transferred to the afternoon service leaving Victoria at 2 p.m. (and, from the change of time in October, at 1 p.m.). This means a diversion from Dover to Folkestone, and, owing to the circuitous Folkestone–Calais route, a deceleration from 6 hours 52 minutes to 7 hours 34 minutes in the running time from London to Paris. The return working *via* Calais-Dover remains unchanged, however, at 12.30 p.m. from Paris, and 7.30 p.m. (6.30 p.m. from the change of time) into Victoria. Thus the pre-war arrangement, outward *via* Dover and inward *via* Folkestone, has been exactly reversed.

28–The "Granite City," the "Bon Accord," and the "Saint Mungo"

In 1905, as a result of spirited competition between the then Caledonian and North British Railways for the traffic between Glasgow and Edinburgh, in the south, and Dundee and Aberdeen, in the north, some magnificent new twelve-wheeled " Grampian Corridor " stock was introduced by the Caledonian for its principal services. This was formed into set trains ; in general, four coaches worked between Glasgow and Aberdeen, with restaurant car ; through coaches from Glasgow to Dundee, detached at Perth, were replaced there by through coaches from Edinburgh to Aberdeen. These morning and evening services both ways continued more or less unchanged, except for acceleration and the substitution of modern L.M.S.R. rolling stock, until the beginning of the Second World War.

In Caledonian days, the restaurant car catering was taken over by the Pullman Car Company, whose contract extended to 1933, well into the L.M.S.R. era ; on its expiry, the L.M.S.R. bought the cars, and painted them in the L.M.S.R. crimson livery. Later on, standard L.M.S.R. cars of the latest type were substituted for the Pullman vehicles.

With the general outbreak of train naming on the L.M.S.R., one of these trains received the permanent name, winter and summer alike, of the " Granite City." It was the 10.5 a.m. express from Glasgow to Aberdeen, returning from the Granite City, as Aberdeen is often known, at 5.35 in the evening. As a result of acceleration, which eventually brought the Glasgow-Aberdeen time of the north-bound train down to 3½ hours, including eight intermediate stops in the 153 miles, some very tight point-to-point timings were in force. For example, the 15·8 miles from Perth to Coupar Angus, with a steeply rising start, had to be run in 20 minutes, the 16·7 miles from there to Forfar in 18 minutes, and the 15·4 miles from Forfar to Bridge of Dun in 19 minutes. Coming south, the " Granite City " was expected to cover the 32·5 miles from Forfar to Perth in 35 minutes ; this train took 3 hours, 39 minutes, reaching Buchanan Street Station in Glasgow at 9.14 p.m.   It is of interest to recall that for many years the 5.30 p.m. from Aberdeen (as it was then) ran round through Coatbridge into Glasgow Central Station, instead of into Buchanan Street.

These timings had to be maintained over a route with long and arduous gradients throughout its length, save only for the racing stretch between Perth and Forfar.   Out of Buchanan Street there is a very steep climb of $2\frac{1}{2}$ miles at 1 in 79-98 through St. Rollox to Robroyston ; between Cumbernauld and Larbert there are over 5 miles down at 1 in 98 to 1 in 128.   Then from Stirling northwards the trains face a $6\frac{1}{2}$-mile climb mostly at 1 in 75-100 up to Kinbuck ; with a corresponding 7-mile descent from Gleneagles northwards. From Bridge of Dun to Drumlithie, $10\frac{1}{2}$ miles out of $17\frac{1}{2}$ are uphill, followed by the steep 5-mile descent to and past Stonehaven ; in addition to mounting the latter, southbound trains have the even worse start out of Aberdeen, beginning at 1 in 96, and continuing for 7 miles, to beyond Newtonhill.   From nearly all the principal starts— Glasgow, Stirling, Perth, Stonehaven and Aberdeen in particular— the engines are faced with steeply rising gradients, many of them lengthy and difficult.

During the last summer seasons before the Second World War, some much more elaborate arrangements were brought into force over this route, and resulted both in the appearance of two additional named trains and in the cutting of the Glasgow-Aberdeen time to the unprecedentedly low figure of 3 hours flat.   The trains concerned were the " Bon Accord " and the " Saint Mungo," strictly limited, because of their speed, to eight-coach formations, restaurant car included, weighing about 260 tons empty, and worked, as usual, by " 5XP " 4-6-0 locomotives.

The northbound "Bon Accord " went out of Buchanan Street at the winter " Granite City's " time of 10.5 a.m., and ran the difficult stretch of 63·2 miles non-stop to Perth in 77 minutes.   After a 5-minute halt there, it was allowed 76 minutes for the 73·7 miles on to Stonehaven ; the final scenic stretch of 16·1 miles round the rugged cliffs to Aberdeen was run in 21 minutes, bringing the train into the Granite City at 1.5 p.m.   After $2\frac{1}{4}$ hours in Aberdeen, the " Bon Accord " began the return journey at 3.20 p.m., and with the same stops reached Buchanan Street, Glasgow, at 6.20 p.m. ; the fastest run in this direction was over the 73·7 miles from Stonehaven to Perth in 76 minutes.   The " Saint Mungo " began its working day at Aberdeen at 9.35 in the morning, and stopped at Forfar instead of Stonehaven, making a very fast run over the 32·5 miles from there to Perth in 33 minutes.   Reaching Glasgow at 12.35 p.m., it returned at 1.30 p.m., with the same stops and times on the northbound trip as the " Bon Accord," and reached Aberdeen at 4.30 p.m.   Neither the " Bon Accord " nor the " Saint Mungo " ran on Saturdays.

In the war timetables only the " Granite City " workings survived, and, of course, without their names ; the restaurant cars were continued up to the time of the general withdrawal. Scottish schedules in general have suffered less than those in other parts of the country, and for a time certain point-to-point bookings of these trains were among the fastest wartime schedules in Great Britain. From Glasgow the northbound train has continued to start at 10 a.m., and is due in Aberdeen at 1.53 p.m.; it returns at 5.30 p.m., reaching Buchanan Street at 9.37 p.m. Thus the overall timing has been lengthened by 23 minutes going north, and 28 minutes coming south, over the normal peacetime figure. Restaurant cars returned on October 1st, 1945.

In 1949 the three names were all revived, but two of them have been transferred to other trains. The 10 a.m. from Buchanan Street and the 5.30 p.m. from Aberdeen are still the "Granite City"; but the old-established 1.35 p.m. from Glasgow to Aberdeen, with the 6.25 a.m. from Aberdeen to Glasgow, have become the "Bon Accord"; and the name "Saint Mungo" has been assumed by the 9.35 a.m. southbound and the 5 p.m. northbound. In each case the one set of stock makes the return journey in the day.

29—The "Granville Express"

At Ramsgate there is a well-known hostelry called the Granville Hotel, which was opened in the 1870's, and extensively advertised. In 1877 the proprietor arranged with the then South Eastern Railway to run special trains for his week-end visitors, down on Friday afternoons and up at a gentlemanly hour on Monday mornings, and the upshot was the "Granville Express," which began to run in March, 1877, between Charing Cross and Ramsgate. Canon R. B. Fellows, the railway historian, believes the S.E.R. "Granville Express" to have been the first train in Great Britain to carry a distinctive title.

The allowance at first was $2\frac{1}{4}$ hours, but after a brilliant inaugural run in $1\frac{3}{4}$ hours, the timing from April onwards was cut to 1 hour 55 minutes down, and 2 hours 10 minutes up. Non-stop runs were made in each direction over the 85 miles between Cannon Street and Ramsgate, *via* Tonbridge and Ashford, and the down journey schedule of 105 minutes demanded a start-to-stop average of 48.6 m.p.h.—a brilliant achievement for the period. From June the train, until then first class only, carried second class passengers, and in July it was extended to Margate. It left Charing Cross at 3.45 p.m., and Ramsgate at 8.40 a.m.

During 1878 deceleration began, and intermediate stops appeared, and the train at times bore the name, and at other times was nameless. In 1888 the title "Granville Express" reappeared in connection with an express leaving Charing Cross at 3.25 p.m.

and Margate at 9.30 a.m., daily except Sundays, but the speed now, excluding stops, had dropped to a fraction over 40 m.p.h. So far as the South Eastern line is concerned, the name was dropped finally on the formation of the S.E. & C.R. in 1899.

A year after the inauguration of the original " Granville Express," the highly competitive London, Chatham & Dover Railway put on, in April, 1878, " The Granville and Westgate-on-Sea Special Express Train," running every weekday and conveying passengers of all three classes. This left Victoria at 3.15 p.m., called at Herne Hill for its connection from Holborn Viaduct, and then ran the 68.4 miles to Westgate non-stop at 46 m.p.h. Margate was reached at 5 p.m., Broadstairs at 5.10 p.m., and Ramsgate at 5.15 p.m. The return service left Ramsgate at 10 a.m. and was due in Victoria at 12 noon. Soon the title was altered simply to " Granville Express."

Before the First World War the " Granville " was leaving Victoria at 3.25 p.m., and calling at Herne Hill to pick up a portion that had come from King's Cross by way of the Metropolitan line, Snow Hill and Ludgate Hill. The latter was in connection with Great Northern expresses from Yorkshire and the Midlands, and the Ludgate Hill stop added a City service to that from the West End given by the main train. The next halt was at Westgate-on-Sea, at 5.5 p.m., and subsequent stops at Margate and Broadstairs preceded the arrival at Ramsgate Harbour at 5.27 p.m. This terminus, of course, ceased to exist when in later years the whole of the operations of the late London, Chatham & Dover and South Eastern Railways were concentrated in a new through station of the Southern Railway at Ramsgate.

The up " Granville " in 1914 still took precisely two hours from Ramsgate to Victoria. Leaving at 10 a.m., with the same stops and the same 90-minute run between Westgate and Herne Hill, it shed at the latter the section for King's Cross, and reached Victoria at 12 noon, unchanged from its arrival time 36 years earlier.

By twenty-five years later, the " Granville " had become a train of corridor stock of the most up-to-date Southern type, with a composite first and third-class Pullman car, which also served refreshments along the length of the train. The through portion from King's Cross never reappeared after the First World War, the stops at Herne Hill and Westgate had gone, and the express was booked to make the run of 73·9 miles to Margate in the excellent time, considering the extreme difficulty of the route, of 90 minutes. With further stops at Broadstairs and Dumpton Park (the latter station of comparatively recent construction) the train reached Ramsgate, 79·3 miles from Victoria, in 1 hour, 50 minutes. The start was at 3.15 p.m. and the arrival at 5.5 p.m. Coming up, the " Granville " was away from Ramsgate at 10.10 a.m., made the same calls and Westgate in addition, running non-stop from there to Victoria in 92 minutes ; arrival was at 12.5 noon.

Mention has been made of the formidable difficulty of this route, and with justice, for no less than 31 miles of its length are as steep as from 1 in 95 to 1 in 110, and there are 12 miles further at 1 in 132, not to mention the extremely severe service slack round the curves at Rochester and slowings of lesser severity at Kent House, Beckenham Junction, Faversham and elsewhere. By far the worst bank is that which faces up trains after slowing through Rochester, for 5 miles up to Sole Street, mostly at 1 in 100. The climb in the other direction, though 6¼ miles long, and including 3 miles at 1 in 100 and a mile at 1 in 132, is more broken, and can be tackled with the impetus gained by the high speed through Farningham Road, often 75 m.p.h. and at times up to 80 m.p.h. and more.

The normal class of engine for the " Granville " ultimately became the 4–4–0 " Schools," though a " King Arthur " 4–6–0 was used from time to time, and a " Lord Nelson " 4–6–0 might make an occasional appearance. Loads varied from 9 to 11 bogie vehicles, according to the season of the year, of a total weight of 310 to 370 tons, including passengers and luggage. Now the West Country Pacifics are available, and the gradients of this hard route have lost their terrors, with such greatly enhanced locomotive power.

There is still a recognisable version of the down " Granville " in the 3.35 p.m. from Victoria, now with restaurant instead of Pullman car, but numerous intermediate stops have been introduced and arrival at Ramsgate is not until 6.8 p.m.—an overall time 43 minutes longer than the pre-war best.

30—The "Heart of Midlothian"

The afternoon services between King's Cross and Edinburgh, by the East Coast route, which were provided with new standard stock and named the " Heart of Midlothian " in honour of the 1951 Festival of Britain, have had a very lengthy history. Before the First World War departures from both King's Cross and Edinburgh were at 2.20 p.m., and with stops at Grantham, York, Darlington, Newcastle, and Berwick—and Doncaster and Peterborough in addition coming south—the journey was a leisurely one, taking 8 hours, 25 minutes in each direction. In the first decade of the present century, the down express was one of the last Great Northern trains to carry a slip coach, which it detached at Doncaster.

In the period between the wars the times of starting were considerably altered, and gradually settled down to 1.20 p.m. from London and 2.5 p.m. from Edinburgh, while the post-1932 accelerations eventually produced the very fast timings of 7 hours, 25 minutes down and 7 hours, 30 minutes up. One particularly notable booking of the down express was over the 124·5 miles from

Newcastle to Edinburgh in 130 minutes; this was made possible by shedding at Newcastle a through portion for principal stations between there and Edinburgh, while the main train ran non-stop—a practice which is still followed during the height of the summer season.

During the Second World War, starting times varied considerably; since the war the King's Cross start, at first 1 p.m., was changed to 1.15 p.m., and now, in accordance with the systematic departure plan, has become 2 p.m., as has also that from Edinburgh to King's Cross. Through the winter timetable the stops in the down direction are at Peterborough, York, Darlington, Newcastle, Berwick and Dunbar, while in the summer, as already mentioned, the Newcastle-Edinburgh run is made non-stop; coming south, they are at Berwick, Newcastle, Darlington, York, and Grantham. The southbound express carries a through portion from Aberdeen, which has started on its journey at 9.55 a.m. A curious feature of the " Heart of Midlothian " workings is that in summer the down train is the faster of the two—7 hours, 50 minutes as against 8 hours, 4 minutes—whereas in winter the up train has the advantage—7 hours, 55 minutes as compared with 8 hours.

31—The "Holiday Camps Expresses"

On the Eastern Region, on Saturdays during the summer season only, there are eight trains titled " Holiday Camps Express." Two of these leave Liverpool Street at 8.5 and 10.15 a.m. respectively, call at Ipswich and Beccles to Lowestoft, arriving at 10.51 a.m. and 1.9 p.m., and continue, after reversal, to Corton, Hopton and Gorleston, reached at 11.22 a.m. and 1.37 p.m.; a third, from Liverpool Street at 11.12 a.m., is slower, because it calls at numerous stations between Ipswich and Beccles and is not due at Gorleston till 2.56 p.m., while a fourth, at 3 p.m., is much faster, for it covers the 117¾ miles to Lowestoft without a stop in 2 hours, 33 minutes, and is into Gorleston by 6.3 p.m. There are only two corresponding up workings; one is at 10.50 a.m. from Gorleston, which picks up at Hopton and Corton, but not at Lowestoft; from here there is a non-stop run to London, reached at 1.52 p.m. The other, at 1.35 p.m. from Gorleston and 2.10 p.m. from Lowestoft, calls at Beccles and Ipswich, and reaches Liverpool Street at 5.1 p.m.

Besides these there is another curious " Holiday Camps " working which takes a different route altogether. It starts from Liverpool Street at 10.50 a.m., and the only publicly advertised stop between London and Potter Heigham, on what was once the

Midland & Great Northern Joint Line (between North Walsham and Yarmouth), is at Wroxham. Actually the train stops at Ely for water, and then continues to Trowse and round the Wensum curve to the Cromer branch; after the Wroxham stop, it runs through North Walsham to Antingham Road Junction, on the Mundesley branch, where it is reversed over the spur on to the M. & G. N. line. It then continues to Potter Heigham, Hemsby, and Caister Camp Halt, and finishes its journey at Caister-on-Sea at 3.21 p.m. In the reverse direction, by the same route and with the same stops, Caister is left at 10.38 a.m., and Liverpool Street is reached at 3.28 p.m. Most of the " Holiday Camps Expresses " are provided with buffet cars.

32—The " Hook Continental," " Antwerp Continental," " Day Continental " and " Scandinavian "

It is generally agreed that the highest level of achievement of the one-time Great Eastern Railway, before its absorption into the London & North Eastern Railway, was reached in its Continental boat services. Of all these the most important was the Hook of Holland service, principal means of communication between England and the whole of North Germany and beyond. To this there was added later the Antwerp service, very popular as a route to and from Belgium because of the smooth stretch along the River Scheldt, on the Continental side, in which the passenger could breakfast in comfort on the way over, or dine on the way back. These services were rendered the more attractive by the miniature ocean liners that the G.E.R. built for the service, on which very comfortable sleeping accommodation was provided. They made possible a late evening departure from Liverpool Street, and, on the return journey, a morning arrival at the very start of the business day.

After the First World War, in order further to popularise the Belgian coast resorts, a service was established between Parkeston Quay and the Belgian port of Zeebrugge. This ran during the summer season only, but it heralded the opening-up of the all-the-year-round freight ferry service between a new terminal at Harwich and Zeebrugge.

In the year 1927 another development of great importance took place at Parkeston Quay. The fine steamers of the Zeeland Shipping Company, which for many years had worked between the Dutch port of Flushing and Queenborough, in the Thames, and then to avoid the inconvenience of the latter and the fogs in the Thames had transferred to Folkestone, for the second time changed their port on the English side, and this time to Parkeston Quay. A fifth Continental passenger service that had begun to use Parkeston Quay was the Danish service operating to and from Esbjerg, on the western side of Jutland, which after the opening of the Little Belt Bridge in 1935 was provided with a high-speed diesel streamline train to make the connection between Esbjerg and Copenhagen.

All these flourishing services concentrated on Parkeston Quay required the provision of a fleet of connecting trains over the 69 miles between this Essex port and Liverpool Street. Here again the old Great Eastern Railway did well by putting on in 1904 a specially built corridor train for the Hook of Holland service, with restaurant cars in which there was established a catering tradition that became justly famed. The train of nine bogie vehicles, three six-wheelers, and four-wheel truck for the registered luggage-boxes, weighed 287 tons. At first the time allowed for the journey in the down direction was 85 minutes; then this was increased to 87 minutes; but with the advent in 1912 of the first 4-6-0 locomotives of the "1500" class (later L.N.E.R. class "B12") the time was cut to 82 minutes.

In 1914 there came to the G.E.R., as General Manager, Mr. H. W. Thornton, who had been in the service of the Pennsylvania Railroad of the United States. An early result, when the necessary vehicles could be obtained after the First World War, was the introduction of Pullman cars on Great Eastern metals. Two first-class Pullmans were attached to the Hook of Holland boat train, and continued to run in the formation until the Second World War. In 1924 the L.N.E.R., as the G.E.R. had now become, built a new train of standard L.N.E.R. stock for the Hook service, and the job of haulage now became one for expert enginemen only.

The train was one of thirteen bogie vehicles, including the Pullmans, and weighed about 430 tons empty. With passengers and luggage, a total weight of 455 tons had to be run from Liverpool Street to Parkeston Quay at an average speed of 50·4 m.p.h. from start to stop. This included the initial climb to Bethnal Green, the long pull up Brentwood bank, the slacks through Stratford, Chelmsford, and Colchester, and a dead slowing over the turnout from the main line at Manningtree, followed by a sharp incline up which to recover speed. Four engine-crews at Parkeston shed constituted the "top link" responsible for these duties, and they were masters of their work. The "1500" class 4-6-0's were used exclusively.

In 1936 a new and still more luxurious train was built for the Hook of Holland service, and the weight was increased further to 443 tons tare. The formation in the outward direction, from the engine backwards, was third-class brake, two second-class compartment coaches, open second, second restaurant, kitchen car, first restaurant, semi-open first, compartment first, two Pullman cars, and two bogie brakes, thirteen vehicles in all, occasionally swollen to fourteen, with a gross weight of 500 tons.

By now, however, the timing had been eased, and was back at the earlier 87 minutes. Also the three-cylinder Gresley 4-6-0's of the "Sandringham" or "B17" class had been introduced, though it is doubtful if the work that they did was ever greatly superior to that of the capable G.E.R. " 1500's," especially after the latter had been fitted with larger boilers, and had had their valve-setting improved on modern lines to allow of earlier cut-off working.

The down " Hook Continental," as it became known officially in later L.N.E.R. days, for many years was booked out of Liverpool Street at 8.30 p.m. In the heyday of its speed, it was scheduled to pass Colchester, 51·7 miles, in 61 minutes, and to reach Parkeston Quay at 9.52 p.m.; after the slowing, the start from Liverpool Street was altered to 8.15 p.m., and the Parkeston Quay arrival to 9.42 p.m. In the up direction, the booked departure from Parkeston was at 6.20 a.m., but the necessity for fitting the working into the dense suburban traffic from Gidea Park onwards made the up timing easier, and the " Hook Continental " was not due in Liverpool Street until 7.53 a.m. Various alternative paths were laid down in the working timetables for the up train, in the event of the steamer having been delayed by bad weather.

The Antwerp train, which in later L.N.E.R. days became the " Antwerp Continental," used to follow the " Hook Continental " out of Liverpool Street at an interval of 10 minutes, at 8.40 p.m., and was allowed the same time to Parkeston Quay—an arrangement which meant smart work on the part of the station staff at Parkeston in getting the Hook train clear, as both normally used the same platform. But when the " Hook " departure was altered to 8.15 p.m., the " Antwerp " train took the 8.30 p.m. path. The " Antwerp Continental " continued to Dovercourt Bay and Harwich, and so carried ordinary as well as boat passengers. It was due at Harwich at 10.14 p.m.

In the morning the starting time from Parkeston Quay of the up " Antwerp Continental " saw a certain amount of variation, and was varied also as between summer and winter. Immediately before the war it left at 7 a.m., and reached Liverpool Street at 8.38 a.m. When the Zeebrugge service was in operation, Zeebrugge passengers were carried on the " Antwerp Continental." At the depth of the depression period, one train, known as the " Hook and Antwerp Continental," sufficed for both routes.

In the year 1905, the Great Eastern Railway also provided its Antwerp passengers with a corridor restaurant car train. In busy summer seasons, more particularly at week-ends, the stock was used to form a restaurant car train from Liverpool Street to Clacton-on-Sea and back between its arrival from Parkeston and its return working at 8.40 p.m. In later L.N.E.R. days, catering on this train was turned over to the Pullman Car Company, and Pullman restaurant cars, three in number, were substituted for the L.N.E.R. cars. A first-class Pullman of the drawing-room type was also run on the train. The composition varied according to season, but rose to a maximum of twelve bogies in the summer, which including the four Pullmans weighed about 390 tons.

A similar formation, with first-class Pullman car and Pullman restaurant cars, was run for the " Flushing Continental." Of this train the running times varied considerably. In the last year before the war it left Liverpool Street in winter at 9.30 a.m., reaching Parkeston Quay West at 10.55 a.m., and continuing into Parkeston main station. In summer departure was at 10 a.m., and arrivals were at 11.30 a.m. and 11.38 a.m., respectively. On the up journey the train left Parkeston Quay at 6.30 p.m., and Parkeston Quay West 15 minutes later, reaching Liverpool Street at 8.13 p.m. in winter ; the summer departures were 7.45 and 7.55 p.m., and arrival in London was not until 9.30 p.m.

During the winter months, the " Scandinavian " passengers had to be content with a portion on the rear of the 3.10 p.m. Yarmouth buffet car express from Liverpool Street, which was detached at Manningtree and run from there independently to Parkeston Quay West, arriving at 4.45 p.m. But in summer, before the war, the " Scandinavian " blossomed out into an independent train with Pullman restaurant cars, due to depart from Liverpool Street at 4.10 p.m., reaching Parkeston Quay non-stop at 5.45 p.m., and running on with ordinary passengers to Harwich, where arrival was at 6.6 p.m. In the up direction the " Scandinavian " left Parkeston Quay on one of the many " conditional " paths arranged in the working timetables, according to the arrival of the boat.

All the L.N.E.R. Continental services were withdrawn in 1939 ; the " Hook Continental " was reinstated, three times weekly, in November, 1945, and daily a year later. Departure from Liverpool Street had now become 8 p.m., and at first the allowance to Parkeston Quay was a leisurely 100 minutes, but with the summer timetable of 1951, and with the new standard " Britannia " class Pacifics replacing the " B1 " 4–6–0's used until then, the journey time was reduced to 90 minutes, which includes a 3-minute recovery margin between Manningtree and Parkeston Quay. During the summer, a relief train is run from Liverpool Street at 8.5 p.m., mainly for second-class passengers who have overflowed from the 8 p.m. ; this has a buffet car in place of restaurant cars. In winter the main train has to leave London at 7.30 p.m., because of difference between British and Continental time during this period.

Much of the pre-war stock, of the L.N.E.R. streamliner type, has reappeared. There are thirteen vehicles, two of them bogie brakes (at the rear end from London), two combined kitchen and restaurant cars in the first- and second-class sections of the train, and the remainder mostly open stock, the whole forming one of the most palatial boat trains in the country. The empty weight is about 460 tons. Plenty of seating accommodation with tables is essential, for on the morning run in summer it is nothing unusual to serve between 150 and 200 breakfasts at one sitting. Incidentally, in 1952 the departure from Parkeston Quay, on the inward run, was put back to 7.42 a.m., and the arrival in Liverpool Street is now 9.14 a.m.

Above : " Royal Scot " Class 4–6–0 No. 46127 *Old Contemptibles* hauls the down L.M.R. " Irish Mail " westwards out of Chester

[*E. Treacy*

Below : Approaching Hatton North Junction with the up " Inter-City " is W.R. " Castle " Class 4–6–0 No. 5008 *Raglan Castle*

[*J. C. Flemons*

Above : Climbing Grayrigg Bank—L.M.R. 2–6–4 tank No. 42457 with the Keswick portion of the "Lakes Express"
[*E. D. Bruton*

Above right : The "Lewisman" leaves Kyle of Lochalsh behind "Clan Goods" 4–6–0 No. 17955
[*F. R. Hebron*

Right : Distant "on" for the down "Master Cutler" as it threads Princes Risborough with "B1" 4–6–0 No. 61199 in charge
[*H. K. Harman*

[*J. C. Flemons*]

The Diesel intruder—L.M.R. Diesel-electric unit No. 10001 hurries the northbound "Manxman" over Bushey troughs on its non-stop Euston-Liverpool run

[*F. R. Hebron*

In former days—Two L.M.S.R. rebuilt "Claughton" Class 4–6–0s, Nos. 5908 *Alfred Fletcher* and 5981, climb the 1 in 75 of Camden bank with the northbound "Lancastrian"

[*J. C. Flemons*

Post-war innovation—The up "Midlander" emerges from Watford tunnel behind "Jubilee" Class 4–6–0 No. 45703 *Thunderer*

As to the other Continental trains from Liverpool Street, the "Day Continental" (before the war the "Flushing Continental," but since the war routed *via* the Hook, like the night service), leaves at 10.5 a.m. in summer and 9.33 a.m. in winter, running non-stop to Parkeston Quay West. The "Scandinavian," with passengers for Denmark, goes out at 3.10 p.m. during the summer, but during the winter passengers for the Esbjerg steamer are taken down by the morning "Day Continental." The up "Day Continental" departs from Parkeston Quay West at 6.55 p.m. in summer and 5.40 p.m. in winter.

33--The "Irish Mails"

For many years past, save in wartime, the principal Irish mail trains have left Euston at times between 8 and 9 in the morning and at a corresponding hour in the evening, and have been due back in London round about 6 o'clock morning and evening. In London & North Western days, 8.30 a.m. and 8.45 p.m. were the departures for the Holyhead–Kingstown service; two boat trains were run from Euston in connection with the North Wall boats, first at 11 a.m. and later at 1.20 p.m., and also at 10.15 p.m.; and yet a fifth for the Holyhead–Greenore route to Northern Ireland, at 7.30 in the evening. But the Greenore services were not revived after the First World War.

The day "Irish Mails" between Euston and Holyhead carried restaurant cars of which the service was renowned as something quite superlative, even to L.M.S.R. standards. The night trains included first-and third-class sleeping cars, out of which their patrons had to turn at the most uncomfortable hour of 2.20 a.m. on the down journey, though coming up, the passenger who had endured the unpleasantness of the Irish Sea was off the boat and into his cosy berth by midnight, and could remain in it until 8 a.m., if he so desired. Both day and night services incorporated in their formations two Post Office sorting coaches for handling the mails, and so were "Irish Mails" in every sense of the term.

The mail services between Euston and Holyhead, though at one time known unofficially as the "Wild Irishmen," have always been distinguished more for weight than for speed. Indeed, between Chester and Holyhead particularly, the loads handled on these trains have often been greater than permitted anywhere else on the L.M.S.R. system without pilot assistance. Even in the piping times of peace, it was nothing unusual for a "Royal Scot" 4-6-0 to be expected to handle trains up to 16 or 17 bogies, with a full weight of 510 to 540 tons, over the North Wales main line. The present working timetable lays down a limit of 495 tons empty.

By 1939 the down morning "Irish Mail" from Euston had

strayed by 15 minutes from its earlier 8.30 a.m. departure, which was now given over to a Liverpool and Manchester train, and had become 8.45 a.m. A one-minute stop was made at Watford to pick up passengers, and the next 65·1 miles to Rugby were run in 68 minutes. The Rugby times were 10.18 to 10.21 a.m. ; then came a run over the 75·5 miles to Crewe in 83 minutes, and a stop of 9 minutes there. Away from Crewe at 11.53 a.m., the Irishman made its last stop at Chester from 12.19 to 12.27 p.m., and then ran the 84·4 miles on to Holyhead in the easy time of 98 minutes. On the journey the postal apparatus was in use at Nuneaton, Llandudno Junction, and finally at Menai Bridge, just before crossing the Britannia Tubular Bridge into Anglesey.

The evening " Irish Mail " was also publicly advertised to leave Euston at 8.45, but the actual working departure was 8.50 p.m. Running times were easier—93 minutes to Rugby (with no Watford stop), 90 minutes on to Crewe, 26 minutes from there to Chester, and 97 minutes from Chester to Holyhead—and with longer station stops the Holyhead arrival was not till 2.20 a.m. Every Friday night during the summer, and nightly during the height of the season, this train was relieved by an 8.45 p.m. express which ran the entire 263·6 miles from Euston to Holyhead without a stop in 5 hours, 10 minutes. The morning " Irish Mail " was similarly relieved on Fridays with a non-stop at 8.30 a.m., which completed the journey in 5¼ hours.

Of the up " Irish Mails," the night train was the slower. At 13 minutes after midnight it drew out of Holyhead, and was allowed 97 minutes to Chester, 27 minutes on to Crewe, 83 minutes from Crewe to Rugby, and 84 minutes over the 82·6 miles from Rugby to Euston, where the arrival was at 5.30 a.m. The postal apparatus on this train had a busy time, and was in action at Bangor, Rhyl, Stafford, Tamworth, Nuneaton, Bletchley, Hemel Hempsted and Harrow.

As for the up day " Irish Mail," it was booked out of Holyhead at 12.40 p.m., and allowed only 94 minutes for the 84·4 miles to Chester, where there was a 10-minute stop, followed by a booking of 27 minutes to Crewe. Here there was an allowance of no less than 11 minutes—chiefly to deal with mails—and then an 82-minute run to Rugby was followed by a brilliant 82 minutes for the final 82·6 miles to Euston (just over 60 m.p.h.), bringing the train into London at 5.50 p.m., in 5 hours, 10 minutes from Holyhead. With the invariably heavy load, this timing meant very hard work for a " Royal Scot." At summer week-ends this train also was relieved by a non-stop to Euston in 5 hours, 3 minutes, at 52·2 m.p.h.

For a long time past there have been through engine workings between Euston and Holyhead, manned exclusively by Holyhead engine-crews in both directions. " Pacifics " were used for a short time, but now the " Irish Mail " has been turned over to the highly capable rebuilt " Royal Scots ".

During most of the war, the day " Irish Mail " was run in each direction, but not the night service : from London it left at 8.15 a.m., with a portion for Manchester on the rear, and with additional stops at Colwyn Bay and Bangor reached Holyhead at 2.34 p.m. In the reverse direction the start from Holyhead was at 1.45 p.m., and the only stops were at Chester, Crewe, and Watford, bringing the train into Euston at 7.40 p.m.—a slowing down of no more than 45 minutes on the pre-war schedule.

It is now the night service, restored in October, 1946, which is maintained throughout the year, with the day service running during the currency of the summer timetable only. In the 1952-1953 winter timetables, the "Irish Mail" is booked out of Euston at 8.45 p.m. in the public timetables (but the working departure is still 8.50 p.m.) and is due in Holyhead at 2.25 a.m., only 5 minutes later than before the war. Owing to time lost by customs formalities, the up train cannot now leave Holyhead till 1.10 a.m. (instead of the pre-war 12.13 a.m.), and is booked into Euston at 6.30 a.m., a journey 2 minutes longer than before the war. A post-war innovation in both directions, from 1950 onwards, has been the provision of a buffet car for refreshment service throughout the run. Every Friday night the down "Irish Mail" starts from Euston at 8.45 p.m., and runs non-stop to Holyhead in 5½ hours, with a "relief" at 8.52 p.m. to make the usual intermediate stops. In the summer, the down day "Irish Mail" is away from Euston as early as 8.10 a.m., and reaches Holyhead at 1.45 p.m., 20 minutes after the up "Irish Mail" has left for London. The latter is due in Euston at 6.35 p.m.

34—The "Irish Mail via Fishguard" and the "Red Dragon"

It was in 1906, after immense expenditure in blasting away a rocky hillside to make the necessary shelf on which to lay out the station, that the Great Western Railway brought into use their new port of Fishguard, in West Wales. The aim was to operate direct services between England and Southern Ireland, and G.W.R. steamers began to run both by day and night between Fishguard and another new port which had been created at Rosslare, just across the St. George's Channel. Connecting restaurant car trains were put in service between Rosslare, Waterford and Cork, and another connecting service was introduced between Rosslare and Wexford. Direct steamers ran also from Fishguard to Cork and Waterford.

The prospects of Fishguard grew still brighter when the Cunard Steamship Company decided to make this a port of call for their steamers coming across the Atlantic from New York to Liverpool. Disembarkation at Fishguard, with fast rail travel over the G.W.R. from there to Paddington, made possible a far earlier arrival in

London than was possible after the normal steaming up the Irish Sea into the Mersey. The possibilities of this traffic were so great that the G.W.R. bestirred itself into making a costly new line to avoid the traffic handicaps in the vicinity of Swansea ; the " Swansea District Lines," as they are called, leave the South Wales main line at Court Sart, east of Neath, cross the Neath River south of that place, then tunnel under the main line and strike due west through Felin Fran to Morlais East Junction, where a turn is made due south to rejoin the main line near Llanelly. Actually this line saves only ½-mile, but it avoids some severe gradients and congestion on the old main line.

Originally the plan was to continue westwards from Morlais to Pembrey, on the main line beyond Llanelly, which would have made a wonderfully direct route to Fishguard. But meantime the claims of the great port of Southampton on all the leading Transatlantic services had become so strong—partly because the use of Southampton made possible also a call at Cherbourg, across the English Channel, for the traffic to and from the mainland of Europe—that the Cunard decided to transfer its liners from Liverpool to Southampton. This transfer put Fishguard completely out of the picture, and as a result the remainder of the Swansea District Lines scheme was never completed. So Fishguard was left with its Irish services ; these never grew beyond relatively moderate passenger dimensions, though freight traffic, chiefly agricultural, was on a large scale.

At first the boat trains left Paddington at 8.45 both morning and evening, and each was allowed 5½ hours to make the journey of 261·4 miles from Paddington to Fishguard Harbour. With various special trains, at different times, the G.W.R. has run the entire distance non-stop, but in ordinary daily working the largest intermediate towns were of too great importance to be missed out in this way. So both trains called at Newport and Cardiff ; in order to obtain a direct run past Swansea without reversal, the stop here was made at Landore, 1¼ miles away. In addition, the morning boat train called at Reading and the evening one at Swindon. Engines were changed once only, at Cardiff. Restaurant cars were run on both services, and the evening train in addition carried a first-class sleeping car, from the warmth and comfort of which its occupants were required to turn at the uninviting hour of 2.15 a.m., on arrival at Fishguard.

During the 1914—1919 war the night boat service between Fishguard and Rosslare survived, but not the day service, and the latter has never since been reinstated, so that the morning express from Paddington became a train to Pembroke Dock and Neyland, but no longer an " Irish Mail via Fishguard." In the recovery period after the 1914—1919 war, the Great Western Railway decided to standardise its main line departures out of Paddington, and as the South Wales starting times were fixed at 5 minutes to the hour, the exit of the evening boat train was advanced to 7.55 p.m. The original stop at Swindon was exchanged for one at Didcot, and eventually the latter gave place to a stop at Reading instead. By now Swansea had become too important to bypass, and the train was running into Swansea and out again, instead of taking the direct spur from Landore ; a further nightly stop had been added at Llanelly, and the train was prepared also to stop at both Severn Tunnel Junction and Neath if passengers wished to alight.

Up to 1939, therefore, the " Irish Mail *via* Fishguard," leaving Paddington at 7.55 p.m., ran the 36 miles to Reading in the then standard allowance of 40 minutes, and was booked to stand there 6 minutes, dealing with a considerable volume of luggage, parcels and mails. Away again at 8.41 p.m., it ran through Didcot and Swindon to Wootton Bassett, where the finely engineered junction made it possible to take the diverging line to Badminton at as high a speed as 50 m.p.h. For most of the distance between here and the summit at Badminton the line rises at 1 in 300, and it then passes through the 2½ miles of Sodbury Tunnel before descending at the same inclination to the junction with the Bristol-South Wales main line at Patchway.

At Stoke Gifford East Box, just before Patchway, two slip coaches were detached, to be worked by a waiting tank engine into Bristol, and so providing a late evening service from London to that city. From Patchway the descent steepens to 1 in 68, and then, after a level strip, to the 3 miles at 1 in 100 which lead to the middle of the Severn Tunnel. In the opposite direction this is the worst bank on the route, for although the 1 in 68 is flattened on the up line to 1 in 100, up trains are faced with 6 miles at 1 in 100 between the middle of the tunnel and Pilning, and with a further 12 miles at 1 in 300 before the summit is breasted at Badminton—an arduous task.

Including the " conditional " stop at Severn Tunnel Junction, the down " Irish Mail *via* Fishguard " was allowed 106 minutes to run the 97·4 miles from Reading to Newport. Here a stop of 4 minutes was scheduled, and a short run of 16 minutes brought the train into Cardiff at 10.47 p.m., for a wait of 8 minutes and a change of engine. There are awkward grades between Cardiff and Swansea, and this length of 45·8 miles was allowed exactly one hour, bringing the train into Swansea at 11.55 p.m. Here reversal took place, and on the stroke of midnight the train, after a second change of engine, was due out westwards. From Swansea for 1¾ miles the line climbs at 1 in 60 and 1 in 52 to Cockett tunnel, so that an assistant engine was provided either to the summit or to Llanelly, where a stop of one minute was made from 12.22 to 12.23 a.m. Then came a schedule of 77 minutes over the remaining 60·3 miles, including some heavy grades, to Fishguard Harbour, reached at 1.40 a.m.

In the reverse direction the start on the up journey of the " Irish Mail *via* Fishguard " was made 2¼ hours later, at 3.55 a.m. Banking assistance was needed from the start, for the single-track line out of Fishguard climbs at 1 in 50 for 1¾ miles past Manorowen halt. The first scheduled stop was at Gowerton, 67 miles from Fishguard, at 5.18 a.m., to take on another assisting engine for the 2¼-mile climb at 1 in 50 to Cockett. Fifteen minutes later the train was in Swansea.

Leaving Swansea at 5.37 a.m., as in the reverse direction there was an allowance of exactly an hour to Cardiff, and the start from there was at 6.45 a.m., and from Newport at 7.5 a.m. An easy allowance followed of 113 minutes to Reading, and after a 5-minute stop there, the schedule was as long as 44 minutes to Paddington, for the boat train had to be fitted in between other morning arrivals. Into London at 9.47 a.m., the up " Irish Mail " had thus taken 5 hours, 52 minutes for the 263·6 miles from Fishguard *via* Swansea, as compared with 5¾ hours in the opposite direction.

The make-up of the train included composite sleeping car, composite restaurant car, corridor first, about three corridor thirds and a third brake, two or three long brake-vans, and the Bristol slip coaches in the down direction, eleven or twelve bogies in all out of Paddington, and two less in the reverse direction. Between London and Cardiff a "Castle" 4–6–0 was the invariable rule; west of Cardiff either 4-cylinder or 2-cylinder 4–6–0's might be used. The Fishguard-Rosslare service did not long survive the outbreak of war, and with its withdrawal the boat trains in each direction were cancelled also, though the 8.55 a.m. from Paddington continued to run to Pembroke Dock.

From October 1st, 1945, however, the 7.55 p.m. down was restored as far as Swansea, and the 8.55 a.m. down had a through portion for Fishguard reinstated on Tuesdays, Thursdays and Saturdays. For a time the latter was relieved as far as Swansea by an 8.50 a.m. breakfast-car train, which called only at Newport and Cardiff, and reached Swansea at 1 p.m. but this was withdrawn in the coal crisis, and since its reinstatement has run only on Saturdays and during the summer season. Irish boat passengers *via* Fishguard now leave Paddington on the 6.55 p.m. express, which is the present version of the old 7.55 p.m. down, but the boat portion runs on Mondays, Wednesdays and Fridays only ; on other days the express terminates its journey at Swansea at 11.25 p.m., after having called at Reading, Newport and Cardiff. The time to Swansea thus exceeds that of pre-war days by 30 minutes.

When the boat portion is run, it leaves Swansea at 11.30 p.m., and with one intermediate halt, at Llanelly, makes its way into Fishguard Harbour at 1.15 a.m., as compared with the pre-war 1.40 a.m. At Fishguard, the train has a turn-around time of 3¾ hours, and then is away on Tuesdays, Thursdays and Saturdays, back to Paddington at 4.55 a.m. In this direction, after leaving Llanelly, the train avoids Swansea altogether by taking the direct line through Morlais and Felin Fran, already mentioned, crossing under the main line between Skewen and Neath and then passing over the Neath River swingbridge to regain the main line at Court Sart Junction, near Briton Ferry. Cardiff is reached at 8.7 a.m., in time for attachment to the daily 8.15 a.m. for Paddington, but this makes so many stops that the boat passengers are not into London until 11.40 a.m.—a run slower by 53 minutes than in pre-war days.

With the introduction of the 1950–1951 winter timetable,

another train over this route had a title conferred on it—the " Red Dragon." This is the popular 8.45 a.m. from Swansea, which is due in Paddington at 1.5 p.m., and returns as the 5.55 p.m. from Paddington to Swansea. Both trains have a Carmarthen section ; in the up direction this makes an early start, at 7.30 a.m., for an " all stations " run to Swansea, where it is attached to the main train. Stops are made at Cardiff and Newport, followed by a non-stop run over the 133½ miles to Paddington in 165 minutes. The return journey is rather more lethargic ; there are additional stops at Swindon and Badminton, so that Cardiff and Swansea are not reached until 9.15 and 10.45 p.m. respectively, and it is ten minutes to midnight before the last of the " Red Dragon's " tail drags its weary way into Carmarthen.

35—The " Irishman " and the " Fast Belfast "

It would be difficult to find a more remarkable route, from the gradient point of view, than that by which the " Irishman " and the " Fast Belfast " make their way from Glasgow to the port of Stranraer, in south-west Scotland. For the first 41¼ miles, to Ayr, it is nearly level ; over the final 37 miles, from Girvan to Stranraer, it is the exact opposite, and the 3¾-mile climb at 1 in 54 and 1 in 56 from Girvan up to Pinmore tunnel is a fitting introduction to the fearsome switchback that follows. The objective at Stranraer, of course, is the steamer service to and from Larne, in Northern Ireland, which explains the names " Irishman " and " Fast Belfast."

Of the two trains, only the " Irishman " ran throughout the year. But while the Glasgow-bound passenger in peacetime, with its help, could leave Belfast as late as 6.25 p.m., and be in Glasgow just before midnight, it was a different proposition going south. For the " Irishman," leaving Glasgow St. Enoch at 8.5 p.m., deposited him at Stranraer by 10.57 p.m., with all night to wait before the Larne steamer started at about 6.30 on the following morning, though he could console himself with a very comfortable cabin on board. Thus the southbound journey between Glasgow and Belfast took nearly 13 hours, as compared with 5½ hours going north.

In peacetime summers the boat service was duplicated, and it then became possible to make a much faster trip from Glasgow to Belfast. The " Fast Belfast " came into operation, leaving St. Enoch at 3.50 p.m., and its passengers crossed to Larne the same evening and reached Belfast by 10 p.m. In the reverse direction, departure from Belfast was at 9.28 a.m., and the " Fast Belfast " ran into St. Enoch precisely 6 hours later. Both the " Irishman " and the " Fast Belfast " were restaurant car trains of corridor stock, and normally were limited to about six bogie vehicles south of Girvan, as the difficulty of the route is so great that piloting is essential between Girvan and Stranraer if this load is exceeded. From the Glasgow & South Western 4–4–0 classes originally used, locomotive power changed by degrees to the Midland 4–4–0 compounds, then to 2–6–0's, Class " 5 " 4–6–0's, and finally to Class " 6 " 4–6–0's, which are still largely used over this route.

The " Irishman," southbound, got away from St. Enoch station in Glasgow at 8.5 p.m., and with stops at Paisley, Troon and Prestwick, reached Ayr, 41·3 miles away, in 56 minutes. From Ayr to Girvan there are some severe ups-and-downs, at gradients between 1 in 63 and 1 in 72, and five separate summits, of which the highest is Maybole, where the train stops. Including this stop, the " Irishman " ran the 21·4 miles from Ayr to Girvan in 34 minutes.

At Girvan the real tug-of-war begins, with the terrific 1 in 54–56 climb already mentioned, and over single track, which entails reduced speed through every passing loop, for tablet-exchange purposes. From Pinmore tunnel there is a sharp descent to Pinwherry ; then follows a still longer climb, 8½ miles of it, and mostly at about 1 in 70, through Barrhill to the highest summit, at milepost 16½. Through wild country the train now swings downwards, slowing for Glenwhilly, and then for the S-shaped " Swan's Neck," which is the terror of northbound drivers when making their way up a long 1 in 57 grade to the summit. More slacks at Challoch Junction, Dunragit, Castle Kennedy, and a final one at Stranraer Junction, and the " Irishman " was into Stranraer Harbour at 10.57 p.m., having taken 74 minutes for the final 37·9 miles from Girvan.

Of the 74-minute allowance, 6 minutes were allowed at Pinwherry, where the two " Irishmen " were booked to meet. The northbound train had the " right-of-way " here, and needed it, with an allowance of only 63 minutes to get through from Stranraer Harbour to Girvan—a tough task indeed through such exposed country on a wild winter's night. After a 5-minute wait at Girvan to take water—and breath !—the " Irishman " had a smart booking of 28 minutes for the 21·4 miles over Maybole summit into Ayr, and finished with a 56-minute run over the 41·3 miles into St. Enoch, arriving at 11.50 p.m. This last timing was fairly easy, for certain " conditional " stops were permitted between Stranraer and Ayr for passengers through from Ireland who wished to alight, and the final timing allowed the " Irishman " to recover some at least of the lost time. If no additional stops were called, it was due in St. Enoch at 11.45 p.m. To railwaymen this train has always been known as " The Paddy."

The " Fast Belfast " had somewhat similar peacetime schedules. There were intermediate halts at Paisley, Irvine, Ayr, Girvan and Dunragit, and Stranraer was reached at 6.45 p.m., after a 66-minute run from Girvan. Northbound, the " Fast Belfast," getting away from Stranraer Harbour at 12.50 p.m., had the same Dunragit stop and 66-minute timing to Girvan, then stops at Maybole, Ayr, and

Paisley were scheduled, with an arrival in St. Enoch at 3.28 p.m.

Of these expresses the only recognisable example that wartime left was the northbound " Irishman," but its departure from Stranraer Harbour was put back to 10.15 p.m., and with many conditional stops added to the regular stops, its weary passengers were not due to make their appearance in Glasgow until the distressingly " small hours "—actually at 1.5 the following morning. In the summer of 1945 the southbound " Irishman " returned to the timetable, leaving St. Enoch as before at 8.5 p.m., but not due in Stranraer Harbour until five minutes before midnight. Since then it has been considerably accelerated, and though not leaving Glasgow till 8.45 p.m., it makes Stranraer Harbour by 11.57 p.m. Conversely, the northbound " Irishman " has been made much earlier, and getting away from Stranraer Harbour by 9.15 p.m., and with all conditional stops between Ayr and Paisley cut out, it comes to rest in St. Enoch only 5 minutes later than in pre-war days, at 11.50 p.m. Restaurant cars are no longer run over this route. The name " Irishman " has been restored to both these trains.

During the war years this route became of considerable importance, and a good deal of work was done on lengthening the single-line passing loops between Girvan and Stranraer, and in easing the curves at the entry to and exit from each loop, so greatly speeding up the working. Also the new Class " 6 " Pacifics of the " Clan " type are at work on the principal trains.

36—The "Kentish Belle"

A fourth was added to the list of all-Pullman trains on the Southern Railway, as it then was, when the " Thanet Belle " entered service in May, 1948, joining the " Brighton Belle," the " Bournemouth Belle" and the " Devon Belle." The " Thanet Belle," like the " Devon Belle," ran during the currency of the summer time-table only. For a long time before the Second World War individual Pullman cars were run in Southern trains between Victoria and the Kent Coast, but in the recovery period after the war their places were taken by restaurant cars. Then came the announcement of the all-Pullman " Thanet Belle " ; also, during the winter months, when the " Belle " is withdrawn, Pullmans once again are running during the winter on the 11.35 a.m. from Victoria to Ramsgate, and the 5.5 p.m. from Ramsgate to Victoria. With the introduction of the 1951 summer timetable the " Thanet Belle " was provided with through Pullmans to and from Canterbury, and its name was changed to " Kentish Belle," but the Canterbury cars were not well patronised, and did not reappear in 1952.

Apart from its Pullman formation, normally one of eight cars, there is no distinction about the schedule of the "Kentish Belle," which falls far short of the one-time 90–minute booking of the "Granville Express" from Victoria to Margate. The 11.30 a.m. "Belle" is allowed 107 minutes for the same run, though certainly this includes stops at both Whitstable and Herne Bay. So Margate is reached at 1.17 p.m., Broadstairs at 1.28 p.m., and Ramsgate at 1.34 p.m. On Saturdays the start is deferred until 3.5 p.m., and the schedule to Whitstable is 85 instead of 82 minutes ; with the same stops at Herne Bay, Margate and Broadstairs, the arrival time at Ramsgate is 5.15 p.m. The pre-war 3.15 p.m. from Victoria, without the Whitstable and Herne Bay stops, made the run to Ramsgate in 1 hour, 50 minutes, or 14 minutes less.

Coming up, on the summer service, the "Kentish Belle" leaves Ramsgate at 5.5 p.m. on weekdays, Broadstairs at 5.11 p.m., Margate at 5.20 p.m., Herne Bay at 5.37 p.m. and Whitstable at 5.46 p.m., and a non-stop run from there gets the "Belle" into Victoria at 7.5 p.m. On Saturdays the Ramsgate start is 70 minutes later, and the Victoria arrival 75 minutes later at 8.20 p.m. In this case the running compares more favourably with that of the pre-war 5.15 p.m. from Ramsgate, which, with an additional stop at Dumpton Park, but none at Herne Bay and Whitstable, also was booked into Victoria at 7.5 p.m. When the Canterbury portion was run, in 1951, an additional stop was necessary to Faversham, to detach and attach these cars.

On Saturdays in 1950, between July 3rd and September 1st, the "Thanet Belle" was booked to make an additional round trip, out of Victoria at 7.55 a.m. and into Ramsgate at 10.13 a.m. ; return was at 11.15 a.m., with an arrival in Victoria at 1.28 p.m. On these Saturdays, therefore, the set of cars ran a total of 318 miles in the day. Since the war, of course, there has been a considerable increase in motive power, for the "West Country" Pacifics have replaced the "King Arthur" 4–6–0's and the 3–cylinder 4–4–0 "Schools" on the principal services, such as the one under review.

37—The "Lakes Express"

In earlier years the train which ultimately became the "Lakes Express" ran during the summer season only, but eventually its popularity was such as to call for week-end running throughout the year, and by 1939 it was a permanent service down on Fridays and Saturdays, so far as concerned the main Euston-Windermere section, and up on Saturdays and Mondays. In summer, when the daily working began, a through portion was added for the Keswick line. This express shared in the general L.M.S.R. acceleration which began in 1932, and ultimately had some smart timings. Leaving Euston at 12 noon, it stopped first at Rugby, 82·6 miles in 88 minutes, and spent 8 minutes there. Missing Stafford, Crewe and Warrington, it called next at Wigan, and was allowed 117 minutes for the 111·4 miles from Rugby to this point. The Wigan stop was made both to give a connection to Southport, which here is only 17 miles away, and to detach a through portion for Preston and Blackpool. Departure from Wigan was at 3.37 p.m. and the next stop, 4.20 p.m. at Lancaster, was to get rid of a through section for Barrow-in-Furness and the coast line up to Whitehaven, Workington and Maryport.

Next came a stop at Oxenholme, at 4.48 p.m., and from here the Keswick portion was first away, at 4.53 p.m., running on to Shap and Penrith, and there reversing (5.40 to 5.47 p.m.). Curiously enough, this part of the train crossed Cumberland *via* Keswick to reach Workington at 7.26 p.m., 38 minutes in front of the coaches which had meandered round the coast *via* Barrow, on their way to come finally to rest at Maryport at 8.17 p.m.

However, any passenger in a hurry to reach Maryport would hardly make the 8¼-hour journey offered by the " Lakes Express," for he could leave Euston luxuriously on the " Coronation Scot " streamliner at 1.30 p.m., make a " snap " 5-minute connection at Carlisle with the 6.18 p.m., and be in the Cumberland port at 7.19 p.m., a shorter journey by 2½ hours ! Long before this the main portion of the " Lakes Express " had left Oxenholme, called at Kendal, and run into Windermere at 5.25 p.m.

Coming up, the first part of the " Lakes Express " to start was that from Workington, at 9.5 a.m. Getting away from Keswick at 9.59 and Penrith at 10.47 a.m., it ran into Oxenholme at 11.35 a.m., there to await the main train from Windermere, which started at 11.15 a.m. The complete train, restarting at 11.53 a.m., called at Lancaster and next at Preston (12.43 to 12.51 p.m.), attaching the through Blackpool section there. A non-stop run followed to Crewe, where a stop was made from 1.49 to 1.56 p.m.

On the way from Crewe to Euston the only stop was at Bletchley ; the express was allowed exactly 2 hours to run the 111·4 miles from Crewe to this point, and 51 minutes for the final 46·7 miles to Euston, so arriving at 4.50 p.m. There were thus several differences in the stops going down and coming up ; on the latter, Bletchley, Preston and Tebay replaced Rugby, Wigan and Shap on the former. The journey over the whole 259½ miles from Euston to Windermere took 5 hours, 25 minutes, and 10 minutes longer was needed for the return.

The " Lakes Express " included a set of three restaurant cars— open first, kitchen, and open third—in the Windermere portion, with first-class brake, two third corridors, and third brake ; but this might be expanded somewhat in the summer season. The Keswick and Workington section (the only part of the train which actually saw one of the English Lakes at close quarters, for it skirted the whole length of Bassenthwaite Lake) was normally three coaches, composite corridor and two third brakes. Then there was the two-coach Blackpool portion, and on the down journey a further two coaches for the Furness line. A " 5XP " 4–6–0 worked through between Euston and Windermere, and returned the next day.

Between Oxenholme and Windermere a 4–4–2 or 4–6–2 *ex*-L.N.W.R. tank often provided the motive power, followed later by a standard 2–6–4 tank, but between Keswick and Workington, with severe weight restrictions over the bridges of the one-time Cockermouth, Keswick & Penrith Railway, a veteran in the shape of a Webb " Cauliflower " 0–6–0 had to suffice, notwithstanding such gradients as the 4 miles of 1 in 62 from Threlkeld up to Troutbeck, to be negotiated by the up train. Now the new light 2–6–0 locomotives are available.

During the war, through midday service was provided between Euston and Windermere and *vice versa*, and in the later war summers to and from the Keswick line also, but as a part of other trains ; in the down direction the service was on the 10.25 a.m. from Euston, taking 7 hours, 20 minutes to Windermere and about an hour less at summer week-ends. In the up direction the wartime version of the " Lakes Express " left Windermere at 11.10 a.m., and during the earlier years was detained for 48 minutes at Crewe to await the North Wales express due in Euston at 6.42 p.m. ; but, first at week-ends, and then daily, in the last war years, the Windermere and Blackpool train assumed sufficient importance to be worked up independently from Crewe and to reach London at 5.55 p.m.

In the summer the " Lakes Express " is now back in service, leaving Euston at 11.50 a.m. (working time 11.52), and appearing in the public timetable as though still non-stop to Wigan. But this is not the case, as a stop is made at Crewe from 2.54 to 3.2 p.m. to drop the Barrow and Whitehaven section, complete with its own restaurant car. This is a curious arrangement, as both portions then stop on each other's tails at Wigan, Preston and Lancaster. The " Lakes Express " proper reaches Windermere at 6.5 p.m., and the Workington portion is into Keswick at 7.3 p.m. and Workington at 8.9 p.m. In the reverse direction the earliest departures are from Workington at 8.35 a.m. and Keswick at 9.38 a.m. ; while the main train makes its way out of Windermere at 10.50 a.m. In this direction, as in earlier years, there is no Barrow portion, but a Blackpool section is attached at Preston ; Euston is reached at 5.15 p.m., except on Saturdays, when the Wigan and Warrington stops are omitted and the arrival is 10 minutes earlier. Between Euston and Windermere, therefore, to-day's journey is 50 minutes longer than in pre-war days.

38—The "Lancastrian" and the "Mancunian"

Most popular of all the trains on the express service between London and Manchester, with little doubt, is the 6 p.m. from Euston, which assumed the title " Lancastrian " in the year 1927. In London and North Western days, for many years the 5.30 p.m. from Euston provided the evening business service from London to Manchester and Liverpool, but growth in traffic compelled division into various independent sections, of which the 6 p.m. to Manchester, later 6.5 p.m., was one. From that time onwards the Manchester train was booked non-stop over the 183 miles to Stockport, where the rear portion, with through coaches for Colne and Rochdale, was detached. The 6.5 p.m. was due in Manchester at 9.35 p.m., and was one of the first trains to bring this Lancashire city within 3½ hours of London.

On the opening in 1909 of the new line from Wilmslow to Levenshulme, avoiding Stockport, the 6.5 p.m. down was transferred to it and the first stop then became Wilmslow, 176·9 miles from Euston, where the train divided.

When the 1932 accelerations took place, it was decided to cut the time allowance to 3¼ hours from Euston to London Road, and this made necessary a mile-a-minute schedule to Wilmslow, 176·9 miles in 176 minutes. In order to ensure a clear road for the " Lancastrian," it was made to change places with the Liverpool train, which had become the " Merseyside Express " ; instead of 6.5 and 5.55 p.m., the departure times became 6.0 and 6.5 p.m. respectively. Also, in order to keep the " Lancastrian's " load within the " XL Limit " of the working timetables, the East Lancashire section was cut off this express, and transferred to the Heysham boat train at 6.10 p.m. from Euston. The " Lancastrian " continued to call at Wilmslow, but no division of the train now took place there. It was booked to pass Crewe at 8.36 p.m., call at Wilmslow from 8.56 to 8.59 p.m., and reach Manchester London Road, 188·5 miles from Euston, at 9.15 p.m.

The down " Lancastrian " was usually made up to about twelve bogie vehicles. From the rear end were first-class brake, first, open first, first class restaurant car, kitchen car, third restaurant car, and the remainder third-class, partly open and partly compartment stock. This made up a total tare weight of approximately 360 tons, well within the compass of " Royal Scot " haulage. The maximum load permitted was 415 tare tons. After 4–6–0 No. 6170, *British Legion*, had been rebuilt with taper boiler, forerunner of the highly successful " Royal Scot " rebuildings of later years, it was used frequently on this train. In the years immediately preceding the Second World War, engines of the first Pacific series began to make their appearance on the " Lancastrian."

On the southbound journey, the stock of the 6.0 p.m. from Euston returned from Manchester on the noon service, and when the former train became the "Lancastrian," the 12.5 p.m. from London Road assumed the same title. This meant that the train followed a different route when travelling south from that used in the north-bound direction ; and the different route meant a different type of engine, for nothing heavier than a "5XP" 4-6-0 was permitted to work over the Stoke-on-Trent route. The southbound "Lancastrian" called first at Stockport, arriving at 12.15 p.m., and here 6 minutes were allowed for the attaching in front of the East Lancashire portion from Colne, Burnley, Blackburn, Bolton, and Manchester Victoria.

Leaving Stockport at 12.21 p.m., and diverging from the Crewe line at Cheadle Hulme, 2¼ miles to the south, the "Lancastrian" then climbed to Macclesfield, where a stop was made at Hibel Road station from 12.40 to 12.43 p.m. An even steeper climb follows, from the Central station at Macclesfield up to Macclesfield Moss box, which for 1¼ miles is at 1 in 102, and up this banking assistance was invariably provided. The only remaining stop was at Stoke-on-Trent, reached at 1.10 and left at 1.15 p.m., and from here to London once again a mile-a-minute run was scheduled— 145·9 miles in 145 minutes—for an arrival in Euston at 3.40 p.m. The up train regained at Colwich, 6·4 miles south of Stafford, the main route followed by the down "Lancastrian." For an engine of the "5XP" type this was no easy task with a load that was usually between 400 and 440 tons, but excellent time was kept by the Longsight drivers, and the spotless condition of the engines turned out by this shed for the run was always a pleasure to see.

It is of interest to recall that in earlier days, when the train, then unnamed, left Manchester London Road at 12.10 p.m., and was due in Euston at 4 p.m., motive power was provided by the then North Staffordshire Railway between Manchester and Stoke. The N.S.R. had some fine superheated 4-4-2 tanks, similar in appearance to the Brighton "I3" class, and although the load was less in those days than it became later, these tanks, and their 0-6-4 successors, did some magnificent work on this first stage, to Stoke, where the tank would be replaced by a "George the Fifth" 4-4-0 of the London & North Western for the non-stop run of 140·4 miles to Willesden Junction in 148 minutes.

The full load from Stockport, immediately before the outbreak of war, was usually about fourteen bogies. From the engine there were first the four East Lancashire coaches—a composite brake, composite, and two thirds—then first-class brake, two firsts, first restaurant, kitchen, third restaurant, three thirds, third brake, and a bogie van on the rear for mails.

The "Mancunian" workings were the precise opposite of those of the "Lancastrian," for the up "Mancunian" was a 3¼-hour train between Manchester and Euston, non-stop from Wilmslow, and the down "Mancunian" took the Stoke-on-Trent route, with the same stops as the up "Lancastrian," and four others in addition. Out of Manchester the main train, starting from London Road at 9.45 a.m., was usually worked to Wilmslow by a 2–6–4 tank locomotive, arriving at 10.2 a.m. The express engine, which had picked up at Stockport through coaches from Colne, Huddersfield and Rochdale, was waiting at Wilmslow, and there transferred them to the front of the Manchester portion. The combined train then left at 10.8 a.m. and was due to make the run of 176·9 miles to Euston in 172 minutes, at an average of 61·7 m.p.h. As with the down " Lancastrian," a " Royal Scot " 4–6–0 was normally used on this service, though latterly Pacifics had begun to appear on the train.

Going north, the down " Mancunian," like the up " Lancastrian," had to be content with a " 5XP " 4–6–0, on account of travelling *via* Stoke-on-Trent. But this was a lighter train, as although it carried a through portion for Northampton, this came off early in the journey, at Bletchley, and there were no through coaches for the East Lancashire towns. Departure from Euston was at 4.10 p.m., and Bletchley was reached at 5.2 and left at 5.5 p.m. After this some smart running was needed, as the allowances were only 38 and 36 minutes respectively for the 35·9 mile and 33·7-mile Bletchley—Rugby and Rugby—Lichfield stages. Only 2 minutes was allowed at each of these stops. Stoke-on-Trent was reached at 7 p.m., and with halts at Congleton, Macclesfield, and Stockport, the " Mancunian " was due in Manchester London Road at 8.5 p.m.

After the outbreak of the Second World War, recognisable versions of two of these four trains, though much slower than in peacetime, and without their distinctive names, remained. A train resembling the down " Lancastrian " was split off from what at first was a combined express from Euston to Liverpool and Manchester at 5.30 p.m. Except on Saturdays, the Manchester section left Euston at 5.38 p.m., calling at Stafford, Wilmslow and Stockport, and reaching London Road at 9.47 p.m., and with its journey of 4 hours 9 minutes, was 54 minutes slower than in peacetime. Then, from October 7th, 1946, the down express resumed its pre-war 6 p.m. departure, and its non-stop run to Wilmslow; continuing *via* Styal, it was due in Manchester at 9.45 p.m., in 3¾ hours from Euston. The Colne portion was detached at Wilmslow, as in former days, and continued *via* Stockport. From mid-September, 1952, however, the down " Lancastrian " once again lost its Colne section, was put on to a " Special Limit " timing, and with the Euston-Wilmslow timing cut to 187 minutes, it is now brought into Manchester at 9.30 p.m., in 3½ hours from London. This change has reduced its load to 12 coaches.

In the morning, the traffic from Manchester is heavy enough to require two trains. The 9.45 a.m. from London Road travels *via* Styal, and, running non-stop over the 188·5 miles to Euston, is due in London at 1.20 p.m.; the 9.52 a.m., later 10 a.m., and now 10.5 a.m., works up *via* Stoke, attaching through Colne coaches at Stockport, and stopping after that at Macclesfield and Stoke-on-Trent, and is due in London at 2.0 p.m. Loads up to fifteen and sixteen bogies are worked by rebuilt " Royal Scot " 4–6–0's. The

6 p.m. from Euston and the 9.45 a.m. from Manchester have resumed the name " Mancunian," but there is no longer a " Lancastrian " in either direction.

39—The "Leeds, Bradford and Morecambe Residential Express"

In point of distance by rail, Leeds and Bradford are roughly equi-distant between the East Coast at Bridlington and Scarborough and the West Coast at Morecambe. These two coasts are both at about the limit of distance for daily travel to and fro by business men, and there has been considerable competition in the railway facilities offered. In winter the attraction of the East Coast was limited by low temperatures ; but in summer the late North Eastern Railway had some remarkable city-to-coast schedules, covering the $67\frac{1}{2}$ miles from Leeds to Scarborough non-stop in 75 minutes, and the $63\frac{1}{4}$ miles to Bridlington in 70 minutes. In view of the gradients and service slacks on each route, the working of these trains, often with 4–2–2 single-drivers, required locomotive performance of a very high order.

The Midland Railway, on its part, developed corresponding fast services between Bradford and Leeds and Morecambe, and the equable temperatures of the West Coast made it a paying proposition to run their express all the year round for residential purposes. Thus the " Leeds, Bradford & Morecambe Residential Express " came into operation. Before the war this was an official title and appeared in the timetables ; to-day the " Residential " is still a name in current use by the railway staff of the train concerned.

Of such importance is this express regarded that it was one of the first since the Second World War to be restored to " Limited Load " timings in each direction, with the result that by May, 1946, once again it was running at full pre-war speed in each direction. It begins its journey in the Promenade station at Morecambe at 7.40 a.m., for the Yorkshire businessman likes to reach his work early, and is enabled to do so by the fact that the " Residential " deposits him in the Forster Square station at Bradford, $60\frac{1}{2}$ miles away, at 9.15 a.m. The intermediate stops are at Lancaster (Green Ayre), Clapham, Hellifield, and Skipton ; at the last mentioned the three Leeds coaches split off from the four for Bradford, and leaving 6 minutes later, at 8.55 a.m., and calling at Keighley, are into Leeds City station at 9.32 a.m. The Leeds journey is 8 miles further than that to Bradford.

When returning home at night, the Leeds traveller must be ready by 4.55 p.m., and his train, calling at Keighley, is due in Skipton at 5.32 p.m. Four minutes later the Bradford section, which has started at 5.10 p.m., and has called at Shipley, follows in.

and by 5.42 p.m. the combined train is ready to re-start. There was no Hellifield stop in this direction, but it has now been reinstated ; the next stop to Lancaster, and Morecambe is reached at 6.50 p.m.

As to the gradients on this route, much the toughest proposition is that of climbing from the sea level of the Lune Valley up to the watershed east of Clapham. The ascent begins 7½ miles east of Lancaster, and continues unbroken for 11½ miles, of which 7 miles are at between 1 in 100 and 1 in 150. The summit is a mile east of Clapham station. In the reverse direction the worst obstacle is the climb between Skipton and Hellifield, 6 miles long past Gargrave and Bell Busk, and as steep in parts as 1 in 131. Between Leeds and Settle Junction, of course, the " Leeds, Bradford & Morecambe Residential Express " shares the route with the express trains between St. Pancras and Scotland.

40—The " Lewisman " and the " Hebridean "

It is not quite clear why such trains as the " Lewisman " and the " Hebridean " should have earned the dignity of names. The reason is hardly speed, seeing that the journey of 82 miles covered by each required 3¼ to 3½ hours for its completion, and over most of the distance included stops at all intermediate stations. Sole distinction that these trains boasted, perhaps, was that, in company with the West Highland trains of the L.N.E.R. to Fort William and Mallaig, they brought restaurant car service to some of the most remote regions of the British Isles.

As the titles suggest, the " Lewisman " and the " Hebridean " provided connection with the Hebrides, which was made by way of the Kyle of Lochalsh, opposite the island of Skye. This port is linked to the main Highland system by means of a single line branch, the Dingwall and Skye line, which branches from the Inverness-Wick line at Dingwall, and crosses Scotland, through country growing ever wilder and more mountainous, for 63½ miles until, amid the fjord-like scenery of the Western Highlands, it reaches the Kyle of Lochalsh. Here the L.M.S.R. thoroughly modernised what had been previously a Highland Railway hotel.

It was from Kyle, in the very " small hours," at 5.5 a.m. on a summer morning in peacetime, that the " Lewisman " started its journey. On this trip, singularly enough, when the sleepy traveller was the most in need of the comfort of refreshments, the restaurant car was absent. A through coach for Glasgow was attached, and after arrival of the " Lewisman " in Inverness at 8.10 a.m., was transferred to the 8.35 a.m. express for the south, on which the passenger from Kyle was able to obtain his belated breakfast. This through coach reached Glasgow (Buchanan Street), 263 miles from

Kyle, at 1.44 p.m. The "Lewisman" itself, after a wait of two hours at Inverness, and now having acquired its restaurant car, started back at 10.15 a.m., and finished its day at Kyle of Lochalsh at 1.40 p.m.

It had been preceded in this direction by the "Hebridean." The latter was booked to leave Inverness, as a breakfast car train, at 7.25 a.m., complete with a through coach for Kyle which had left Glasgow on the sleeping car train for Inverness at 10.45 p.m. on the previous evening. The "Hebridean" reached Kyle of Lochalsh at 10.31 a.m., and the eastbound "Hebridean" was due to start 14 minutes later, at 10.45 a.m., for Inverness, arriving back there at 2 p.m.

During the winter months two of these four workings were withdrawn. The westbound "Lewisman," at 10.15 a.m. from Inverness, ran with its timing unchanged, and the eastbound "Hebridean," apart from starting five minutes earlier, at 10.40 a.m., and reaching Inverness 18 minutes later, continued on its way throughout the year. But so far as the timetable was concerned, neither of these trains ever returned to its starting-point! For some years one restaurant car was used for both workings, and this meant transferring it from the "Lewisman" to the "Hebridean" at the passing loop at Achnasheen, where the two trains were scheduled to meet. Passengers on the "Lewisman" who had not finished their lunch by 12.13 p.m. were liable to lose the last course or two, as the car was due to be on the way back to Inverness six minutes later!

Both trains continued to run through the war period, though without names or restaurant cars, and on later timings; the overall times have remained practically unchanged, however, as they could hardly be much slower than they were. The westbound service now leaves Inverness at 10.30 a.m., and 15 minutes later the eastbound starts away from Kyle of Lochalsh; arrivals are at 1.59 and 2.24 p.m. at Kyle and Inverness respectively. Latterly the working of the Dingwall and Skye line was mainly in charge of the ex-Highland Cumming 4–6–0's, but now the ubiquitous class "5" 4–6–0's have appeared on the scene, and have had little difficulty, despite difficult gradients, with loads of about four corridor bogies and the restaurant car, which, with its change-over at Achnasheen, has been reinstated.

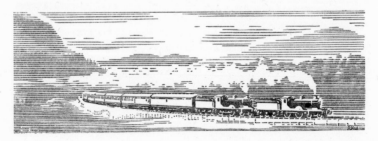

41—The "Llandudno Club Train"

The "Llandudno Club Train" made the longest journey of any of the Manchester club services. The club saloons appeared before the First World War, and eventually this particular "club" became the proud possessor of two of the magnificent 12-wheel first-class saloons built originally by the L.N.W.R. for the American boat services between London and Liverpool. These were marshalled in a train of standard L.M.S.R. corridor stock.

In its heyday, this train had some very fast timings in relation to the difficult route covered. Up to 1914 it left Manchester Exchange at 4.55 p.m., ran non-stop over the 40 miles to Chester in 48 minutes, including severe slowings through Earlestown Junction and Warrington, and the climb to Halton tunnel, and was allowed 34 minutes for the 30 miles on to Rhyl, reached in 85 minutes from Manchester. After making further stops at Abergele, Colwyn Bay and Llandudno Junction, the express made its way into Llandudno at 7.3 p.m., in 2 hours, 8 minutes from Manchester, 87¾ miles distant. A portion for Bangor was detached at Llandudno Junction and reached its destination at 7.30 p.m.

Before the outbreak of the 1914-1918 war, with eleven 8-wheelers of some 320 tons loaded weight, the "George the Fifth" 4-4-0 or "Prince of Wales" 4-6-0 rostered for this duty had no easy task to keep time. The return morning service had even smarter times, and made the Llandudno-Manchester run in precisely 2 hours, leaving at 8.10 a.m. and arriving in Exchange terminus at 10.10 a.m.

By 1939, the Manchester business men residing on the North Wales Coast were evidently taking life more easily, and found that they could get away from their offices earlier in the afternoon. The "Llandudno Club Train," therefore, was now leaving Exchange 25 minutes earlier, at 4.30 p.m., and the benefits of the service were extended to Warrington, where a stop was made to pick up passengers. The overall time, however, was still 2 hours, 8 minutes, and Llandudno was reached at 6.38 p.m. Corridor stock had come into use throughout the train, but the weight had not greatly increased, for an additional service, with more intermediate stops, was leaving Manchester Exchange for Llandudno at the old starting time of 4.55 p.m. What the business men had gained in the afternoons they lost in the mornings, however, for the start from Llandudno was at 7.48 instead of 8.10 a.m., and the journey was 9 minutes longer.

Through the war period the service still continued, but without any club saloons, and badly slowed down, for the 4.30 p.m. from Exchange, though with only one additional stop at Frodsham, was not due in Llandudno till 7.20 p.m.; and it needed a start from the popular seaside resort as early as 7.15 in the morning to be in Manchester by 10 a.m. But in May, 1946, there came a speed-up, bringing the 4.30 into Llandudno at 6.50 p.m., while a morning start at 7.40 instead of 7.15 gets the business man into Manchester by 10 a.m. Since then, further acceleration has brought the Llandudno arrival forward to 6.48 p.m., and the Manchester arrival of the 7.40 a.m. eastbound now is 3 minutes earlier, at 9.57 a.m.

42—The "Lothian Coast Express" and "Fife Coast Express"

It is a custom of Scottish schools to shut their doors at the beginning of July and to remain closed until early in September. During this period families remove themselves *en masse* to the Highlands and to the coast ; but unfortunately the Scottish businessman cannot leave his business to its own devices for an equally long period. In the days of peace, therefore, the railways in Scotland made strong efforts to attract the family moves to their own particular resorts by providing fast services which would enable *paterfamilias* to spend the nights and week-ends with his family, getting him to his business betimes without too early a start, and getting him back quickly at night.

The North British Railway served an attractive range of resorts on the North Sea coast round from Berwickshire and across the Forth to Fife, and it was with the intention of making these accessible to the Glasgow people that the " Lothian Coast Express " and the " Fifeshire Coast Express " were introduced, the former in 1912, and the latter in 1910. The " Lothian Coast Express " was to provide rapid communication between Glasgow and the seaside towns south of the Firth of Forth, and the " Fifeshire Coast Express," as its name implied, connected Glasgow with the coast towns from Leven round to Crail.

A minor distinction of the " Lothian Coast Express " was that of being the first train to run daily between Glasgow and Edinburgh in the even hour. The distance by the North British route—later, of course, the L.N.E.R.— is 47¼ miles, and a speed of 47·3 m.p.h. would not excite comment were it not for the formidable bank at the Glasgow end. Cowlairs incline, as it is called, starts directly out of Queen Street terminus in Glasgow, and for 1¼ miles is inclined at 1 in 41. As is well known, in earlier years a winding-house at the top of the bank hauled the trains up by wire ropes ; for the descent special brake-trucks were attached, as the control of the ordinary brakes was thought to be inadequate. From November, 1908, onwards, however, ordinary locomotive power has been used, with assistance given by banking engines to eastbound trains starting up the bank from Glasgow.

Allowing for the time lost in climbing from Queen Street to Cowlairs, therefore, and equally in making the descent—which is always very cautious—the " Lothian Coast Express " had to maintain a mile-a-minute gait for much of the distance between Cowlairs and Edinburgh, especially as this length of line is seldom free from at least three speed restrictions, often severe, due to coal-mining and shale-mining subsidences.

From its introduction on June 3rd, 1912, the "Lothian Coast Express" consisted of three sections, corridor throughout. The first to start in the morning was a two-coach set from Dunbar at 7.55 a.m., which travelled along the main line to Drem. Here it picked up the main train from North Berwick at 8 a.m., made up of a three-coach set with restaurant car. A short run brought the train to Longniddry Junction, where there were attached two more through coaches, from Gullane, also at 8 a.m. The complete set of eight vehicles, with a " Scott " class 4-4-0 at the head, then ran to Edinburgh (Waverley) in 18 minutes, and after a 6-minute halt, proceeded at 8.49 a.m. to make the 60-minute run to Glasgow, reaching Queen Street at 9.49 a.m.

The "Lothian Coast Express" started back from Queen Street at 3.50 p.m., and as far as Edinburgh acted as a relief to the popular 4 p.m. "diner" from Glasgow to Leeds. Reaching Waverley at 4.50 p.m., and restarting at 4.56 p.m., it split up into its component parts at Longniddry and Drem, and the arrivals were 5.34 p.m. at Gullane, 5.40 p.m. at North Berwick, and 5.45 p.m. at Dunbar. From Glasgow to Dunbar the total distance covered was 76½ miles. In the first year the express did not run on Saturdays, but in 1913 a Saturday working was introduced, with the return train as a luncheon car express from Glasgow at 12.37 p.m., which reached North Berwick at 2.23 p.m. and Dunbar at 2.27 p.m. Also the 3.50 p.m. was started 3 minutes later, and the time to North Berwick cut to 1¾ hours. Suspended during the First World War, the "Lothian Coast Express" reappeared during the summer season for some years from 1921 onwards, and by 1929 had attained the dignity of a Pullman restaurant car, but later the train faded out of existence. By 1939 no through coaches were being run between Glasgow and either North Berwick or Gullane.

The "Fifeshire Coast Express" had two years' start of its "Lothian Coast" relation, for it began to run in 1910, at first only on Fridays outwards and on Mondays in the reverse direction. In the following year, however, it became a daily service during the height of the season, leaving Glasgow (Queen Street) at 4.20 p.m., and running without a single intermediate stop over the 66½ miles to Leven. This took the express along the Edinburgh main line as far as Winchburgh Junction, then by the spur to Dalmeny, after which the Aberdeen main line was used across the Forth Bridge and on through Kirkcaldy to Thornton Junction. Leven, where the coast was reached, is the second station beyond Thornton on the line to Crail; at Crail, 84 miles from Glasgow, the "Fifeshire Coast Express" terminated.

By 1939 the "Fifeshire Coast Express," though still retaining its title, was a considerably slower train; moreover, it now ran from

Glasgow to Dundee, with a through section for Crail. The working of the train was interesting. After calling at Polmont, the next stop, at Dalmeny, at the south end of the Forth Bridge, was a " shadow " halt not shown in the public timetables, from 4.59 to 5.2 p.m. Immediately following was the 4.50 p.m. " Fifeshire Coast Express " from Edinburgh to Dundee, which also made a " shadow " stop, from 5.5 to 5.8 p.m. The purpose of both stops was to transfer the Glasgow-Crail section from the first train to the second.

The 4.6 p.m. from Glasgow then ran on to Thornton Junction, and with a number of intermediate stops reached Dundee at 6.29 p.m. Then the 4.50 p.m. from Edinburgh, a few minutes behind, called at Kirkcaldy, and, passing Thornton, made its next call at Leven. Leaving the Glasgow coaches at Crail, reached at 6.42 p.m., it continued a leisurely journey round the coast through St. Andrews back to the main line at Leuchars Junction, and finished its run in Dundee at 8.6 p.m., 97 minutes after the express which it had followed so closely to Thornton.

The morning working was simpler. A single " Fifeshire Coast Express " left Crail at the early hour of 7.5 a.m., and called at all the seaside stations round to Thornton Junction, by departure from which the clock had got round to 8.8 a.m. After calling at Kirkcaldy, the train then stopped at Dalmeny to divide, and brought its passengers into Edinburgh at 9.3 a.m., and Glasgow at 9.46 a.m.

Since the Second World War the train has been revived as a Glasgow–St. Andrews express only, and with the shorter title of "Fife Coast Express " ; departure from Queen Street is at 4.7 p.m., and there are stops at Burntisland, Kirkcaldy, Leven, Elie and Anstruther before St. Andrews is reached at 6.53 p.m. In the city-bound direction the " Fife Coast Express " is away from St. Andrews at 7.15 a.m., and, in this direction without the Burntisland stop, is into Glasgow by 9.50 a.m. A melancholy reminder of pre-war speed is that this train for some time past has been made up of five coaches from the pre-war " Silver Jubilee " streamliner. During the winter a nameless down express runs from Glasgow at 4.7 p.m., in the same times, but as far as Leven only ; and there is no corresponding return service.

43—The "Master Cutler" and the "South Yorkshireman"

As the antecedents of these two expresses were rather mixed up with one another, it is convenient to deal with them both together. Both run over what in earlier days was the Great Central main line—now the Great Central Section of the Eastern Region of British Railways. Although two ex-G.C. trains—the " Sheffield Special " and the " Ports-to-Ports " express, are included in this book, their names were unofficial, and were never carried on head-boards. The " Master Cutler," therefore, was the first properly " titled train " to run over this route ; moreover, it was the first entirely new name to be conferred on any Eastern Region train after the conclusion of the Second World War.

Between the two wars there was a popular breakfast car express which left Sheffield for Marylebone at 7.30 a.m., and with stops only at Nottingham and Leicester, was into London by 10.40 a.m. For the final 103.1 miles from Leicester to Marylebone the time allowed was no more than 109 minutes ; this included the by no means easy gradients of the Great Central line proper, but also the much more difficult Metropolitan line grades, such as the tremendous climb from Aylesbury up past Wendover, and then the entry to London through the dense Metropolitan electric service between Rickmansworth and Harrow. Nevertheless this train at first, usually, with G.C. Director 4–4–0's, and later with the L.N.E.R. " B17's " and loads of eight or nine coaches, kept very good time.

After the Second World War a morning express from Sheffield to Marylebone reappeared, and with the introduction of the 1947 winter timetable received the name of " Master Cutler." It was a popular and heavily-patronised service, as it was faster than the corresponding London Midland Region train, and so had grown to a formation of ten or eleven bogie vehicles of the latest stock. The only additional stop was Rugby, but the speed had declined sadly from pre-war days. On its first restoration, departure from Sheffield was at 7.35 a.m., and Marylebone was not reached until 11.25 a.m. ; but concurrently with the name " Master Cutler " being conferred, there was a 15–minute acceleration. Sheffield now was left at 7.40 a.m., and Marylebone was reached at 11.15 a.m., and although the time was still 25 minutes slower than pre-war, the up " Master Cutler " had become the fastest train operating between London and Sheffield by either competing route. But to ensure better timekeeping it has been necessary to slow up the journey by 12 minutes, and the Marylebone arrival is now at 11.27 a.m.

The return of the " Master Cutler " was at 6.15 p.m. from Marylebone. Before the war, this was an express to Bradford, which left London at 6.20 p.m., and was one of the hardest of all Great Central trains to work. Because of the congestion of the Metropolitan line during the evening rush hour, the 6.20 took the longer loop route through High Wycombe and Princes Risborough, but even so was allowed only 113 minutes for the 107.6 miles from Marylebone to Leicester. In Great Central Atlantic days, the haulage of a 9-coach load out of Marylebone was an exceedingly tough proposition, but the Leicester drivers kept wonderful time with this train. The load was reduced progressively by the detaching of two slip coaches, one at Finmere and the other at Woodford. Later, the " slips " were withdrawn and stops at both stations were substituted, and this made the working harder still, for the extra time conceded to Leicester was no more than 6 minutes, and the 34 mile run from

Woodford to Leicester had to be made in 34 minutes, start-to-stop. But by now the 3-cylinder " B17 " 4–6–0's of the " Sandringham " class had arrived, and with speeds of from 80 to 90 m.p.h. where conditions permitted, time was still kept.

On its post-war restoration, the starting time of this express from Marylebone was altered from 6.20 to 6.15 p.m. ; the Wycombe route once again was followed, and, as on the up journey, a Rugby stop was introduced. But Sheffield was not reached until 10.14 p.m., as compared with the 9.38 p.m. of pre-war days. With the conferring of the name " Master Cutler " in October, 1947, there was an improvement, and the Sheffield arrival was advanced to 10.2 p.m. ; by September, 1949, this had been further improved to 9.58 p.m. By this time the restaurant cars on this train had been replaced by new combined restaurant and tavern cars of Southern design, which aroused such stormy protests, however, that they were later withdrawn. The ubiquitous " B1 " 4–6–0's handled the train for some time, but Gresley Pacifics have now returned to the Great Central Section for these and other of the harder workings. Like the up " Master Cutler," the down working has also been decelerated, and the Sheffield arrival now is back to 10.8 p.m.

The " South Yorkshireman " appeared in the post-war time-tables, complete with name, in May, 1948. As a through train from Marylebone to Bradford, it took over the function of the pre-war 6.20 p.m. down Bradford express ; in the up direction, leaving Bradford (Exchange) at 10 a.m., it is the post-war counterpart of the pre-war 10 a.m. from Bradford to Marylebone, though with fewer stops. But whereas the latter train returned from Marylebone to Bradford at 6.20 p.m., the " South Yorkshireman " starts north at 4.50 p.m., and as far as Sheffield is a post-war substitute for the 4.55 p.m. down Manchester express of pre-war days. This used to run the 103.1 miles from Marylebone to Leicester in no more than 108 minutes, and had the very smart timing of 24 minutes for the 23.5 miles from Leicester to Nottingham, so getting to Sheffield at 8.1 p.m., in no more than 3 hours, 6 minutes from London.

The " South Yorkshireman " has an extra stop at Aylesbury, and from there, with its ten coaches instead of the six of pre-war days, for a time it had a very smart post-war booking of 69 minutes over the 65.2 miles from Aylesbury to Leicester, and 26 minutes for the 23.5 miles thence to Nottingham, since increased to 73 and 29 minutes respectively. At first the " South Yorkshireman " was taken round the loop from Heath in order to call at Chesterfield, but the patronage was not sufficient to justify the continuance of this halt, and when it was taken out of the schedule, and the train was given a straight run from Heath to Staveley Town, the Sheffield arrival was brought forward from 8.42 p.m. to 8.26 p.m., in 3 hours, 36 minutes from Marylebone. This has since been altered to 8.40 p.m., and the journey is longer by 44 minutes than that of the pre-war 4.55 p.m. down.

At Sheffield three of the ten coaches, with the two restaurant cars, are dropped, and the Eastern Region " B1 " 4–6–0 is replaced by a London Midland Region class " 5 " for the continuation with the five remaining vehicles to Bradford. Incidentally, the L.M.R. engine carries an E.R. headboard for this part of the run. Then follows the stiff climb from Sheffield to Penistone, where a halt is made, and over the moors to Huddersfield ; conditional stops are allowed for at Heckmondwike, Liversedge and Cleckheaton, and with one remaining regular stop, at Low Moor, the " South York-shireman " wends its way into Bradford Exchange station at 10.20 p.m., having taken 5 hours, 30 minutes for the journey from Marylebone, London.

Southbound, the Class " 5 " 4–6–0 is ready for the steep pull out of Bradford at 10 a.m. ; in this direction the Penistone stop is omitted, but the " South Yorkshireman " will call at Brockholes and Shepley, between Huddersfield and Penistone, if there are through passengers to pick up. The train runs into Sheffield at 11.20 a.m., where the Class " 5 " makes way for a " B1 " 4–6–0. It is of interest that the former no longer wastes time waiting about in Sheffield for a return trip ; it follows the " South Yorkshireman " over E.R. metals to Leicester with the through York to Bournemouth express, and returns to Sheffield with the northbound train from Bourne-mouth, in readiness to complete its return journey to Bradford with the down " South Yorkshireman." Meantime the up " South Yorkshireman," leaving Sheffield at 11.27 a.m., and calling in this direction at Loughborough and Rugby in addition to Nottingham, Leicester and Aylesbury, is due in Marylebone at 3.30 p.m., a total journey time of 5 hours, 30 minutes from Bradford. For some time no stop was made at Aylesbury, and the London arrival was at 3.10 p.m., but timekeeping was not good, and a 20–minute deceleration followed, partly through the difficulty of finding a later path through the dense electric service after Rickmansworth. The Aylesbury stop was then added, in part to justify this considerable increase in running time. But the speed is a sad decline from the the the smart running of Great Central days.

44–The "Merseyside Express," the "Manxman" and the "Red Rose"

In earlier London & North Western days a single express from Euston at 5.30 p.m. was sufficient to carry the evening traffic from London to Liverpool and Manchester, and to various other parts of Lancashire as well. But as the extent of the traffic and the luxury of the accommodation grew, and especially as more and more passen-gers demanded to be fed *en route*, the 5.30 p.m. by degrees split into various independent trains. First of all, the Manchester pas-sengers were given a separate 6 p.m. express, and the 5.30 p.m.

became a train for Liverpool and Fleetwood. Then, in 1905, an express at 5.55 p.m. down was allocated exclusively to Liverpool, making a non-stop run to Edge Hill. Later a stop was added at Mossley Hill, a more convenient alighting point for many residents in the southern suburbs of Liverpool.

The name "London–Merseyside Express" was conferred on this train in 1927, soon to be abbreviated to the simpler "Merseyside Express." In 1932, when the 6.5 p.m. down "Lancastrian" was accelerated to make a 3¼-hour run to Manchester, the two trains changed places, and the 5.55 p.m." Merseyside " start was altered to 6.5 p.m. The latter train was booked to run the 189·7 miles to Mossley Hill in 200 minutes, at 56·9 m.p.h., and so continued to the outbreak of war; then, after calling at Edge Hill, Lime Street was reached at 9.40 p.m. The Edge Hill stop was to detach the two rear Southport coaches, which were worked round through Walton to Bootle, on the electric Liverpool–Southport line, and reached Southport, after making certain intermediate stops, at 10.30 p.m.

In the up direction the " Merseyside Express," which for some years left Liverpool Lime Street at 10 a.m., and was due into Euston at 1.30 p.m., was also accelerated to start 10 minutes later, and to make the journey to London in 3 hours, 20 minutes. In this direction the Southport coaches, leaving Chapel Street station at 8.50 a.m., were worked through into Lime Street, and attached to the front of the London express there. This arrangement enabled the " Merseyside " to dispense with an Edge Hill stop, and to call only at Mossley Hill, from which the run of 189·7 miles to Euston was booked non-stop in 189 minutes, at just over a mile a minute throughout—to be precise, at 60·2 m.p.h. Often between Crewe and Stafford the up " Merseyside," running on the fast road, would overtake the " Pines Express " from Manchester to Bournemouth, on the slow road, and at times a lively race would develop, especially over the falling gradients south of Whitmore. This is a reminder that the down " Merseyside " has often had a similar race with the 6.6 p.m. from Euston to Northampton, which runs non-stop to King's Langley; but the latter now has a minute's start, and generally shows the heavier train a clean pair of heels.

Latterly the " Merseyside " became a very heavy train for its fast schedule; it was seldom less than 14 or 15 coaches and, if the latter, weighed about 490 tons empty and 525 tons with passengers and luggage. Two complete sets of dining cars were provided—a kitchen car flanked by two open first-class cars, and a twelve-wheeled third and kitchen with an open third, five vehicles in all. The first-class accommodation included one of the lounge brake cars, furnished with armchairs, that were built originally for the " Royal Scot."

During the war the 5.30 p.m. departure from Euston of much earlier history was resumed; for some time the Liverpool and Manchester trains were worked as one combined formation again, but eventually, except on Saturdays, this became too heavy a single engine load, and the Manchester train thereafter was run separately. With stops at Crewe and Mossley Hill, the 5.30 p.m. down reached Liverpool Lime Street at 9.46 p.m. ; coming up, the start was at 10 a.m., and with stops at Mossley Hill, Crewe and Watford, London was reached at 2.22 p.m.—a slowing-down by one hour of the peacetime schedule. On October 7th, 1946, the Euston departure was altered to 5.45 p.m., and the journey time was cut to 3 hours, 55 minutes : in September, 1949, the historic 6.5 p.m. (working time 6.7 p.m.) departure was reverted to, following instead of preceding the " Lancastrian," an Edge Hill stop was introduced to detach the Southport coaches, and Lime Street now is reached at 9.50 p.m. The up express, starting at 10.10 a.m., has come down to a public timing of 3 hours, 40 minutes (3 hours, 37 minutes working time).

The morning express from Euston to Liverpool, at 10.40 a.m., also in earlier years used to run combined with a Manchester train, and started at 10.30 a.m., but latterly it became a separate departure at 10.40 a.m. In summer it carried the name of " Manxman," by reason of connecting at Liverpool with the Isle of Man boats. Through sections were run to Southport, like that of the evening train, and also—an oddity for a train travelling north-westward out of London—to Swansea ; the latter coaches, attached in rear, were taken off at Stafford and worked to Shrewsbury, whence they made the lengthy cross-country journey by way of the Central Wales spas to reach Swansea Victoria at 6.35 p.m. The " Manxman," calling only at Stafford and missing Crewe, was due in Liverpool Lime Street at 2.18 p.m.

The up " Manxman " was the express leaving Lime Street at 2.10 p.m., calling at Mossley Hill and Crewe, and then making a very fast run over the 156 miles from Crewe to Euston in 152 minutes, and so reaching London at 5.30 p.m. During the war period, the 2 p.m. from Liverpool did not reach London until 6.15 p.m., but now this popular express, which calls at Rugby only, has been speeded up to a run of 3 hours, 45 minutes, reaching Euston at 5.45 p.m. The morning train from Euston, now 10.30 a.m., has had all the intermediate stops cut out, and takes the same $3\frac{3}{4}$ hours for a non-stop journey of 193·7 miles, but runs during the summer service only.

The Festival of Britain in 1951 was made the occasion of naming a third train on the Euston-Liverpool service, and equipping it with new standard stock throughout. This was the 12.5 p.m. from Euston to Liverpool and the 5.25 p.m. back. In years gone by the up express had a distinguished record, as for some years it was one of the fastest trains on the L.M.S.R. It was timed over the 152·7 miles from Crewe to Willesden Junction in 142 minutes (64·5 m.p.h.) from 1932 onwards, and when, later, the Willesden stop was taken out, the timing became 148 minutes for the 158·1 miles from Crewe to Euston (64·1 m.p.h.). Up to the outbreak of war, this express was running from Liverpool to Euston in 3¼ hours—the fastest regular time on record.

The new name given this train was " Red Rose," Lancashire counterpart of the Yorkshire " White Rose" between Leeds and King's Cross. At that time it was reaching Euston at 9.10 p.m., but in September, 1952, the arrival was advanced to 9 p.m., with a 165-minute run up from Crewe, bringing the overall time down to 3 hours, 35 minutes. As already mentioned, the down " White Rose " at first was the 12.5 p.m. from Euston to Liverpool, but with some timetable rearrangement in 1951, the departure was altered to 12.30 p.m., and the train was made non-stop over the 193¾ miles from Euston to Liverpool (Lime Street) in 3 hours, 45 minutes, as with the " Manxman."

45—The " Midday Scot "

Among the titled trains of Great Britain the " Midday Scot " has had a comparatively short reign, for although it began to run in 1889, it did not receive an official name until 1927. For many years it was known to the railway staff as " The Corridor," from the time when, in July, 1893, it became one of the first London & North Western expresses to be formed of corridor stock throughout. It had been provided with a first-class dining car from 1891 ; in 1893 second class was withdrawn, and both first-and third-class passengers were provided with restaurant car accommodation. It is remarkable that when, from its first journey in 1889, the up train left Glasgow Central at 2 p.m. and reached London Euston at 10.50 p.m., the time was not varied by more than 5 minutes in the next 25 years.

A great day in the history of " The Corridor " was July 11th, 1908, when there was introduced to the service one of the finest sets of passenger stock that the country had seen up to that time, or, indeed, for years afterwards. This was a magnificent train of 12-wheel cars, marred only by the inclusion of two considerably older West Coast Joint Stock dining cars. The formation going north at that time, from the engine, was brake third, composite restaurant car, composite coach, and brake third for Glasgow ; composite restaurant car, composite and third brake for Edinburgh ; and composite brake for Aberdeen ; to which were added a composite brake for Whitehaven, and a composite for Altrincham.

The last-mentioned vehicle—a most curious working—came off at Crewe, and was worked from there *via* Sandbach and over the Cheshire Lines Committee's route. The Whitehaven and Aberdeen coaches were detached at Preston, and continued from there on the back of a following express from Liverpool and Manchester to Glasgow. Leaving Euston at 2 p.m., the main train had called already at Willesden Junction, Rugby and Crewe ; from Preston it was run non-stop to Carlisle, where it had now become the regular procedure to attach the McIntosh inside-cylinder 4–6–0 No. 903 *Cardean*. In her light blue livery, the famous Caledonian 4–6–0, with her train of chocolate-and-white 12-wheelers, made an *ensemble* quite unmatched at that time. The Scottish stops were at Beattock, for banking assistance to Summit, and in the open country at Strawfrank Junction, outside Carstairs, to detach the section for Edinburgh. The Glasgow section was into Central station by 10.20 p.m., and the Edinburgh portion reached Princes Street 10 minutes later.

Coming south, both parts of the train started simultaneously at 2 p.m., from Glasgow and Edinburgh, and both included, on the rear, sections for Liverpool and Manchester. The Edinburgh train, notwithstanding a stop at Symington to pick up the Aberdeen coach, kept ahead of the Glasgow all the way to Preston. From Glasgow the main part of " The Corridor," headed by *Cardean*, ran the 102·3 miles to Carlisle without a stop—the only 100-mile run made by the train in either direction—and then called at Penrith as the only stop between Carlisle and Preston. At Preston the Edinburgh, Aberdeen and Glasgow coaches, having shed their Liverpool and Manchester " tails," were joined up, and proceeded to call at Crewe, Rugby and Willesden Junction before reaching Euston at 10.45 p.m. At this period, " The Corridor " dropped a slip-coach (attached at Crewe) at Nuneaton, to replace a previous Nuneaton stop.

As to London & North Western motive power, in the earliest phase of its history " The Corridor " was associated with the famous Webb 3-cylinder compound *Jeanie Deans*, which used to work it daily from Euston to Crewe and back—a tough task for a 2–2–2–0 locomotive of such modest dimensions. By 1908 the Webb 4–4–0 compounds had given place to the " Precursor " 4–4–0's and the " Experiment " 4–6–0's, followed by their superheated " George the Fifth " and " Prince of Wales " variants ; and before the outbreak of the First World War the 4-cylinder 4–6–0 " Claughtons " were available for the working of a train which was now a minimum formation of 400 tons between London and Preston.

During the latter part of the 1914–1919 war " The Corridor," shorn of its dining cars, was the only L.N.W.R. day service between London and Glasgow ; the starting time had changed from 2 to 1 p.m., and with slower running and additional stops, the down train did not reach Central till 11.10 p.m., while the up train ran into Euston 10 minutes later. Recovering in the post-war period, by 1923, the year the L.M.S.R. came into being, " The Corridor " was leaving Euston at 1.30 p.m., and reaching Glasgow at 10 p.m., while the up train had precisely the same times. The stops going north were now Rugby, Crewe, Lancaster, Carlisle and Carstairs ; on the southbound run the Glasgow train was stopping at Symington to collect the Edinburgh portion, and calling only at Carlisle and

Crewe between there and London. The Aberdeen section followed from Law Junction as a separate train, and made the calls that in earlier years had been made by the up " Corridor."

So matters continued until 1932, when the L.M.S.R. and L.N.E.R. at length broke loose from the bonds of the agreement which for 32 years had restricted the overall times of their Anglo-Scottish day trains to a minimum of 8¼ hours. The " Midday Scot "—as " The Corridor " had become five years earlier—was one of the trains to share in the acceleration. At first the times came down to 8 hours, 5 minutes northbound and 8 hours southbound ; later the up train was accelerated to 7 hours, 55 minutes, despite an additional stop at Lancaster from 1933 onwards. The Stanier Pacifics had now appeared on the scene, and not only ousted the " Royal Scot " 4–6–0's, which had been changed *en route* at Crewe only, but were working the " Midday Scot " through in each direction unchanged over the 401½ miles between Euston and Glasgow. In the northbound direction, also, the train acquired at Crewe a Great Western composite brake running through from Penzance to Glasgow, attached next the engine.

In the fourteen months from May, 1936, to June, 1937, inclusive, the " Midday Scot " reached the height of its fame. In the down direction it reverted to its historic departure hour of 2 p.m. from Euston, and was relieved by a new express from London at 1.30 p.m., so that it could run non-stop over the 158 miles to Crewe in 163 minutes. A new stop was made at Penrith, and the timing of 59 minutes for the 51·2 miles over Shap Summit from Lancaster to Penrith, with a minimum trainload of 14 bogies (about 445 tons) and often more, was the hardest, from the locomotive point of view, that has ever been included in the train's schedule. At Carlisle, reached at 7.35 p.m., the train divided, and the Glasgow section was run non-stop from there to Central in the then unprecedented time of 116 minutes, arriving at 9.35 p.m. The Edinburgh and Aberdeen portions continued together to Lockerbie, and there they also parted company ; Lockerbie to Edinburgh non-stop brought that section in at 9.55 p.m., and Perth passengers enjoyed a total acceleration of 72 minutes by getting into that city at 11.28 p.m. The up " Midday Scot," but little altered, reached Euston at 9.20 p.m.

Then came the upheaval caused by the introduction of the " Coronation Scot " streamliner in July, 1937. For the first time in its history the " Midday Scot " ceased—officially—any longer to provide an advertised service between London and Glasgow, although it was provided with Glasgow coaches in order to accommodate passengers to and from intermediate stations. Still leaving Euston at 2 p.m., the train shrunk to no more than six coaches—third brake, third restaurant and kitchen, semi-open first, and third brake for Edinburgh, and composite and third brake for Glasgow—which, nevertheless, boasted the services of a Pacific for its haulage. To Crewe there was now a booking of over a mile-a-minute—158 miles in 156 minutes—and here the G.W.R. coach was picked up. After leaving Crewe at 4.45 p.m., the next stop was at Wigan, where through coaches from Manchester to Glasgow and Edinburgh were marshalled in the centre of the train ; this took from 5.23 to 5.32 p.m. Passing Preston, the " Midday Scot " proceeded to Lancaster, where a stop from 6.19 to 6.24 p.m. was needed to add a portion from Liverpool to Glasgow, bringing the load up to 14 vehicles.

At Carlisle, reached at 7.44 p.m., the express split up into its Edinburgh and Glasgow sections. The Pacific came off, and was replaced by a " 5XP " 4-6-0, which took the six-coach Edinburgh portion—four from London and two from Manchester—out at 7.49 p.m., and was due to run into Princes Street at 9.45 p.m., in 7¾ hours from Euston. Then the Pacific backed down at Carlisle on to the remaining eight—which might be nine or ten if more through Glasgow coaches had been run from London—and leaving at 7.56 p.m., made Glasgow Central at 9.55 p.m. Glasgow passengers had to be careful to get their dinners betimes, as they had no restaurant car service from Carlisle onwards.

In the reverse direction, the locomotive task was distinctly harder. The Pacific locomotive moved out of Glasgow Central at 1.35 p.m., 5 minutes behind the " Coronation Scot," with a load of from four to six bogies. At Law Junction, 18·3 miles away, there was waiting the London portion of the 10.5 a.m. express from Aberdeen, a four-coach restaurant car set similar to that from Edinburgh, and hungry Glasgow passengers could then get their lunch. Meantime the " Midday Scot " proper had left Edinburgh at 1.40 p.m., and awaited the Glasgow and Aberdeen portions at Symington.

The full train of 12 to 14 vehicles, including two pairs of restaurant cars, leaving Symington, after a 4-minute stop, at 2.36 p.m., was next booked to make a 72-minute run over the 66·9 miles from Symington to Carlisle, including the climb to Beattock summit, and in the summer months added further to its load at the Border city by acquiring two through coaches from Stranraer, which made it possible to get through from Northern Ireland to London in the compass of a single day. The load might now be anything up to 16 coaches, with a tare weight of 500 tons or more, and this had to be worked over the 141 miles from Carlisle to Crewe, including Lancaster stop, in 176 minutes, and finally over the 158 miles from Crewe to Euston in the very smart time of 160 minutes. The up " Midday Scot " was thus brought into London at 9.30 p.m.

Through most of the Second World War, though suspended for several lengthy periods, the " Midday Scot " continued to run. Once again it became a London–Glasgow train, and with no Edinburgh or other portions. It was also a very heavily-patronised service, and in the northbound direction almost daily needed formations of 15 or more coaches, crowded to capacity. Leaving Euston at 1 p.m., it stopped only at Rugby and Crewe to Carlisle, and then at Carstairs (to give connection to Edinburgh,

Perth and the North) and at Motherwell ; Glasgow was reached at 9.58 p.m. In the other direction, also leaving Glasgow at 1 p.m., the wartime version of the " Midday Scot " called at Motherwell, Carstairs, Carlisle, and Crewe, and then made a call unknown in peacetime, at Watford, to set down passengers—a convenience for residents in the north-west suburbs introduced at the time of the London *blitz*. Arrival in London was at 9.56 p.m., 2 minutes before the Glasgow arrival of the northbound train. The through Pacific workings continued unchanged. Restaurant cars were restored to the train both ways on October 1st, 1945, and the up Watford stop was excised in May, 1946. From October 7th, 1946, the down train was altered to leave at 1.15 p.m., but the Glasgow arrival was put back to 10.5 p.m. ; the up express, however, was accelerated to reach Euston at 9.50 p.m.

Since then the up " Midday Scot " has had its Glasgow start altered to 1.30 p.m., to bring it into Carstairs behind instead of in front of the through Perth portion, and from there the " Scot " makes a spirited dash over the 73·5 miles to Carlisle, including Beattock summit, in 75 minutes. South of the Border there is a stop at Preston as well as Lancaster, and the Watford stop has been reinstated, Euston being reached at 10 p.m., after 8½ hours *en voyage*. The northbound "Midday Scot," with stops unchanged, is now allowed 8 hours, 20 minutes, and is into Glasgow by 9.35 p.m. During the winter the latter acquires, as far as Crewe, a through Blackpool portion which in summer leaves Euston as an independent restaurant car train at 1.30 p.m.

46—The "Midlander"

It was as far back as 1902 that the London & North Western Railway first timed a non-stop train to cover the 112.9 miles between London and Birmingham in the even two hours ; it was the 5 p.m. from New Street to Euston. The route was ideal for the purpose ; apart from the initial climb of 1¼ miles from the platform end at Euston to Camden, at 1 in 70 to 1 in 105, and the short and sharp rise into New Street, Birmingham, the old London & Birmingham Railway was so magnificently engineered that there is no other gradient steeper than 1 in 330 throughout its length. Moreover, the only speed reduction enforced at any point was the 40 m.p.h. through Rugby.

Within two years of the first two-hour timing, a complete service of two-hour trains, four in each direction daily, had come into existence. In those years, Coventry had not attained to its later motor manufacturing eminence, and before the First World War, two of the down Birmingham two-hour trains (the 8.40 a.m. and the

Right : Light task for an E.R. Class " A1 " Pacific—No. 60118 *Archibald Sturrock* at speed with the down " Harrogate Sunday Pullman " north of Peterborough

[*P. H. Wells*

Above : Class " 5 " 4–6–0 No. 45292 leaves Halton Tunnel with the westbound " Llandudno Club Train "

[*R. Whitfield*

Right : From Morecambe to Bradford— the morning " residential " leaves Skipton with Caprotti Class " 5 " 4–6–0 No. 44757

[*H. Weston*

3

Above : An E.R. flyer —Class " A2 " Pacific No. 60526 *Sugar Palm* hurries the up " Norseman ", past Essendine

[*P. H. Wells*

Left : Getting away from the Rugby stop— L.M.R. Pacific No. 46256 *Sir William A. Stanier, F.R.S.* with the down " Midday Scot ".

[*H. Weston*

[E. D. Bruton

[S. Oborne

Nearing journey's end—The up "Northumbrian," in charge of "A4" Pacific No. 60029 *Woodcock*, passing Red Hall box, Hatfield.
Inset above : The short-lived "Northern Belle" tourist sleeping-car train at Crianlarich, in the West Highlands, behind Class "K4" 2-6-0
No. 3446 (original numbering) *Macleod of Macleod*

131

[E. R. Wethersett

Climbing the 1 in 42 of Cowlairs Bank—Class " A3 " Pacific No. 60096 *Papyrus* does some hard work with the Leeds-bound " North Briton "

[K. W. Wightman

Climbing the 1 in 122 to Sevenoaks Tunnel—" Merchant Navy " Class Pacific No. 35030 *Elder Dempster Lines* with the through Paris-London sleepers and vans of the " Night Ferry "

6.55 p.m.) provided a service to Coventry by slip coaches, which were stopped clear of the platform loops and then drawn into the platforms by waiting locomotives or horses. Eventually, in the last year before 1914, the L.N.W.R. specially built vestibuled slip coaches for this service, to give Coventry passengers access to the restaurant cars up to the moment of severing the train.

The most rapid development of the L.N.W.R. Birmingham and Wolverhampton service was during the years when the G.W.R. was building its shortened Birmingham route *via* Bicester, and the former company thus was being threatened for the first time with competition for this important traffic on more or less equal terms. One striking L.N.W.R. experiment in 1910 was the introduction of a " City-to-City " service between Birmingham and Broad Street, in the heart of the City of London, leaving New Street at 8.20 a.m. and reaching Broad Street at 10.35 a.m.; returning, the express left Broad Street at 5.25 p.m. for a 2¼-hour run back to Birmingham. The four-coach train included a restaurant car, and was worked by one of the rebuilt and simplified Webb compound 4-4-0's of the " Renown " class. A typewriting compartment with typist was provided for businessmen desiring to dictate their correspondence *en route* (as also on the 4.45 a.m. from Euston to Birmingham and the 8.40 a.m. up express to Euston); intermediate stops were made at Willesden Junction and Coventry. But old customs are difficult to alter, and as the city magnates could not be induced in any numbers to change their custom from Euston to Broad Street, the " City-to-City " disappeared on the outbreak of war in 1914.

After the First World War, the Coventry slip coaches were never reintroduced, but as the importance of Coventry was increasing steadily, measures had to be taken to provide an adequate service. This had been done in part by running local trains over the short distance between Coventry and Rugby to connect at the latter station with expresses from and to the North, but by degrees Coventry stops began to appear also in the schedules of the Birmingham two-hour trains. As more powerful locomotives became available it was found that with faster running, notwithstanding the increased weight of the trains, an intermediate stop could be included in the two-hour schedule without any detriment to time-keeping. Among the earliest of the two-hour one-stop trains were the 9.10 a.m. from Euston and the 4.50 p.m. from Birmingham, both of which called at Willesden Junction. Coventry stops now appeared in other two-hour schedules ; and after the advent to the service of the 3-cylinder " 5XP " 4-6-0's, which ousted the 4-4-0 Midland compounds just as they, in their turn, had displaced the L.N.W.R. " George the Fifth " 4-4-0's, the two-hour timing came down to 115 minutes (all but a mile-a-minute for the 112.9 miles), Coventry stop included.

These timings meant a start-to-stop average of over 60 m.p.h. between Euston and Coventry in both directions. Three down and three up expresses were booked to cover the 94.0 miles in 92 minutes,

The 4.50 p.m. up contrived to cover the distance in two hours stopping at both Coventry and Willesden and running the 88.6 miles between them in 86 minutes; the 9.15 a.m. down ran the 107.5 miles from Willesden to Birmingham in 104 minutes, and the 8.10 a.m. down the 76·5 miles from Watford to Coventry in 73 minutes. But the most startling performance was that of the 6.20 p.m. up, which ran from New Street to Euston in two hours notwithstanding *three* intermediate stops—at Coventry, Rugby and Watford Junction. The 65·1 m.p.h. timing of this express from Rugby to Watford—65·1 miles in the hour exactly—was the fastest start-to-stop schedule in the L.M.S.R. time-tables up to the Second World War.

It should be added that all the Birmingham two-hour trains began or ended their journeys at Wolverhampton, some travelling *via* Dudley Port and stopping there to give communication to and from Dudley, and others by the heavily-graded and slightly longer route through Soho Road, Bescot and Darlaston. Some called at Bescot in order to connect to and from Walsall, and Walsall was served by one lone through coach attached to the 4.35 p.m. from Euston and the 11.45 a.m. from Birmingham.

The Second World War wrought havoc with the L.M.S.R. Birmingham service, and as yet it is far from recovery. The trains are certainly a good deal heavier, loading as many of them now do to from 11 to 13 bogies regularly, but the one-stop trains, of which the best during the war (the 6 p.m. down) was allowed 2 hours, 24 minutes, as yet have not got below 2 hours, 8 minutes on the fastest service of the day. This is the "Midlander," reinstated in October, 1950, and the first train on the London Midland Birmingham service to earn the dignity of a title. At first this was the pre-war 11.12 a.m. from Wolverhampton and 11.45 a.m. from Birmingham, starting at 10.55 a.m., and from New Street 11.30 a.m., which with an arrival at Euston at 1.44 p.m. gave an overall time of 2 hours, 49 minutes—an addition of 21 minutes to the pre-war allowance. But the train concerned has been withdrawn, and the title is now carried by the 9.45 a.m. from Wolverhampton (10.30 a.m. from Birmingham), which calls at Coventry, then takes the Northampton loop to call at that town, and is due in Euston at 12.45 p.m. This usually has a load of nine bogies, for which a "6P" 4-6-0 provides more than adequate power. On its return journey the "Midlander" stock forms the 5.45 p.m. from Euston to Wolverhampton, which calls at Coventry and reaches Birmingham at 7.53 p.m. and Wolverhampton at 8.27 p.m., also "6P" 4-6-0 hauled. Certain other expresses on this service from time to time have rebuilt "Royal Scots" as their motive power.

47—The "Night Ferry"

In the past there have been a number of proposals for providing transport for passengers and freight between Great Britain and the mainland of Europe without change of carriage or wagon. The first such scheme was abortive ; it was the Channel Tunnel, work on which was actually begun between Folkestone and Dover, at the English end, but which was later abandoned. Then followed the train ferry idea, already well developed in Scandinavia for providing communication between the mainland and islands of Denmark and both Germany and Sweden. Across the English Channel this first took shape in the 1914–1918 war, when train-ferries were established both between Richborough in East Kent and Dunkerque, and also between Southampton and Le Havre, greatly facilitating the movement of war material.

After the war, the two initial cross-Channel train ferries went out of use, but were succeeded by a permanent train-ferry between Harwich and Zeebrugge in Belgium, which came into operation in April, 1924. But once again this ferry was for freight only, except that it was used to transport to Europe dining, sleeping and Pullman cars that had been built in Britain for Continental use. At last, in 1936, the dream of years took shape by the completion of a train-ferry terminal at Dover which, with the remodelled Dunkerque terminal of earlier years, made it possible to establish the first passenger service between London and Paris without change of carriage. The first through train ran on the night of October 14th in that year.

The aim has been to provide, not faster transport than the day services *via* Dover-Calais and Folkestone-Boulogne, but a comfortable night route which permits the passenger to go to bed on leaving London, and to wake up on the French side in time to dress, breakfast on the train, and reach Paris at the beginning of the business day. The same facilities are provided in the reverse direction. As a result, for the first time in history the blue sleeping cars of the International Sleeping Car Company are now seen in a London terminus every day. The sleeping cars and a brake-van alone run through ; passengers in ordinary first and second class compartments have to change at Dover and Dunkerque on and off the ferry-steamers, on which comfortable passenger accommodation is provided, in the same way as they do on the day service.

As the service is a night one, the first journey in the day of the " Night Ferry " train is up from Dover to Victoria, which is reached at 9.10 a.m. all the year round. In the reverse direction the start from Victoria is at 9.0 p.m. in winter and 10.0 p.m. in summer. For the 78.0 miles between Victoria and the Dover ferry terminal the time allowed is 100 minutes down and 110 minutes up. From 1936 until the war two 4-4-0 locomotives were used to work the train ; from its post-war revival " West Country " Pacifics took charge, but the increase in accommodation eventually made it necessary for these locomotives to be piloted also. Since then a number of the larger " Merchant Navy " Pacifics have been drafted to Dover shed to handle the " Night Ferry " and other Continental trains. The " Night Ferry " also has been handled by standard Class " 7 " Pacifics of the " Britannia " type.

The formation of the train from Dover to Victoria from the engine backwards is, first, one or two vans and four or five sleeping cars, all of International Sleeping Car Company's stock working through from Paris to London ; then, attached at Dover, a restaurant and kitchen car, buffet car, corridor first, corridor second, another restaurant and kitchen car, and a first class brake—six or seven Continental and six S.R. vehicles, with a total tare weight of 475 to 515 tons. The sleepers are of the usual Continental type, though shortened from the Wagons-Lits standard length and reduced in width in order to conform to S.R. loading gauge restrictions.

48—The "Night Scot"

At one time the train which later became the " Night Scot " provided the fastest daily service between London and Glasgow. In the days when the East and West Coast companies were still bound by their agreement not to cut the times of the day trains below a minimum of 8 hours, 15 minutes from London to either Glasgow or Edinburgh, there was no such restriction on the night services. While the Great Northern, North Eastern and North British companies were timing their down night express to Aberdeen to reach Edinburgh in 7¾ hours from London, therefore, the London & North Western scheduled their principal night Scottish service, at 11.50 p.m. from Euston, to reach Glasgow Central at 7.50 a.m., 8 hours later, calling at Crewe, Carlisle and Carstairs.

In the years after the First World War, however, the train by degrees grew considerably heavier, and the speed was much reduced. Departure time finally became 11.45 p.m. from London Euston, and arrival in Glasgow was 9.35 a.m. But the traveller was compensated for this later arrival by the insertion at Carlisle, in the centre of the train, of a couple of restaurant cars, which enabled him to have breakfast in comfort before alighting. The formation of the train from Carlisle might include from six or more 12-wheel first-class sleeping cars, two third-class sleepers, a composite coach, two corridor thirds, and two brakes, with a 12-wheel dining car and an adjacent open car for meal service, making an empty weight of at least 530 tons.

The stops on the down journey were now at Rugby, Crewe, Preston and Carlisle, where the " Night Scot " was due at 6.28 a.m., and had a booked stop of 22 minutes to give time for the marshalling of the restaurant cars in the centre of the train. A curious feature of the working was that this express, while waiting at Carlisle, was overtaken by another train which had left Euston at 12.20 a.m., 35 minutes later, and was due in Carlisle at 6.35 a.m. From Carlisle, leaving at 6.50 a.m., the " Night Scot " had a most leisurely allowance of 2¾ hours for the 102·3 miles on to Glasgow. Any gain on schedule was impossible, for the train was due to pass Lockerbie 8 minutes after the Glasgow-bound " Tinto," which called at all stations to Carstairs before beginning to run " express passenger," had left. So if the northbound " Night Scot " was on time, constant signal checks were almost inevitable over a considerable part of its journey in Scotland, though the timing certainly had the merit of making a late arrival in Glasgow extremely unlikely. A scheduled stop was made at Symington, where a supply of morning newspapers was put on board the train ; the timetable also showed a " conditional " stop at Lockerbie to set down passengers, and a stop at Beattock was necessary for banking assistance.

In the up direction the " Night Scot," before the war, had become a train of distinction by being booked to make the run of 243·3 miles from Glasgow to Crewe without any intermediate stop. This meant that a load often equal to that of the down journey— for, although no restaurant cars were run on the southbound working, their place might be taken by more sleeping accommodation, which frequently reached a total of eight first-class 12-wheelers and two third-class cars—had to be worked by the one engine, first over the 1,015 foot altitude of Beattock summit, then down virtually to sea level north of Carlisle, and after that up on to Shap, 915 feet above the sea, in the compass of this one non-stop break.

Departure from Glasgow was at 10.45 p.m., and 5 hours, 5 minutes was allowed for the run to Crewe ; in all the circumstances, the scheduled average of 47·9 m.p.h. was not to be despised, especially in rough winter weather. There was an allowance of 10 minutes at Crewe, and whereas the public timetable booked the " Night Scot " into Euston at 7.15 a.m., in 8¾ hours from Glasgow, the working time of arrival was 10 minutes earlier, at 7.5 a.m.

As to locomotives, the " Royal Scots " had a fairly lengthy reign on the " Night Scot," until the advent of the " Pacifics " ; with the latter, through workings from Crewe to Glasgow and back to Crewe were first arranged, but with the introduction of through locomotive workings between Euston and Glasgow, the " Night Scot " became one of the trains to be rostered regularly for a Pacific throughout in each direction. In the latter case no attempt was made, of course, to induce a single engine-crew to work the train all the way ; this would be much too arduous a turn of duty. Drivers and firemen were changed, therefore, at Crewe.

Wartime witnessed some striking developments in the working of the " Night Scot." The name went, but the train remained, and was one of the most popular on the service. The main portion left

Euston 2¼ hours earlier than in peacetime, at 9.15 p.m., with an average load of 15 bogies, a number of them sleeping cars. Stopping at Crewe from 12.27 to 12.37 a.m., it was booked to make its next halt at Beattock, in Southern Scotland, at 4.39 a.m., for assistance up the famous 10-mile bank to Beattock summit.

It is the greater steepness of the inclination on this side, from 1 in 69 to 1 in 88 throughout, that makes a "banker" necessary with a train of this weight, even though the train may be headed by a Pacific, to save time on the climb ; in the opposite direction the gradients are more widely distributed, and the steepest of them is 1 in 99 for 2½ miles, also to Beattock summit. From Beattock, left at 4.46 a.m., to Glasgow was a non-stop run of 62·6 miles, and Glasgow Central was reached at 6.15 a.m., in 9 hours from London. The wartime "Night Scot" was thus 50 minutes quicker than the peacetime service—a most unusual inversion of the normal order of things.

But the traffic was so heavy that during most of the war three trains in all were necessary in each direction, at about the same departure hour, to handle all the passengers, and each of them usually a 15-coach formation. The first down service, at 8.40 p.m., later 8.50, was reserved exclusively for Service passengers. This was of considerable note in being booked nightly to make the longest war-time non-stop run in the world, over the 301·1 miles from Euston to Kingmoor, 2 miles north of Carlisle, where there was a stop to change enginemen and examine the train. The time allowed was 6 hours, 25 minutes, so that no more than moderate speed was called for.

Following the 9.15 p.m. there was also the 9.20 p.m. for Glasgow ; this train, without sleeping-car accommodation, called at Crewe from 12.40 to 12.50 a.m., and next at Kingmoor, like the 8.40 p.m. down, from 4.2 to 4.9 a.m. ; from there it also travelled by the Glasgow & South Western line, but non-stop over the 113·5 miles to St. Enoch, which was reached at 6.50 a.m. in 9½ hours from London. In the public timetable both the 9.15 and 9.20 p.m. were advertised as non-stop from Euston to Glasgow, their intermediate stops being for operational purposes only.

In the reverse direction the arrangements were somewhat similar, except that the wartime version of the southbound "Night Scot," at 9.30 p.m. from Glasgow Central, was unique in Great Britain as being composed only of first-class and third-class sleeping cars. It was preceded at 9.5 p.m. (9.8 p.m. working time) by a relief train without sleeping accommodation. The latter ran through Carlisle, but stopped at No. 12 box, south of the station, to change enginemen, from 11.37 to 11.42 p.m. ; after that the only stop was at Crewe, from 3.4 to 3.7 a.m., and Euston was reached at 6.25 a.m. Ten minutes later the "Night Scot" arrived, after having run non-stop from Glasgow to Crewe, and halted there from 3.13 to 3.24 a.m.

The strangest of these schedules, however, were those of the southbound Services sleeping car special and a third section of the

" Night Scot," which performed some odd feats of passing and repassing one another on the way to London. The former left Glasgow St. Enoch at 9.27 p.m., and called at Kilmarnock and Dumfries on the way down to Carlisle, only to find, on passing Gretna Junction, that the 9.38 p.m. from Central, stopping at Motherwell to pick up passengers, had got through 6 minutes ahead. Both trains ran through Carlisle, and changed engine-crews at Carlisle No. 12 box, from which the train from Central got away at 12.14 a.m., and the Services sleeper at 12.25 a.m.

But while the 9.38 p.m. from Central was making a leisurely stop at Crewe from 3.27 to 3.50 a.m., the sleeping car train slipped by at 3.38 a.m., and got ahead, and notwithstanding a " set down " stop at Watford which was inserted in the schedule in the later months of the war, reached Euston at 6.55 a.m. The 9.38 a.m. from Central made a call at Rugby and was into Euston 13 minutes later. It is a fitting commentary on the amazing growth of long-distance traffic in war-time that four expresses, composed of a total of at least 60 coaches and filled to capacity, should have been required to leave Glasgow every night between 9.8 and 9.38 p.m., and to reach Euston between 6.25 and 7.8 a.m., doing little else than to convey through traffic. All the express trains mentioned in this chapter normally were through Pacific workings between London and Glasgow.

From May, 1946, there was a complete revision of the night service between Euston and Glasgow. The principal down " sleeper " reverted to its pre-war 11.35 p.m. departure, now acquired a couple of breakfast cars at Carlisle, and reached Glasgow Central at 9.45 a.m.—a journey of 10 hours, 10 minutes. The up run took 80 minutes less—10.35 p.m. from Glasgow and 7.25 a.m. into Euston ; it was still an all-sleeping car train.

To-day the " Night Scot," no longer named, has settled down to a departure from Euston at 11.40 p.m. The first stop is made at Carlisle, at 6.10 a.m. From here, after a 20-minute wait, during which the two breakfast cars are marshalled into the train, departure is at 6.30 a.m., now by the Glasgow & South Western route, with stops at Dumfries and Kilmarnock to set down sleeping car passeng-ers. At Kilmarnock a pilot is attached to help this heavy train up Stewarton bank, and there is a special stop at Lugton to detach it ; beyond Strathbungo the sleeper is switched back to the Caledonian line, and ends its journey in Glasgow Central at 9.30 a.m., an overall journey of 9 hours, 50 minutes. In the reverse direction the all-sleeping car train leaves Glasgow Central at 10.20 p.m., via Carstairs, and the only stop is at Carlisle No. 12 box, south of the station, to change enginemen ; the express is booked into Euston in the working timetable at 7.3 a.m. and in the public book 12 minutes later. It is followed by a 10.30 p.m. sleeper from Glasgow Central, which takes the G. & S.W. route, calls at Kilmarnock to pick up passengers, and then, like its immediate predecessor, at Carlisle No. 12 only to London, which it reaches 20 minutes after the 10.10 p.m. sleeper.

The overall time of 8 hours, 53 minutes is roughly one hour less than that of the northbound train.

49—The "Night Scotsman"

Like its rival, the "Night Scot" from Euston to Glasgow, the "Night Scotsman" was a considerably faster train in earlier years than it became in the period before the Second World War. In 1914 it was leaving King's Cross at 11.30 p.m., and taking a level 8 hours to Edinburgh; by 1939 the departure time had come forward to 10.25 p.m. and the arrival in Edinburgh Waverley had been retarded to 7.15 a.m., making a journey of 8 hours, 50 minutes. Moreover, by 1939 the business done by the "Night Scotsman" to and from Scottish cities north and west of Edinburgh had grown to such dimensions that Edinburgh passengers from London were no longer welcome on it, but had to take the following 10.35 p.m. sleeping car train from King's Cross.

Stops were made by the "Night Scotsman" at Grantham, York and Newcastle, to pick up passengers only. On arrival at Waverley at 7.15 a.m., like the "Aberdonian" the "Night Scotsman" split into three component parts—Glasgow, Perth and Aberdeen. Each of the three sections formed part of a breakfast car train; two of these trains started simultaneously at 7.35 a.m. to Aberdeen, due at 11.12 a.m., and to Glasgow, due in Queen Street at 8.49 a.m.; while the third left at 7.30 a.m. for Perth, due at 8.55 a.m. The last-named had a Pullman restaurant car, of which several were at work on the L.N.E.R. in Scotland before the Second World War.

In the reverse direction, curiously enough, no train up to 1939 officially carried the title "Night Scotsman," though the southbound counterpart of the northbound 7.30 p.m. from London was doubtless the 11 p.m. from Edinburgh Waverley, running just ahead of the "Aberdonian," and conveying through coaches and sleeping cars from Dundee (9 p.m.), Inverness (4.15 p.m.) and Perth (8.10 p.m.). This train had stops at Berwick, Newcastle, York and Grantham, and was due in King's Cross at 7.15 a.m. In both directions the "Night Scotsman," like all the L.N.E.R. night expresses, was a train of great weight, usually made up to thirteen or fourteen vehicles, with six to eight of them first- or third-class sleeping cars. Pacific haulage was provided between London and Edinburgh.

Over the whole length of the East Coast main line the worst bank is Cockburnspath, which faces southbound trains, and begins at Innerwick, 4½ miles south of Dunbar. It is introduced by 1¾ miles at 1 in 210, and then steepens to 4¼ miles continuously at 1 in 96. The steepest incline on the route is 1¼ miles at 1 in 78 up into

Edinburgh Waverley, but this can be taken by northbound trains " at the double," and causes little difficulty. Much worse in its effect is the start out of King's Cross, averaging 1 in 107 for 1½ miles through two tunnels in which the rails are invariably slippery.

But there are also long and gruelling stretches of more moderate gradient, such as 8 miles at 1 in 200 up to Potter's Bar, 9 miles mostly at 1 in 200 and 178 up to Stoke Summit (5½ miles south of Grantham), 4¼ miles at 1 in 190 northwards from Berwick, and another 6 miles at 1 in 200 a little further north to Grantshouse, at the summit of Cockburnspath bank. Coming south, apart from the last-mentioned, the worst pulls are from Newark past Grantham to Stoke Summit, finishing with 5 miles at 1 in 200, and from Arlesey past Hitchin to Stevenage, concluding with 5 miles at the same inclination. Such banks as these must be taken into account in assessing the locomotive work on such heavy trains as these.

During the Second World War this train retained its title. It was a through train between King's Cross and Edinburgh only, leaving London at 10.15 p.m. and due in Waverley at 7.42 a.m., and this was no more than 37 minutes slower than in peacetime. Also it was preceded nightly, in the last year of the war, by a relief express at 10 p.m., calling only at Grantham and Newcastle (except a momentary stop at York to change engine crews), and reaching Edinburgh at 6.57 a.m. This timing was only 7 minutes slower than that of peace. In October, 1946, the Edinburgh arrival was altered to 7.5 a.m., so restoring the pre-war timing of 8 hours, 50 minutes.

Curiously enough, in the up direction the train which in the peacetime timetable had no name has been officially titled the " Night Scotsman," and has carried the roof-boards of that train. Leaving Edinburgh Waverley at 9.40 p.m., it called at Dunbar, Berwick, Newcastle and Darlington to pick up passengers only, then at Grantham and Peterborough, running into King's Cross at 7.10 a.m.—a much slower journey of 9½ hours. In October, 1946, the start from Waverley was altered to 10 p.m., and the journey time to King's Cross was cut to 8½ hours.

To-day the " Night Scotsman " is a train of considerable distinction. All stops between King's Cross and Newcastle have been cut out, and the non-stop run of 268.3 miles is the longest made throughout the year on Eastern and North Eastern Region metals, though beaten in summer, of course, by the London–Edinburgh run of the " Capitals Limited." Moreover, it is far faster than the pre-war " Night Scotsman," for with departure from King's Cross at 10.15 p.m. and arrival in Edinburgh at 6.21 a.m., the overall time has come down to 8 hours, 6 minutes. Southbound, with departure from Edinburgh at 10.40 p.m. and arrival in London at 6.57 a.m., additional stops at York and Grantham make the overall time 8 hours, 17 minutes ; it is a relief " sleeper " at 10.20 p.m. from Edinburgh that does the Newcastle–London non-stop run and completes the journey in 8 hours.

50—The "Norfolk Coast Express"

Actually the title of " Norfolk Coast Express " did not reappear after the London & North-Eastern Railway absorbed the Great Eastern Railway, on which it originated, in 1907. In fact, the title went out with the First World War. In later years, too, the train retained but a pale shadow of its glory in Great Eastern days ; from a daily service it was restricted to Mondays, Fridays and Saturdays only, and its running times were eased out. But when the set of corridor stock, with restaurant cars, was first brought into service by the G.E.R., the problem set the locomotives of that day, in relation to their dimensions, was one of the most exacting that this country has ever known.

It was after the G.E.R. had installed two sets of water troughs on its Colchester main line, at Halifax Junction, south of Ipswich, and at Tivetshall, that the idea was conceived of running a special express from London to the Norfolk Coast during the currency of the summer timetables. In 1897 the service was first brought into operation, with a non-stop run over the 130·2 miles between Liverpool Street and North Walsham. In the following year the 4–2–2 locomotives of the " 10 " class came into service, and were used on a train of mixed six-wheel and bogie stock, but without corridors. The year 1900 saw the introduction of the first Holden 4–4–0 locomotives—the famous " Claud Hamilton " series—and the earliest of these, like the single-drivers, were fired with oil-fuel.

The corridor restaurant car train came into being in 1907, and was given the title of " Norfolk Coast Express " ; and from now on the haulage of the train became a task requiring the highest degree of locomotive performance, and the utmost skill in handling. Engine-crews from the top links at Stratford, Ipswich and Norwich sheds alternated in the working of the train, and there was keen competition between all three sheds as to which could maintain the best timekeeping record. A representative of Stratford Works always accompanied the crew on the footplate, and took notes of the running ; this was a pleasant species of summer outing that usually fell to works pupils.

The minimum formation of the " Norfolk Coast Express " was twelve bogie vehicles. Of these the first eight, including three restaurant cars, were for Cromer ; the next two were for Sheringham, by connection between the Great Eastern and Midland & Great Northern Joint Line from Cromer Junction, opened in the previous year ; and the rear two, detached at North Walsham, were for Mundesley-on-Sea, and continued round the joint coast line to Overstrand. The total empty weight of this formation was 317 tons. But at busy summer week-ends the make-up might rise to thirteen, fourteen, and even fifteen bogies ; and even then, with a tare weight of all but 400 tons, and a full weight of 430 to 440 tons, time was seldom lost. Yet the locomotives employed, at that date innocent of superheating or other modern requirements of design, weighed no more than 50 tons without their tenders.

In these circumstances, as will be realised by all those who know the difficulties of this route, the maintenance of schedule was a miracle of competence. Shortly after leaving Liverpool Street the engines had to face the 1 in 70 rise to Bethnal Green Junction. Just as they were getting away nicely with their train there came the slowing through Stratford, 4 miles out, nominally to 25 m.p.h. Then, after continuously rising grades, there came the formidable climb up Brentwood bank, $3\frac{1}{4}$ miles long, and with $2\frac{1}{2}$ miles at 1 in 85-103, to Ingrave summit. From here to Colchester, though continuously undulating, the line had no difficult gradients, though there were the complications of 30 and 40 m.p.h. slacks through Chelmsford and Colchester respectively. Swinging ups and downs between Colchester and Ipswich ended with a bad slowing through Ipswich, usually observed with more strictness than the unduly severe limits earlier in the journey.

Between Ipswich and Norwich there were more heavy grades, but the worst obstacle of the entire journey was the running through Norwich, entailing two miles of reduced speed, and a walking pace over Trowse swing-bridge. Immediately after this, from Whitlingham, came a climb of a mile at 1 in 80 on to some of the high ground of Norfolk. Thus there was no respite anywhere on the journey, and the schedule of 158 minutes for the 130·2 miles from Liverpool Street to North Walsham meant far more than its apparently moderate average of 49·4 m.p.h. might indicate. From Shenfield to Trowse, including the Chelmsford, Colchester and Ipswich slacks, the distance of 93·8 miles had to be run in 105 minutes, at an average speed of 53·6 m.p.h. throughout.

At different periods of Great Eastern history the down "Norfolk Coast Express" left Liverpool Street at 1.0 and 1.30 p.m., but the time allowed to Cromer was unvaried at 2 hours, 55 minutes in each direction for the 138·1 miles. In the up direction the start from Cromer was always at 1 p.m., and Liverpool Street was reached at 3.55 p.m.

The advent of the 4-6-0's of the "1500" class in 1912 was shortly followed by their introduction to the "Norfolk Coast Express," and from then on the working was somewhat simplified. Under London & North-Eastern auspices, as previously mentioned, the name disappeared, the operation was cut down to three times weekly, the start from Liverpool Street was altered to 12.25 p.m., and the allowance to North Walsham increased to 159 minutes. Cromer was reached in 2 hours, 57 minutes. On the up journey departure from Cromer was at 12.50 p.m., and from North Walsham at 1.8 p.m., and Liverpool Street was reached at 3.49 p.m., in one minute under three hours. There has been no regular non-stop running between Liverpool Street and North Walsham since the war, and the water-troughs at Tivetshall have been taken up, so the practice is not likely to be revived.

51—The "Normandy Express," "The Cunarder" & "The Statesman"

On the Southern Region, names are displayed on certain boat trains between Waterloo and Southampton. Trains which work between Waterloo and Southampton Docks in connection with the St. Malo and Havre steamer sailings carry the title "Normandy Express," and as in winter the Havre boat passengers share the same train as those to the Channel Islands (9 p.m. from Waterloo), the latter come under the Normandy heading also. Between Waterloo and the Ocean Quay at Southampton, the last special train connecting with a sailing of the *Queen Mary* or the *Queen Elizabeth*, and the first train up, both usually all-Pullman formations, carry headboards inscribed "The Cunarder"; and the corresponding trains in connection with the sailings of the American *United States* are named "The Statesman."

52—The "Norseman"

One of the fastest post-war expresses over the East Coast route, which first began service in the summer of 1950, is the "Norseman," which runs on Wednesdays and Saturdays only for the exclusive benefit of Norwegian boat passengers between King's Cross and Tyne Commission Quay at Newcastle. It is limited in weight to a total of ten bogie vehicles—350 tons—and runs during the three mid-summer months only. At first it left King's Cross at 9.10 a.m., but in 1952 the departure time was altered to 9 a.m. The first stop is at York, and the 188·2 miles from London must be covered in 201 minutes. After a stop here of 6 minutes, to pick up passengers only, the "Norseman" is away at 12.27 p.m. on a non-stop run of 87 minutes to Newcastle, 80·2 miles, reached at 1.54 p.m. Here a 4-6-2 tank usually replaces the Pacific haulage. Out of Newcastle Central the train is worked over the Tynemouth branch as far as Percy Main North Junction, where a 5-minute stop is made for reversal, after which a cautious run has to be made down a steep gradient, over some tortuous tracks, to the Quay, which is reached at 2.30 p.m., 30 minutes after leaving Newcastle.

In the southbound direction, the "Norseman" is due away from the Quay at 11.42 a.m., for a similar 30-minute run back to Newcastle. From here it makes one of the fastest runs on the North Eastern Region, for the allowance for the 80·2 miles to York is no more than 81 minutes (59·4 m.p.h.), after the train has stood at Newcastle Central from 12.12 to 12.25 p.m. The halt at York is from 1.46 to 1.52 p.m., to set down passengers only, and for the non-stop run from there to King's Cross the allowance is 208 minutes, with an arrival in London at 5.20 p.m. The entire journey thus takes 5½ hours down, and 8 minutes longer up.

53—The "North Briton"

In the first decade of the present century competition between railways to secure passenger traffic was keen. It developed between individual railways and groups of railways working in association ; and it was made all the livier because the more progressive companies were awakening to a realisation of their capacity to run fast—stirred up in the first place, no doubt, by the amazing exploits of the 1895 " Race to Aberdeen "—and were determined to develop this capacity in full measure.

This competitive idea, no doubt, was behind the decision of the North Eastern Railway, in conjunction with the North British, to put on a new train in the morning from Leeds to York, Newcastle and Edinburgh, with connections to Glasgow, Perth and Aberdeen; after five hours' turn-around time in the Scottish capital, it would return by the way it had come, and be back into Leeds the same night. The actual extension of the train's run to Glasgow and back came in later years. Such was the genesis of the train which in the post-war spate of new train names was dubbed the " North Briton."

The competitor against which this train was to operate, needless to say, was the Midland, and the traffic angled for was that between the West Riding of Yorkshire and Edinburgh. From Leeds to Edinburgh *via* Newcastle is 230¼ miles, whereas the Midland and North British route *via* Carlisle is 211¼ miles ; but the North Eastern had a vast advantage over the rival in the matter of gradients. In addition the new train had a valuable function in getting West Riding business men and people from York into Newcastle by mid-morning, and in providing a fine fast mid-morning service from Newcastle to Edinburgh and beyond. Coming south, however, the new train ran too late to perform quite the same useful functions, and through its history it has never been heavily patronised from Newcastle to York and Leeds.

A time-table of 1904 shows the then " North Briton "—at that time, of course, unnamed—as leaving Leeds New station at 8.50 a.m., and running the 25½ miles to York in 35 minutes. After an unaccountably long wait of 13 minutes under the curved roof of the great station, the express then set out on a run which, all conditions considered, I am inclined to think must have required the fastest running in the whole of Great Britain at that period. For to cover the 80¾ miles from York to Newcastle Central (which, be it remembered, required the use of the tortuous Gateshead connections and over the old High Level Bridge (for the King Edward Bridge was not yet open) the timetable allowed no more than 82 minutes.

True, the line is beautifully straight and level from York to Darlington. But after that come the sharp ups-and-downs of North Durham, the severe slowing over Durham viaduct, the slow travelling at the end of the run, as already mentioned, and possibly even then the first permanent way slowings due to pitfalls had begun to appear. It was not long before this 82 minute schedule began to be eased out, first to 84 minutes and then by a wider margin, and it is significant that nothing so fast ever reappeared in North Eastern time-tables until the coming of the first streamliner in 1935. But think of the difference—the seven-coach " Silver Jubilee " with a big 4-6-2 capable of doing 90 m.p.h. on the level with the greatest ease, and the N.E.R. " R " class 4-4-0 of 1904 with its five-coach load ! Time was certainly kept, and it needed a most creditable performance.

At Newcastle Central the train was reversed and provided with a composite restaurant car and composite corridor brake for the remainder of the journey. The non-stop timing of 142 minutes for the 124½ miles from Newcastle to Edinburgh was easily the fastest of the day, and brought the flyer into Waverley by 1.30 p.m. Here it remained until 6.25 p.m., when it started south again. After stopping in this direction at Berwick also, it reached Newcastle at 9.5 p.m., and dropped the dining car and its companion vehicles. Another additional stop in the southbound direction was Darlington ; York was reached at 10.55 p.m., and Leeds, after a very lengthy York wait of 15 minutes, at the late hour of 11.45 p.m.

While the times of the " North Briton " on its northbound journey have changed relatively little throughout its history—except during the war periods and after, of course—on reinstatement after the First World War, to make the southbound service more attractive by doing away with excessively late arrivals, the starting time from Edinburgh was put forward by more than an hour. By 1910 the train was working through to and fro between Leeds and Glasgow, 277½ miles each way, or 555 miles all told. Moreover it had become a corridor restaurant car train throughout, and so far as I can trace, the restaurant cars and their staffs made a longer continuous journey in a single day than any other cars in Great Britain, serving breakfast, luncheon, tea and dinner.

By 1914 the " North Briton " left Leeds at 9 a.m., was in Edinburgh by 1.32 p.m. (with 84 minutes from York to Newcastle and 138 minutes from there to Edinburgh) ; at 1.52 p.m., in charge of the North British, the train was continuing to Glasgow, where, after a wait from 3.8 to 5.0 p.m. at Queen Street, it began its long return journey, in readiness to leave Edinburgh for the south at 6.25 p.m. Little improvement had been made in this direction, and the arrivals at York and Leeds, 11.0 and 11.58 p.m., were later than ever. From Leeds and Newcastle, northbound, the engine now was usually one of the large Worsdell " R1 " 4-4-0's, with Atlantic haulage between Newcastle and Edinburgh.

When 1939 came to end the period between the wars, the "North Briton" had increased considerably in weight, with additional coaches and modern stock. For a number of years a Neville Hill "Shire" or "Hunt" 4-4-0 would make a gallant effort with it to Newcastle, where a Pacific would take over; coming south, it was normally Pacific haulage from Edinburgh to York. This working had been transformed; Glasgow now was left at 4 p.m., not 5 p.m., and Edinburgh at 5.10 p.m., not 6.25 p.m.; an additional stop was slipped in at Dunbar; Newcastle was reached at 7.41 and left at 7.48 p.m., and the train ran on to York in a blaze of glory by running the 44.1 miles from Darlington in 43 minutes, start to stop. So York was reached at 9.22 instead of 11 p.m., and Leeds at 10 p.m. instead of midnight—a vast improvement involving a total acceleration of 50 minutes.

From then, and particularly since restoration of the bridges washed away in the floods of 1948 between Berwick and Dunbar, there has been further speeding up. The "North Briton" earned the considerable distinction of being the first post-war train in Britain to get back to a mile-a-minute schedule—44.1 miles from Darlington to York in 44 minutes—the October, 1950, time-table showed the time cut further to 43 minutes, which demanded a start-to-stop average of 61·7 m.p.h., while in the summer of 1952 the time was pared again to 42 minutes, putting the average up further to 63·0 m.p.h. This is done with a train of ten or eleven bogie vehicles, which is the normal formation in both directions.

The 1952–1953 winter time-table shows the "North Briton" as leaving Leeds at its 1939 time of 9.5 a.m., and York at 9.41 a.m., with a fast run from there to Darlington, against the rising tendency of the road, in 46 minutes. Newcastle is reached at 11.14 a.m. and left at 11.20 a.m. for a non-stop run to Edinburgh in 132 minutes—13 minutes less than in 1939 and 6 minutes less than in 1914. Edinburgh thus is made by 1.32 p.m., and the train then is detained 18 minutes at Waverley Station. Arriving in Glasgow at 2.57 p.m., the "North Briton" has a turn-around time of 63 minutes before setting out on the return journey to Leeds at 4 p.m. Leaving Edinburgh at 5.14 p.m., and with additional calls in this direction at Dunbar and Berwick, the express runs into Newcastle at 7.40 p.m., York at 9.20 p.m., and Leeds at 10.2 p.m., only 2 minutes later than in 1939.

54—The "North Country Continental"

A typical example of the enterprise of the one-time Great Eastern Railway, linked with its Continental services based on Parkeston Quay, was the connecting express to and from the Midlands and the North, inaugurated in 1885, which soon acquired the unofficial name of "North Country Continental." It was one of the first long-distance cross-country trains to be put into service in Great Britain, and one of the first British trains, also, to be provided with restaurant car accommodation. Indeed, it is believed to have been the very first train in the country on which, from July, 1891, third-class passengers were admitted to the exclusive precincts of a "dining saloon." The dining-cars in question were six-wheelers, for at that early date the G.E.R. had done little or nothing towards the construction of bogie stock.

In 1906, a modern corridor train was completed at Stratford Works for this service. It consisted of a set of six cars (including composite kitchen car, and adjacent open third and semi-open first), with a six-wheel brake for the Harwich-York section, which was the main part of the train; two bogie vehicles for Manchester and two more for Liverpool; and two at the rear end for Birmingham. Going north, the "North Country Continental" left Parkeston Quay just after 7 a.m., and took the northern spur at Manningtree to reach Ipswich. From here the Norwich main line was followed to Haughley, where the train diverged westwards to Bury St. Edmunds, and then followed a single line from a point just east of Newmarket to Ely. A short run across the Fens brought the train into March, where the first division took place. The two rear cars were detached, to continue to Peterborough, and from there over the L.N.W.R. through Market Harborough to Rugby and Birmingham.

From March the "North Country Continental" had an almost dead level spin for many miles through Lincolnshire, through Spalding and Sleaford to Lincoln, where a second division took place. The Liverpool and Manchester coaches were worked forward from Lincoln by the then Great Central Railway, travelling on separate trains from Sheffield. The main section of the train went on through Gainsborough to Doncaster, where it joined the Great Northern main line, and from there to York. Great Eastern locomotives were used throughout; by the time the new train came into use in 1906, "Claud Hamilton" 4-4-0 engines were available for its haulage.

For a short time, about 1903 and 1904, a connecting express ran from Lincoln over the Lancashire, Derbyshire & East Coast Railway *via* Langwith, Clowne, and the Sheffield District Railway, into the Midland station at Sheffield. This carried also a through coach for Manchester Central, which continued from Sheffield over the Midland Dore & Chinley line.

[*J. Cupit*

Post-war version of the " North Country Continental "—E.R. Class " B17 " 4–6–0 No. 61631 *Serlby Hall* pulls the Harwich-Liverpool through express out of Lincoln

[*R. E. Toop*

Drifting down from Midford Tunnel with the southbound " Pines Express "—Class " 2P " 4–4–0 No. 40563 pilots S.R. Pacific No. 34041 *Wilton*

[C. W. Footer

Above : Steam off for Colchester—Class "7MT" 4-6-2 No. 70002 *Geoffrey Chaucer* crossing Lexden Viaduct with the down "Norfolkman".

[E. Tuddenham

Left : The down "Norfolkman" takes a run at Whitlingham Bank, on its way from Norwich to Cromer, behind Class "D16/3" 4-4-0 No. 62522. The train includes an S.R. Tavern-Restaurant Car set used on this service for some time.

[E. R. Wethersett

High above the Tweed—Class "A1" Pacific No. 60127 *Wilson Worsdell* wheels the northbound "Queen of Scots" Pullman across the Royal Border Bridge

[*H. N. James*

Two " North Wales Cruise " trains at Barmouth, W.R., with L.M.R. Class "2" 2–6–0s Nos. 46430 (*left*) from Llandudno and 46420 (*right*) from Rhyl

[*G. F. Heiron*

Through the cornfields—The down " Red Dragon," W.R., near Badminton behind 4–6–0 No. 5007 *Rougemont Castle*

As far as Black Carr Junction, Doncaster, the G.E.R. engines were working over their own right-of-way, as this far-seeing company was responsible, with the G.N.R., for building the "Great Northern & Great Eastern Joint Line" between Huntingdon, March, Lincoln and Doncaster; north of that point, running powers were exercised over the Great Northern and North Eastern Railways to reach York. Actually, G.E.R. locomotives made four daily appearances in York, as at that time there were three express trains daily in each direction between Liverpool Street, London, and York *via* Cambridge and the so-called "Cathedral Route."

Leaving Parkeston Quay at 7.2 a.m., the "North Country Continental" deposited its passengers in Birmingham at 12.11 p.m., Manchester at 1.38 p.m., Liverpool at 2.45 p.m., and York at 12.32 p.m., in nice time to connect with the northbound "Flying Scotsman." In the southbound direction, the train left York at 4 p.m., picked up at Lincoln the coaches which had left Liverpool at 2.30 p.m. and Manchester at 3.20 p.m., and at March those which had worked out of Birmingham at 4.0 p.m., and arrived at Parkeston Quay at 9.35 p.m., just ahead of the boat trains from London. One set of stock thus sufficed for the double journey each day (except for the Manchester and Liverpool coaches), and made by far the longest daily run of any Great Eastern train.

On the revival of the Great Eastern Continental services after the 1914-1919 war, the working of the "North Country Continental" was somewhat modified. The restaurant cars were transferred to the Manchester and Liverpool section, which in both directions was altered to travel *via* Manchester (Central). A through York section of the train was worked between Lincoln and York in each direction, and the through Birmingham coaches were still detached and attached at March.

In the course of years there was little change in the running times of this train. From its earlier 7.2 a.m. departure, the "North Country Continental" altered to one at 7.25 a.m. With identical stops—at Ipswich, Bury St. Edmunds, March and Spalding, and a new one at Sleaford—Lincoln was reached at 11.20 a.m. as compared with the 10.56 a.m. of the earlier years. The York section left at 11.27 a.m., called at Doncaster at 12.16 to 12.20 p.m., and then had the singular distinction of travelling to York by way of Knottingley— the original main line from London to York before the direct line through Selby had been built—including the use of L.M.S.R. metals between Shaftholme Junction and Knottingley.

This was done to keep the "Continental," when running late, out of the way of the accelerated "Flying Scotsman," which latterly was due in York as early as 1.15 p.m., only 9 minutes after the former train. But the "North Country Continental" was 11 minutes slower from Parkeston Quay to York in 1939 than it had been in 1914, 25 years earlier. Actually, a through composite brake for Glasgow was run in the York portion, but as its passengers could save hours by changing into the "Flying Scotsman" at York, it worked north as ordinary stock, ready for return as a through Glasgow-Harwich coach on the following morning.

Meantime, the Liverpool restaurant car portion got away from Lincoln at 11.32 a.m., stopped at Worksop, Sheffield and Guide Bridge, and reached Manchester Central at 1.55 p.m., and Liverpool Central at 2.43 p.m.—an acceleration of 25 minutes over the 1914 times to Liverpool. One of the most remarkable through cross-country locomotive workings in the country was made by this train, for a 3-cylinder 4–6–0 of the " B17 " or " Sandringham " class took it over at Ipswich and worked it right through, for 216 miles, to Manchester—a continuous journey of 5¾ hours with unchanged engine-crew, varying in characteristics from the extraordinary flat-ness of the Fen country to an altitude of all but 1,000 ft. above the sea on entering Woodhead tunnel; and from the quietude of a single-line country branch to the teeming manufacturing areas of Sheffield and Manchester.

Although the train set and the restaurant car staff were run into Liverpool, they did not remain there for the night. For in order to utilise the stock to the best advantage, each afternoon the train was used to form the 4 p.m. express from Liverpool to Hull, *via* Sheffield and Doncaster, reaching Hull Paragon at 7.34 p.m. And it was from Hull, at 8.55 in the morning, that the stock of the " North Country Continental " set out as a breakfast car train to Liverpool, this time avoiding Manchester by taking the direct line from Godley to Glazebrook, and reaching Liverpool at 12.30 p.m., before taking up its real Continental duties at 2.20 in the afternoon. The first constituent of the southbound " North Country Continental " to get on the move, however, was the through Glasgow coach, coming out of Queen Street terminus at 8.35 a.m. On reaching Edinburgh, this was attached to the 10.15 a.m. train, following the " Flying Scotsman," and brought into York at 2.18 p.m., where it had a 72-minute wait before the York section of the " Continental " started.

From Manchester Central at 3.10 p.m. and York at 3.30 p.m., the two main portions of the train converged at Lincoln, arriving at 5.20 and 5.15 p.m. respectively. An ample stop for marshalling was made here, with a departure at 5.32 p.m., and a non-stop run to Spalding, for there was no halt at Sleaford in this direction. At March the two coaches from Birmingham were attached, and the complete train then pursued its sedate cross-country course to Ipswich, where the locomotive, which had been in continuous steaming from leaving Manchester at 3.10 until 8.37 p.m., was detached, and replaced by another of the same type for the short final stage. Parkeston Quay was reached at 9.12 p.m., and Harwich at 9.25 p.m. Between Harwich and Hull, *via* Liverpool, the main restaurant car train travelled 406 miles daily. In summer months the " North Country Continental " frequently loaded to thirteen or fourteen bogie vehicles between Harwich and March, and at week-ends required duplication.

Needless to say, the " North Country Continental " was withdrawn immediately the Second World War broke out, and was not reinstated until 1949. There are now no longer any through sections or even connections to and from Birmingham and York, and the restaurant car accommodation has been cut down to a buffet car which plies between Harwich and Sheffield only. The times are much slower than before the war ; Liverpool Central is left at 12.50 p.m. and Parkeston Quay reached at 8.43 p.m., while northbound the departure from Parkeston is at 8 a.m., and the Liverpool arrival not till 3.30 p.m.

55—The "Northern Belle"

One of the most attractive railway touring developments in British history was that inaugurated by the London & North Eastern Railway in June, 1933, when a special train was marshalled to provide a " cruise " over the L.N.E.R. system. For a sum of £20 its fortunate participants were given about the maximum value possible in luxurious first-class travel, admirable meals, extensive rail mileage and fine scenery.

The train provided consisted of fourteen vehicles, six of them sleeping cars with berths for the 60 passengers who made up the touring party, and with two shower-bath rooms ; two open restaurant cars seating 60, and a kitchen car ; two lounge cars with buffet, hair-dressing saloon, ladies' retiring room, writing rooms, and a train " office " ; two cars to accommodate the train staff ; and a luggage brake with a locker for each passenger—a complete hotel on wheels.

The itinerary of the train varied on different " cruises," but a specimen, such as the tours beginning on June 1st, 8th, 15th and 22nd, 1934, is worth description. A start was made from King's Cross, at 9 p.m., on the Friday evening, with a Pacific which worked the train as far as Wetherby, in Yorkshire, where part of the night was spent with the train standing in a siding. Next morning, two " K3 " Moguls worked the train to Harrogate, where motor-coaches were waiting to take the party for a tour of Harrogate and Ripon. Here the " Northern Belle " picked them up again, and ran them to Darlington, and on to Barnard Castle for the night.

Owing to the extremely heavy gradients over Stainmore summit from Barnard Castle to Kirkby Stephen, and on to Penrith, it was now necessary to divide the train into its day and night sections (the latter the six " sleepers " and the brake), and to work it forward in halves. From Penrith the passengers were taken on a motor-coach tour of the Lake District, and, re-entraining at 7 p.m., were run over L.M.S.R. metals to Carlisle, and from there by the Waverley route to Corstorphine, outside Edinburgh, for the Sunday night. After a day in Edinburgh, there came a run up the East Coast main line to Montrose, and then a halt on the Inverbervie branch for part of the night, before proceeding next morning to Aberdeen, for a motor-coach tour of Deeside to Braemar.

Tuesday night was occupied by a run from Aberdeen to Balloch, on Loch Lomond, where the passengers took steamer up the lake to Ardlui; here they rejoined the day section of the train, which had been run forward to Ardlui to pick them up, and proceeded up the highly scenic West Highland line through to Mallaig and back to Fort William. The sleeping car section had meantime worked its way to Fort William (over these tremendous grades two 4-4-0 North British " Glens " were needed for each half of the train), and here the party spent Wednesday night.

Thursday was occupied with a run of the day section from Fort William to Craigendoran, and a sail on the s.s. *Waverley* through the Kyles of Bute and back to Craigendoran. There the whole train had been assembled, with two 4-4-0 " Directors " at the head, which relinquished their load at Edinburgh to a Pacific and a G.N. 4-4-0; and the final run from Newcastle to King's Cross, reached at 10.45 a.m. on the Friday morning, was made by a Pacific of the " A3 " class. The train then spent the day in preparing for the start of the next cruise the same evening.

A limited number of tours was made each year by the " Northern Belle," mostly in June, and it is hardly necessary to add that on each " cruise " the train was filled to capacity.

56—The "Northern Irishman"

While the boat service between Stranraer and Larne has always provided the quickest and most direct route between Scotland and Ireland, and also between Tyneside and Northern Ireland, it has also been a considerable attraction to passengers between other parts of England and Northern Ireland because of the shortness of the sea passage across what often can be the very turbulent waters separating the two countries. Of the two-hour voyage between Stranraer and Larne Harbours, almost half is made in the sheltered waters of Loch Ryan, leaving little more than an hour of the open sea.

Access from Carlisle and the south to Stranraer at first was over the metals of the Glasgow & South Western Railway to Dumfries and Castle Douglas, and from there by the independent Portpatrick & Wigtownshire Railway, opened in 1862. In the following year, the Caledonian, which had just opened a branch from its main line at Lockerbie into Dumfries, took over the working of the P. & W., and so matters continued until 1885, when the Glasgow & South Western Railway, which in 1877 had completed its own line from Girvan to Stranraer, and all the time had been restless at the invasion of its territory by the Caledonian, came into part ownership of the Portpatrick & Wigtownshire, or, as it has always been known colloquially, the "Port Road." The Caledonian and the G. & S. W. had a quarter share each, and the other owners were their English partners, the London & North Western and the Midland Railways.

At first the London & North Western showed no particular interest in the Stranraer route, as it had its own Belfast service *via* Holyhead and Greenore, and was directly interested also in the services *via* Liverpool and *via* Fleetwood. The Midland, however, soon was running a sleeping-car express between St. Pancras and Stranraer Harbour, which in the years up to the First World War left St. Pancras either at 8 or 8.15 p.m., with a restaurant car over the first stage of its journey, and provided a good late evening express to Leicester, Nottingham, Sheffield and Leeds as well as for Irish boat passengers.

With the grouping, however, just as the Midland Heysham boat train eventually was transferred from St. Pancras to Euston, so the same happened to the Stranraer boat train. Up to the Second World War this went out of Euston at 7.40 p.m., as a second part of the 7.30 p.m. Highland sleeper. During the war, the Stranraer route became an extremely important means of communication with Ireland, and for a time two sleeping-car trains were run from Euston every evening, the first carrying through boat passengers only, and the second making the same intermediate stops as the old 7.40 p.m. ; but the time of departure from Euston had now become as early as 4.50 p.m., to allow a margin for delays *en route.*

After the war, as train services began to recover, it became possible to retard the start from London to 6.30 p.m. ; the stops were at Crewe, to detach the restaurant cars, Carlisle and Dumfries, Wigan, Preston, Carlisle and Dumfries, and Stranraer Harbour was reached at 4.25 a.m. In the summer of 1951 the departure was made even later, at 7.55 p.m., and Stranraer Harbour was now reached at 5.45 a.m. The following summer the name "Northern Irishman" was given to this train. For the winter of 1952–1953 it was decided to combine the "Northern Irishman" with the second, or Perth, portion of the 7.20 p.m. Highland sleeper, starting at 7.30 p.m., so that the Stranraer service is now back almost exactly where it was before the Second World War. Arrival at Stranraer Harbour is still at 5.45 a.m. Between Carlisle and Stranraer this train is usually worked, over the extremely hard gradients of the "Port Road," by the new Class "6" light Pacifics.

57—The "Northumbrian" and the "Tynesider"

In the down direction the "Northumbrian" is a train of war origin. Soon after the Second World War began, the passenger demands on the 1 p.m. down "Scotsman" from King's Cross to Edinburgh became so excessive that loads of 20 bogie coaches and over were being run almost every day. The limit was reached on April 5th, 1940, when the streamlined "A4" Pacific *Silver Link* headed a train of no fewer than 25 bogie vehicles; indeed, before starting, the engine was actually in Gasworks Tunnel, and a man had to be sent from the platform into the tunnel to give the driver the "right away." It may be added that the engine succeeded in getting this vast assemblage of stock to Newcastle without assistance and with no more than 15 minutes loss of time, of which roughly half went in lifting the train up the initial climb to Finsbury Park.

But trains of such length, in addition to imposing unjustifiable strains on the locomotives, were most difficult to handle at intermediate stations, and notwithstanding the heavy wartime calls on motive power, division of the most heavily-patronised trains became essential. Thus the 12.45 p.m. Newcastle "relief" to the 1 p.m., until then booked to run on Saturdays only, became a daily service from the beginning of May, 1940, and, with brief intermissions when train service cuts were made, has so continued ever since. At a later date it left King's Cross at 12.20 p.m., while the 1.0 p.m. started at 1.15 p.m.—in pursuance of the policy of spreading the long-distance services as evenly as possible, rather than "bunching" them together—and the name "Northumbrian" was conferred at the beginning of the 1949 summer train service. From October, 1950, in pursuance of the systematic departure plan at King's Cross, it became 12.18 p.m.

The "Northumbrian" is a train of no special distinction. It calls at Grantham from 2.22 to 2.28 p.m., and York from 4.7 to 4.13 p.m.; then comes the run over the Great Plain of York to reach Darlington at 5.4 p.m.; there is now a stop at Durham, and the "Northumbrian" reaches the Central Station at 6.0 p.m. It is usually a train of about 13 bogie vehicles, including, of course, a set of restaurant cars.

The southbound "Northumbrian" has a history going back to Great Northern and North Eastern days. Before the First World War a restaurant car express left Newcastle at 10.28 a.m. for King's Cross, calling at Darlington; it was turned over by the North Eastern to the Great Northern at York, and became the latter's "No. 562 up," a heavy and rather lethargic train which left York at 12.15 p.m., called at Selby, Doncaster and Grantham (later, the Grantham stop was replaced by one at Peterborough), and rolled into King's Cross at 4.10 p.m. Moreover, the North Eastern authorities ran a very smart little connection from Edinburgh at 7.45 a.m., with their own restaurant car attached; this called at

Dunbar and Berwick, and was due in Newcastle at 10.19 a.m., in nice time for a couple of through coaches to be attached to the London train. In this way a convenient early morning service was given from Edinburgh to London which had no counterpart in the opposite direction at that time.

Between the wars the same service continued, and by 1939 had been slightly accelerated. The connection from Edinburgh now left Waverley at 8.5 a.m., with a buffet car instead of a restaurant car, and reached Newcastle at 10.33 a.m., connecting with the main train at 10.40 a.m. from Newcastle Central for the south. After stopping at Durham and Darlington, this was scheduled to make a fast spurt to York—44.1 miles in 45 minutes, start-to-stop—arriving at 12.21 p.m., but the Southern Area part of the run was but little less leisurely than before, and required from 12.26 p.m. out of York to 4.15 p.m. into King's Cross to cover the 188.2 miles with stops at Selby, Doncaster and Grantham.

Today the southbound " Northumbrian," which is a very popular train, has the unusual distinction of being slightly faster than its 1939 counterpart, though admittedly with fewer stops. The start from Newcastle is at 10 a.m., and with the Durham stop omitted, and a 47-minute run from Darlington to York, the express is into York by 11.37 a.m.—97 minutes from Newcastle as compared with 101 minutes in 1939. Leaving York at 11.43 a.m., the " Northumbrian " stops only at Grantham—1.21 to 1.26 p.m.— and notwithstanding " recovery margins," is due in King's Cross at 3.32 p.m., in 5 hours, 32 minutes from Newcastle, or 3 minutes less than in 1939. A pre-war revival during the winter months on the southbound journey is the addition at York of a through carriage from Scarborough to London which, curiously enough, has no advertised working in the reverse direction ; on certain days also, a through portion from Tyne Commission Quay, in connection with the B. & N. sailing from Bergen, is attached at Newcastle before the " Northumbrian " begins its journey.

For many years the night traffic between London and Newcastle has been of sufficient importance to justify the running of an independent Newcastle sleeping car express and in the summer of 1950 this was added to the list of British titled trains by being given the name " Tynesider." It is no flyer ; leaving King's Cross a quarter of an hour before midnight, it is three minutes after six in the morning before the sleeper draws into the Central Station at Newcastle, but it has had to make seven intermediate stops. Coming south, the " Tynesider " schedule is six hours precisely—10.35 p.m. from Newcastle and 4.35 a.m. into London, but in this direction with stops at Durham, Darlington, York and Grantham only. At King's Cross the sleeping-car passengers are not turned out in the small hours, of course, but may remain comfortably in their berths until 7.30 a.m.

58—The "Orcadian" and the "John o' Groat"

Railway travel in the Northern Highlands is not distinguished by its high speed. But the lines concerned are almost entirely single track; curves are sharp and gradients are steep; and the sparseness of the traffic calls for numerous stops. One of the earliest benefits to be offered to this region by the L.M.S.R., after the Highland Railway had become absorbed in the L.M.S.R. group, was the introduction of restaurant cars and corridor stock north of Inverness; a further distinction, after the war, was the conferring of titles on some of the principal trains.

The "Orcadian" ran all the year round, linking Inverness with Wick, $161\frac{1}{4}$ miles distant, in the extreme north of Scotland. One of its coaches began its journey overnight, in Buchanan Street Station, Glasgow, as part of the 10.45 p.m. sleeping car train to Inverness, and if it reached the latter city on time, had 55 minutes to wait before the "Orcadian" was ready to start from the north end of the station at 6.40 a.m. This vehicle, a composite corridor brake, had a weary journey of 14 hours in covering the $342\frac{1}{2}$ miles from Glasgow to Wick. Another through coach was carried by the "Orcadian" from Inverness to Thurso.

Going north, this train missed only the first two stations out of Inverness, and one a little later on, calling at all the remainder. On reaching The Mound Junction, $80\frac{1}{2}$ miles from Inverness, at 9.43 a.m., the restaurant car, which had been busy serving breakfasts, was detached; finally the "Orcadian" ran into Wick at 12.45 p.m., having spent just over 6 hours on its run of $161\frac{1}{4}$ miles. Latterly, the engine had been one of the ubiquitous L.M.S.R. Class "5" 6 ft. 4-6-0 locomotives. The Thurso coach, detached at Georgemas Junction, $14\frac{1}{4}$ miles short of Wick, was into the northern port, so familiar in wartime to naval men, at 12.49 p.m.

On the southbound journey, the "Orcadian" did a little better. The start from Wick was at 3.30 p.m., and as the restaurant car off its northbound journey had been picked up by an earlier southbound train, a car was collected further north, at Helmsdale, at 5.35 p.m., in time for high teas and suppers. From Tain onwards, the "Orcadian" stopped once only in 44 miles, at Dingwall, and was into Inverness by 9 p.m., so cutting the journey to $5\frac{1}{2}$ hours. It brought back the through coach from Thurso, but not the Wick–Glasgow coach, which came on the morning train from Wick, and got through to Glasgow the same day.

The "John o' Groat" was a rather more lively affair, and ran only during the currency of the summer timetable: also it was distinguished by taking a restaurant car right up to Wick, the most northerly point in Great Britain reached by one of these vehicles. Beginning its journey at Wick at 10.10 a.m., it reached Inverness in 5 hours, 10 minutes at 3.20 p.m., in time for passengers to catch the important trains to the south. Fifty minutes later, at 4.10 p.m., it began its return journey, and such is the meticulous accuracy of timetable compilation that it was due in Wick, not at 9 p.m., but one minute earlier, at 8.59 ! This timing of 4 hours 49 minutes was the quickest scheduled between Inverness and Wick, and included only ten intermediate stops ; the two " John o' Groat " services both made possible a journey time of just over 10¾ hours from Glasgow to Wick and *vice versa*. A nameless counterpart of the " John o' Groat " has now reappeared in the summer timetables, leaving Wick at 9.45 a.m. for a journey of 5 hours, 5 minutes to Inverness, but the return journey, at 4.15 p.m., has many more stops, and requires 5 hours, 51 minutes.

The " Orcadian " continued through the war, though nameless, and also foodless after the general withdrawal of restaurant cars. Northbound, it started 20 minutes later, at 7 a.m., and reached Wick 55 minutes later, at 1.40 p.m. Coming south there was an earlier start by 5 minutes, at 3.25 p.m., and the journey was one of precisely 6 hours, finishing in Inverness at 9.25 p.m. The through Glasgow-Wick coaches also were withdrawn. Restaurant cars were restored to this service in the summer of 1946. In the present timetables the pre-war times of the " Orcadian " (now without name) are almost exactly restored. The northbound train once again leaves Inverness at 6.40 a.m., reaching Wick at 12.51 p.m. ; southbound, Wick is left 5 minutes later, at 3.35 p.m., and the Inverness arrival is at 9.16 p.m. on Saturdays, and 9.40 p.m. on other days.

59—The "Peak Express" and the "Palatine"

Before the Midland and London & North Western Railways came into the L.M.S.R. group in 1923, the competition between the two companies for the passenger traffic between London and Manchester was the subject of keen rivalry. There was little difference in length between the principal L.N.W.R. route *via* Crewe and the Midland *via* Derby—189 and 190 miles respectively—but there was no comparison between the respective gradients.

Apart from the 1 in 75 climb out of Euston, the L.N.W.R. had hardly an inclination worth mention ; whereas the Midland, save for the 44 level miles from Wigston to Ambergate, was severely graded throughout its length, and finally compelled its hard-worked locomotives to climb to an altitude of 980 feet above sea level at Peak Forest, in the heart of the Peak area of Derbyshire. But the ride through the superb Derbyshire scenery, from Ambergate past Miller's Dale to Chinley and beyond, together with the characteristic excellence of Midland rolling stock and catering, were factors that influenced many regular travellers in favour of the Midland route.

The dignified and deliberate L.N.W.R. had managed to get its best trains down to a run of $3\frac{1}{2}$ hours between Euston and Manchester, though for the most part its times ranged between 3 hours, 40 and 50 minutes. Nevertheless the Midland, even if the lightness of its train-loads be admitted, by 1904 was nearly tieing with the " Premier Line " with overall schedules of 3 hours, 35 to 40 minutes, despite the formidable difficulties of its route. The best Midland trains could not afford the time to stop at Derby, and avoided that town by the Chaddesden curve, stopping only at Leicester on the northbound journey ; coming south, in different years there were non-stop runs over the 175·1 miles from Chinley, and even the 186·9 miles from Cheadle Heath to St. Pancras, in both cases *via* the Dore and Chinley line and Chesterfield. Indeed, in the summer of 1914, after the opening of the Midland Adelphi Hotel at Liverpool, on Friday evenings the Midland ran a non-stop express at 6.10 p.m. from St. Pancras to Liverpool, using the Cheshire Lines system from Cheadle Heath, and taking 4 hours, 10 minutes for the $217\frac{3}{4}$ miles.

After the grouping, the competitive urge between the two routes no longer existed, but in the years before the Second World War, the L.M.S.R. began to realise the advantage of the Midland route as helping to relieve the busy Western Division main line, and accelerated the trains between St. Pancras and Manchester to an extent that restored the best times of competitive days. Derby had now become too important an industrial centre to miss, and stops at Leicester and Derby were both a " must " on every run, while stops at Chinley were added in the case of certain trains carrying through portions to and from Liverpool.

In the further outbreak of L.M.S.R. train naming which took place in 1938, two trains between St. Pancras and Manchester Central received appropriate titles. In the down direction the 10.30 a.m. from St. Pancras became the " Peak Express " and the 4.30 p.m. the " Palatine." In later Midland days the principal down Manchester expresses had all been arranged to leave London at 25 minutes past the hour—in fact, they had become known unofficially as the " Twenty-Fives "—but in the accelerations of October, 1937, the starting-times were altered to the even half-hour in each case. In the reverse direction the " Palatine " was a morning express from Manchester Central, at 10 a.m., and the " Peak Express " provided the principal afternoon departure, at 4.25 p.m.

The down " Peak Express " was the fastest train of the day between St. Pancras and Manchester, and with an additional Derby stop restored the " crack " 3 hours, 35 minutes time of Midland days. It began its journey with a mile-a-minute run to Leicester— 99·1 miles in 99 minutes. Practically the same speed was required on to Derby—29·4 miles in 30 minutes. With 4 minutes at Leicester and 5 minutes at Derby, the train had 77 minutes left for the exceedingly difficult 61·5 miles from Derby over Peak Forest summit to Manchester. In 1939, however, this train was slowed down

21 minutes by the addition of four stops between Derby and Manchester. The down "Palatine" stopped at Bedford, and had an easier timing. To Leicester the allowance was 105 minutes and from there to Derby 33 minutes. Between Derby and Manchester there were stops at Matlock, Chinley and Cheadle Heath, and Central Station was not reached till 8.26 p.m., in 3 hours, 56 minutes from St. Pancras.

Coming up, the 10 a.m. "Palatine," with a Cheadle Heath stop, reached Derby at 11.26 a.m., and left 7 minutes later on a 31-minute run to Leicester. From Leicester to St. Pancras the standard 60 m.p.h. 99-minute time was allowed, and London was reached at 1.48 p.m., in 3 hours, 48 minutes from Manchester. The southbound "Peak Express" at 4.25 p.m. ran non-stop to Derby in 78 minutes, called at Loughborough, Leicester and Luton, and was due in St. Pancras at 8.12 p.m., a journey of 3 hours, 47 minutes.

For the Manchester workings generally, a standard set of cars would be third-class brake, two corridor thirds, third restaurant and kitchen, open first restaurant, and first brake, six coaches in all, with an additional two attached for part of the journey, such as the Manchester Victoria portion on the down "Peak Express," the Liverpool portion on the up and down "Palatines," and the Manchester-Leicester additional accommodation on the up "Peak Express." The down "Palatine" was usually a 7-coach train as far as Chinley and six from there to Manchester. Locomotive power over the Midland had been revolutionised by the coming of the Stanier 4-6-0's, and without their help it would not have been possible to work these loads over such a route in these times. It was customary to use a Class "5XP" between St. Pancras and Derby, and a Class "5" 4-6-0 between there and Manchester, until certain bridges at Chapel-en-le-Frith had been rebuilt, after which the "5XP" 4-6-0's could work through.

The Second World War made havoc of the Midland Manchester services, and lengthened the overall times between St. Pancras and Manchester Central to between 5¼ and 5¾ hours. No recognisable trace of either the "Peak Express" or the "Palatine" remained, until the new timetable of October, 1946, when three of the workings reappeared. They are now at 10.15 a.m. and 4.15 p.m. from St. Pancras, and 4.0 p.m. from Manchester Central. Journey times range from 4 hours, 18 to 38 minutes. There are no longer any through portions to and from Liverpool.

60—The "Pines Express"

From 1904 onwards, when the first through coaches were arranged by the London & North Western and London, Brighton & South Coast Railways to run between Liverpool, Manchester and Brighton, a keen competition began between a number of railways and continued for years with numerous new developments, to provide through service between the great cities of the Midlands and the North and the South, South-East and South-West Coasts. Thus the Great Western and London & South Western inaugurated a new restaurant car express between Birkenhead and Bournemouth, and the G.W.R., by virtue of its right of access to Manchester either *via* Crewe or *via* Warrington, in 1910 began to run a through section of this train to and from Manchester London Road, by the Crewe route, connecting with the main train at Wellington.

This was too much for the London & North Western, and as a result of negotiations with the Midland, the precursor of the "Pines Express" came into service in October, 1910. It was arranged to use L.N.W.R. metals between Manchester and Birmingham, and between these cities it provided a useful new express, with a time of 1¾ hours from Birmingham to Manchester—the fastest ever advertised. At New Street Station in Birmingham it crossed over into the Midland platforms, from which it was worked by that company to Bath—and, incidentally, to avoid reversal was worked out of the east end of New Street and *via* Camp Hill to King's Norton—while at Bath the Somerset & Dorset Joint Railway (Midland and London & South Western) took charge for the final stage of the journey.

After suspension during the First World War, the train was reinstated much in its old times, and received the title of "Pines Express" in 1927. It became even more exclusively L.M.S.R. in 1930, when the L.M.S.R. took over the provision of motive power on the Somerset & Dorset Joint Line, which previously had its own independent locomotives. The only stretch of purely "foreign" territory traversed was 7¾ miles of Southern metals from Broadstone through Poole into Bournemouth.

By 1939 the main restaurant car section of the southbound "Pines Express" was leaving Manchester London Road at 10.10 a.m., and at Crewe was picking up a four-coach set for Birmingham, and through coaches for both Bournemouth and Southampton, which had left Liverpool Lime Street at 9.40 a.m. The combined train was due away from Crewe at 10.49 a.m., and—most unusually for an express—was booked to take the slow road to Stafford, through which it passed on the west side of the station. This was to avoid fouling the path of the up "Merseyside Express," due through Crewe at 10.57 a.m., and the result often was a race from Whitmore down to Stafford, if the "Pines" was behind time. The latter stopped next at Wolverhampton, and then ran across into the Midland Division side at Birmingham New Street, arriving at

12.2 noon. Here the four-coach set from Liverpool was detached, and a Midland Division locomotive took charge of the remainder, usually about six for Bournemouth, one of which was a through coach from Bradford, and the Southampton coach on the rear.

Departure from Birmingham was at 12.13 p.m., and by 1.10 p.m. the express was in Cheltenham, where the Southampton coach was detached; the latter was handed over to the Great Western Railway, to be worked over the one-time Midland & South Western Junction line through Swindon to Andover, and thence over the Southern to Southampton Terminus, arriving at 5.5 p.m. The main train stopped next at Gloucester, and then had 48 minutes for the 41¼ miles to Bath. In the Queen Square station at Bath reversal was necessary.

After Bath came the locomotive tug-of-war, for the tremendous gradients through the Mendips had to be tackled. One result of the L.M.S.R. assumption of locomotive responsibility was the introduction between Bath and Bournemouth of the ubiquitous and capable Class " 5 " 4-6-0's, which greatly eased the power problem. Beginning at Bath junction, there is first a 2-mile climb at 1 in 50 to the north portal of Combe Down tunnel; again from beyond Radstock there are 3 miles up at 1 in 50, followed by another 4 miles almost as steeply inclined to the summit at Masbury, and then by a descent to Evercreech Junction which for 7 miles also is largely at 1 in 50. From Templecombe to Blandford the line is single-track, which, though equipped for automatic tablet-changing, involves slacks through the station loops. In the circumstances, 2 hours, 17 minutes for the 71½ miles from Bath to Bournemouth West, with four intermediate stops, was not bad going. The total time for the run of 252 miles from Manchester to Bournemouth, reached at 4.37 p.m., was 6 hours, 27 minutes.

Northbound, the " Pines Express " left Bournemouth West at 10.35 a.m., and with six intermediate stops made the better time of 2 hours, 5 minutes to Bath. Departure from Bath was at 12.44 p.m., from Gloucester at 1.37 p.m., and from Cheltenham (where the " Pines " picked up from the G.W.R. the through coach which had made its way out of Southampton Terminus at 10.10 a.m.) at 1.51 p.m. From here a very fast run was made to Bromsgrove, 31·1 miles in 31 minutes, at just over a mile a minute. The Bromsgrove stop was necessary for taking banking assistance up the formidable Lickey incline, which climbs two miles at 1 in 37¾ up to Blackwell. From King's Norton the direct line was taken into Birmingham, via Selly Oak, and this meant that the train passed through New Street in the same direction—from west to east—on both southbound and northbound journeys, and even used the same platform at that station.

To avoid reversal in this direction, the Western Division locomotive thus had to take its train out of New Street from the eastern end, and in consequence the train left Birmingham via Aston and Bescot. In this direction, also, Wolverhampton was avoided by taking the straight line northwards from Willenhall to Bushbury. With the 4-coach Liverpool section added, and now a formation of about 11 bogies, the " Pines Express " ran the 54 miles to Crewe non-stop in 70 minutes, arriving at 4.2 p.m. Here the severance of Liverpool and Manchester sections took place ; the Liverpool section reached Lime Street at 5.21 p.m., and the " Pines Express " proper was into Manchester London Road at 4.51 p.m., in a minute over 6¼ hours from Bournemouth.

At summer week-ends, on Mondays, Fridays and Saturdays, the express was divided, and the principal section of the train then followed a very curious route, used by no other regular express train, and avoiding both Wolverhampton and Birmingham. From Bushbury it continued direct to Darlaston and there turned leftwards into Walsall, where the change from Western to Midland Division engine took place. From Walsall the old Midland branch through Sutton Coldfield was used down to Castle Bromwich, on the Derby-Birmingham main line, from which it was a straight run to Saltley and then on through Camp Hill by the train's normal route. The same course was followed in the opposite direction.

The " Pines Express " was withdrawn on the outbreak of the Second World War, but it was restored between Manchester and Bournemouth on October 7th, 1946, with a timing of 7 hours southbound and 7¼ hours northbound. It was later accelerated to 6 hours, 56 minutes southbound and 6 hours, 51 minutes northbound, but the southbound schedule has since been eased to 7 hours, 12 minutes. Restaurant cars have reappeared, and through coaches to and from Sheffield are added to those between Liverpool and Bournemouth. Departure from Manchester is at 10.20 a.m., and from Bournemouth West at 9.45 a.m. ; rather unusually, the latter train finishes its journey, not in London Road, but at Manchester Mayfield. The Southern Region is now responsible for locomotive power between Bath and Bournemouth, and uses its light Pacifics over this section.

61—The "Ports-to-Ports Express"

In 1897 what until then had been the Manchester, Sheffield & Lincolnshire Railway changed its name to Great Central Railway, and greatly enhanced its importance and its range by the new main line opened in 1899 from north of Nottingham to London. The next business was to attract traffic to the new route, and the possibilities were further increased when in 1900 a short spur line was opened from Woodford & Hinton, 34 miles south of Leicester, to Banbury on the Great Western. In course of time various through passenger services were established over this connection between the North-East of England and the West and South.

With one exception, all these through trains continued south-wards over the G.W.R. to Oxford and beyond. This exception was the unofficially-named "Ports-to-Ports Express," for which a more direct route had to be found in order to link Banbury with South Wales. It was planned by making use of a sleepy country branch, single-track throughout, which never previously had seen an express train. This was the line from King's Sutton, just south of Banbury, through the old-world towns of Chipping Norton, Stow-on-the-Wold and Bourton-on-the-Water to Cheltenham, from which town main line running could be resumed through Gloucester to Newport, Cardiff and beyond.

Originally the "Ports-to-Ports Express," which began its career in May, 1906, was designed to run between Newcastle-on-Tyne and the port of Barry. In later years it was extended west-wards to Swansea, though still running between Cardiff and Bridgend by way of Barry instead of by the direct main line. In addition to connecting the ports of Tyneside and Teesside with those of South Wales, in L.N.E.R. days two further ports were linked with the service by the running of a through coach to and from Hull and Goole, attached and detached at Sheffield.

In 1939 the express was leaving Newcastle at 9.30 in the morning, and with stops at Durham, Darlington and Northallerton reached York at 11.32 a.m. On the way it suffered the indignity of being put on to the slow loop south of Eryholme, to let the "Silver Jubilee" streamliner get by. The next stage, from York at 11.42 a.m., was a non-stop run to Sheffield, by way of the Swinton & Knottingley Joint Line through Pontefract, with an arrival in Sheffield at 12.51 p.m. Here reversal was necessary, and with the through coach from Hull—which had left there at 10.35 a.m. and had travelled to Sheffield *via* Doncaster—at the head end, the train left for the south at 1 p.m. A fast run was made over Great Central metals to Banbury, with calls at Nottingham, Loughborough, Leicester and Rugby, and the G.W.R. station was reached at 3.30 p.m.

To this point the locomotive power had been similar to that of the "Aberdeen-Penzance" service, but something much lighter was needed for the Banbury-Cheltenham line, and for years, until the advent of the 4-6-0 "Manors," the G.W.R. used Moguls over this section, through between Banbury and Cardiff. After the fast L.N.E.R. running, the allowance of 82 minutes for the 44¾ miles from Banbury to Cheltenham South came somewhat as an anti-climax, even if the lethargy, in the circumstances, was unavoidable. Stopping at Gloucester and at Chepstow, the "Ports-to-Ports Express" skirted the Severn estuary to reach Newport at 6.30 and Cardiff at 6.51 p.m.

Up to 1922, the Great Western Railway relinquished their charge of the train at Cardiff, and handed over to the Barry Railway for the short run between Cardiff and Barry, but from the grouping, this line, with its extension through Aberthaw to Bridgend, became part of the G.W.R. It is considerably more circuitous, of course, than the direct main line from Cardiff to Bridgend, and the 54 miles from Cardiff to Swansea, with stops at Barry Docks, Barry, Bridgend, Pyle, Port Talbot and Neath, took just over 1¾ hours. Swansea was reached at 8.45 p.m., after a 397-mile journey taking 11¼ hours.

In the northbound direction, the G.W.R. in later years cut out the journey by the Barry loop, and leaving Swansea at 8.15 a.m., ran the " Ports-to-Ports Express " direct to Cardiff, with stops at Neath, Briton Ferry, Port Talbot, Bridgend and Llantrisant. Cardiff was left at 9.40 a.m. and Newport at 10 a.m., and with the same stops on Great Western territory beyond Newport as in the reverse direction, the express found its way into Banbury at 12.40 p.m. Four minutes later the L.N.E.R. were away on the journey to Sheffield, and with halts at Rugby, Leicester, and Nottingham this stretch of 107¼ miles was completed in 2 hours, 19 minutes. The Hull coach, detached at Sheffield, found its way into that port at 4.45 p.m. ; the main train, reversing in Sheffield, got to York by 4.19 p.m. A stop of 11 minutes sufficed here, and again with the same stops as coming south, the end of the journey, at Newcastle, was attained by 6.15 p.m. This was a considerably faster effort than that of the southbound train, and cut the through journey to 10 hours precisely.

For most of the year a 6-coach corridor set, including restaurant car, and the through composite corridor coach to and from Hull, provided comfortably adequate accommodation, though the formation was added to as required during the summer. London & North-Eastern and Great Western stock was used on alternate days. The train was withdrawn on the outbreak of war. The only through passenger trains in wartime continuing to use the Woodford-Banbury " link " between the L.N.E.R. and the G.W.R. were the York-Swindon service, and the through train between Newcastle and Ashford, later diverted to Southampton.

The " Ports-to Ports Express " reappeared in October, 1946, but modified at the G.W.R. end by being run between Banbury and Newport *via* Oxford, Swindon and the Severn Tunnel, a considerably longer route than the previous one *via* Cheltenham. Time is saved at the western end of the run, however, by taking the train both ways over the main line between Cardiff and Bridgend instead of *via* Barry. Except on summer Saturdays, also, at the northern end of the route the terminal point is York and not Newcastle. Leaving York at 12.20 p.m., the " Ports to Ports Express " (though carrying no name) is in Swansea by 9.8 p.m., and coming north, with a departure from Swansea at 8.15 a.m., York is reached at 5.12 p.m.

In the winter of 1952-1953 the working of the train was cut short at Banbury, and to Fridays and Saturdays ; thus it ceased to touch any ports at all. But this was largely because of the establishment of a new and far more direct through service between Cardiff and Newcastle by way of Gloucester and the L.M.R. line through Birmingham and Derby to York ; this has cut the Cardiff-

[E. Treacy

On the 1,000-ft. contour—Pacific No. 46230 *Duchess of Buccleuch* nears Beattock summit with the up " Royal Scot "

4

[R. E. Wilson

Head and tail of the " Red Rose "—The down train (*above*) near Watford is being hauled by " Royal Scot " Class 4–6–0 No. 46137 *The Prince of Wales's Volunteers* (*South Lancashire*) and the down train (*left*) is passing Harrow

[C. R. L. Coles

Below : The down " Royal Wessex " making speed past Winchfield with " Battle of Britain " Class 4–6–2 No. 34109 *Sir Trafford Leigh-Mallory*

[M. W. Earley

[R. K. Evans

Companions at Perth—(Right) Standard Class " 5 " 4–6–0 No. 73009 heads the " Saint Mungo," Aberdeen-Glasgow, and (left) Class " A3 " Pacific No. 60099 Call Boy is about to leave with the 12.8 p.m. for Edinburgh

[B. E. Morrison

Climbing the 1 in 200 past Hadley Wood—E.R. Class " A1 " Pacific No. 60122 Curlew with the down " Scarborough Flyer "

[C. C. B. Herbert

Pre-war flyer—The "Silver Jubilee" streamliner, with Class "A4" 4-6-2 No. 2509 *Silver Link*, taking water from Langley troughs

[O. J. Morris

Above : The "Sunny South Express" on S.R. metals near Purley, hauled by Brighton Atlantic No. 2039 *Hartland Point*

Below : Double-heading the "South Yorkshireman" past Heaton Lodge, Huddersfield, are L.M.R. Class "5" 4-6-0s Nos. 45210 and 44982

[K. Field

Newcastle time to 8 hours, 32 minutes, and that in the reverse direction to 8¼ hours, both far faster than ever previously.

62—The "Queen of Scots"

It is curious to reflect that the one-time Great Eastern Railway, serving a comparatively limited area of agricultural country in the Eastern Counties, should have been the means —indirectly, perhaps, but none the less effectively—of introducing Pullman car trains between London and the cities of the West Riding of Yorkshire, the famous Spa at Harrogate, and as far afield as Newcastle, Edinburgh and Glasgow. The reason was that in 1914 the G.E.R. acquired an American General Manager, Mr.—later Sir—Henry Thornton. Accustomed as he was to Pullman travel in the United States, Thornton not unnaturally thought that Pullman service, already established south of the Thames, ought to be popular on the railway which had now come under his control. So an agreement was made with the Pullman Car Company, and a number of new Pullman cars found their way on to the Great Eastern main line.

But while the cars prospered on the Continental boat trains between Liverpool Street and Parkeston Quay, they were less of a success elsewhere, and when the G.E.R. came into the London & North Eastern group in 1923, with a considerable period of the Pullman agreement still to run, it was an urgent question as to whether a more profitable use for these Pullmans might not be found. Except for the Continental boat trains, therefore, the cars were withdrawn from the Great Eastern, and a set of them was formed into an all-Pullman express, called the " Harrogate Pullman," to run between King's Cross, Leeds, Harrogate and Newcastle, in the summer of 1923. The time of 3 hours, 25 minutes in each direction between King's Cross and Leeds equalled the best that had ever operated between London and Leeds, and this was the longest non-stop run on the L.N.E.R. at that time.

The down " Harrogate Pullman," as the train was called, consisted of six cars, two first-class and four third-class. It left King's Cross at exactly the same time—11.15 a.m.—as the up train left Harrogate, and the journey between London and Harrogate took four hours each way. The down train reached Leeds at 2.40 p.m. ; reversing at the Central station, it then ran round the sharp spur to Geldard Junction, which adjoins the L.M.S.R. (Midland) main line from Leeds to Carlisle, and continued up the long 1 in 100 climb past Headingley and Horsforth to Bramhope tunnel. From Pannal it ran round an extremely sharp curve up on to Crimple viaduct, and up a short 1 in 91 stretch into Harrogate. Leaving here at 3.20 p.m., the train dropped sharply downhill—1 in 66 at first. to Bilton Road

Junction—to Ripon, and after making calls there and at Darlington, reached Newcastle at 5.0 p.m.

Coming south, the "Harrogate Pullman" started from Newcastle at 9.20 a.m., called at Darlington, left the London main line at Northallerton for the Harrogate and Leeds detour, and stopped at Ripon and Harrogate to Leeds. Pulling out of Leeds at 11.50 a.m., and rejoining the Newcastle-London main line at Doncaster, the Pullman reached King's Cross at 3.15 p.m. Two years later the working of the train was extended to Edinburgh, with a stop at Berwick, and the entire journey took 8 hours, 35 minutes ; going north the 11.15 a.m. start was unaltered, but on the southbound journey a departure from Edinburgh at 8.30 a.m. retarded the exit from Harrogate to 1.5 p.m., and from Leeds to 1.40 p.m. ; King's Cross was now reached at 5.5 p.m.

In September, 1925, another change was made. A second all-Pullman train, which later became the "West Riding Pullman," had been trying a variety of routes in order to establish itself in public favour, and it was decided to make this into a special Leeds and Bradford service at 11.10 a.m. from King's Cross. It was thus possible to schedule the "Harrogate Pullman" as a non-stop express over the 198·8 miles from King's Cross to Harrogate ; the start was changed to 11.20 a.m., and the Pullman was booked into Harrogate at 3.3 p.m. This run covered an interesting route, including the use of L.M.S.R. metals from Shaftholme Junction, 4½ miles north of Doncaster, to Knottingley, then by a spur line to L.N.E.R. metals at Ferrybridge, and on through Church Fenton and Tadcaster up to Crimple Viaduct and Harrogate. Edinburgh was now reached at 7.35 p.m., in 8¼ hours. On the southbound run, the "Harrogate Pullman," leaving Edinburgh at 8.30 a.m. and Harrogate at 1.5 p.m. as before, followed the same non-stop course to London and was due at 4.45 p.m.

So matters continued until May, 1928, when a new and very handsome train of seven all-steel Pullmans, all eight-wheelers, appeared on the service, bearing the attractive title of the "Queen of Scots." As the "West Riding Pullman" was from the same date moved to an afternoon departure from London, the "Queen of Scots" reverted to the Leeds route, and left King's Cross at 11.15 a.m. Further, it was extended from Edinburgh to Glasgow, and reached Queen Street at 8.45 in the evening, after completing a route of 450·8 miles in length. Coming south, it started from Glasgow at 10.5 a.m., and Edinburgh at 11.15 a.m., and was booked to reach King's Cross at 7.35 p.m. The timing for the non-stop runs between London and Leeds in each direction was still 3 hours, 25 minutes, as in 1923.

From that time onwards there were no changes other than the speeding-up that began with the general acceleration of all the Anglo-Scottish services in May, 1932. When the "Queen of Scots" was withdrawn on the outbreak of war in September, 1939, the starting time from London was 11.20 a.m., and no more than 191 minutes was allowed for the 185·7 miles from King's Cross to Leeds—an average of 58·3 m.p.h. The up run was a minute quicker (58·5 m.p.h.). Harrogate was reached in 3¾ hours, Edinburgh in 7¼ hours, and Glasgow in 8 hours, 53 minutes. In the reverse direction the " Queen of Scots " was due away from Glasgow at 10.15 a.m. and Edinburgh at 11.20 a.m. ; departure from Harrogate was at 3.23 p.m. and from Leeds (Central) at 3.55 p.m., and King's Cross was reached at 7.5 p.m. An additional stop was made in this direction at Holbeck, ½ mile after leaving Leeds Central, at 3.57 p.m.

Between London and Leeds various types of locomotive were tried on the Pullman workings, including the Great Central 4-cylinder 4-6-0's, which could not maintain their steam pressure on these lengthy runs, and the Great Central " Director " 4-4-0's, which did well, but without adequate reserve. It was the Ivatt Atlantics of the one-time Great Northern, however, which will always be associated with the Pullmans. Some of the most famous L.N.E.R. main line drivers first made their reputations in the Pullman link, and as for the engines, to quote from an historic phrase used in another connection, this was " their finest hour." Time-keeping with the 290-ton load was exemplary, and on many of the runs a considerable amount of time lost by permanent way and signal checks was recovered to achieve a punctual arrival. Latterly the all-conquering Pacifics appeared on the train, and from Leeds northwards it was generally a Pacific working.

Since the war the " Queen of Scots " has been reinstated, and by the winter of 1950–1951 had got back to a non-stop run of 3½ hours in each direction between King's Cross and Leeds, as well as to fast timings of 136 minutes northbound and 135 minutes south-bound over the 124·4 miles between Newcastle and Edinburgh. Since then there have been various trivial alterations in the times of both trains ; the post-war fastest between Leeds and King's Cross was 3 hours, 23 minutes up in the summer of 1952.

In the 1952-1953 winter timetables, the down " Queen of Scots," a ten-car formation of about 400 tons, reaches Leeds in 3½ hours, at 3.30 p.m. Here two cars are detached, and the eight-car remainder is into Newcastle by 5.44 p.m. Between Newcastle and Edinburgh the present timing in both directions is the fastest yet scheduled for one of the Pullmans—124·4 miles in 132 minutes—and Waverley is reached at 8.2 p.m. ; the Glasgow arrival is 9.14 p.m. Coming south, the " Queen of Scots " leaves Glasgow at 10.50 a.m., Edinburgh at 12 noon—in both directions the London and Edinburgh starts are in conformity with the systematic departure plan of the Eastern and North Eastern Regions—Newcastle at 2.18 p.m., and Leeds at 4.36 p.m., with a King's Cross arrival at 8.5 p.m. As in the opposite direction, eight cars are run from Glasgow and ten from Leeds. The engines used are now almost invariably Class " A1 " Pacifics.

63—The "Royal Highlander"

Lineal descendant of the flyer which as far back as 1895 made the fastest time ever known between London and Aberdeen, the "Royal Highlander" received its title in the year 1927. Space does not permit a full description of all the happenings in the historic "Race to Aberdeen" between the West Coast and East Coast Companies. The genesis of the contest was an announcement by the West Coast companies—the London & North Western and Caledonian Railways—that from July 1st, 1895, their 8 p.m. express from Euston would reach Aberdeen at 7.40 a.m., 15 minutes earlier than before. The race had begun.

Night after night the competing trains made faster times, and finally the timetables were scrapped altogether. The West Coast, running an additional train behind their racing express to make the ordinary intermediate stops, reduced their load to three coaches of 70 tons weight, and omitted all stops except Crewe, Carlisle and Perth. On the morning of August 23rd, 1895, their train, which had left Euston at 8 p.m. the previous evening, rolled into Aberdeen Joint Station at 4.32, having cut more than *three hours* from the schedule that precipitated the race ! The distance of 540 miles had been covered in 8 hours, 32 minutes, at an average of 63·3 m.p.h. throughout, including stops.

From Euston to Crewe the engine was *Adriatic*, one of the Webb 2-2-2-0 three-cylinder compounds, which covered the 158·1 miles in 147½ minutes. At Crewe, *Hardwicke*, a "Jumbo" 2-4-0, took over, and achieved the astonishing feat of running the 141 miles to Carlisle, including the 915-ft. altitude of Shap summit, in 126 minutes, at 67·2 m.p.h. From Carlisle the Caledonian Railway provided a 4-4-0 locomotive, which covered the 150·8 miles over Beattock and Kinbuck summits to Perth in 149½ minutes ; and finally another Caledonian 4-4-0 ran the 89·7 miles from Perth to Aberdeen in 80½ minutes, at an average of 66·9 m.p.h. With this epoch-making performance, by common consent the railways concerned regarded the race as finished.

By the time the "Royal Highlander" received its name it had become a much more leisurely train, but its weight had vastly increased. In winter it left Euston at 7.30 p.m., and made calls at Bletchley, Rugby, Crewe, Wigan, Carlisle and Stirling, being due into Perth at 5.24 in the morning. Here the Inverness and Aberdeen sections parted company. The latter got away at 5.40 a.m., and with stops at Forfar, Bridge of Dun, Laurencekirk and Stonehaven was into Aberdeen at 7.40 a.m. But the Inverness section, which had to collect the through sleeping cars and coaches off the rival "Aberdonian" from King's Cross, and to attach a breakfast car for the sustenance of its hungry passengers, was not due to leave Perth until a whole hour after arrival, at 6.25 a.m., and with various regular and conditional stops reached its northerly destination, 568¾ miles from London, at 9.50 a.m.

On its winter working the " Royal Highlander " took out of Euston three pairs of sleeping cars, first-class and third-class, for Inverness, Aberdeen, and Perth, respectively, together with composite coaches for each destination and third-class brakes or long luggage brakes. On the back of the train was a restaurant car, provided to enable the long-distance travellers comfortably to take dinner before reaching Crewe. The whole train might amount to 12 or 13 vehicles from London.

In the height of the summer season, however, such a formation as this was nothing like enough to accommodate the traffic, and three independent trains were run nightly. The normal 7.30 p.m. was put back to 7.40 p.m., and was preceded by a 7.25 to Inverness and Oban, and a 7.20—the " Royal Highlander " proper—to Inverness and Aberdeen. This express was booked to call first at Crewe, from 10.22 to 10.32 p.m., where engines were changed. From here the next publicly-booked stop was at Perth, but in the working timetable a stop was shown at Motherwell to detach parcels vans for Glasgow ; and the run of 230·4 miles from Crewe to Motherwell at that time was among the longest scheduled regularly on L.M.S.R. metals. With such a load as that conveyed on this train, however, unless two engines were in use, a stop also at Beattock, 180·7 miles from Crewe, was necessary for assistance up the famous bank.

Arriving at Perth at 4.46 a.m., the Aberdeen section was away 5 minutes later, and with one intermediate stop only, at Coupar Angus, was due in Aberdeen at 7 a.m., 40 minutes earlier than in winter. The main train, too, waited only 23 minutes, instead of an hour, at Perth, and so was into Inverness at 8.45 a.m., 65 minutes earlier than on the winter working. It is, of course, the difficulty of the 118 miles between Perth and Inverness that accounts for the lengthy allowance of 3 hours, 36 minutes over this stretch. There are 28 miles of single track from Stanley Junction to Blair Atholl, and another 48½ miles from Dalwhinnie to Daviot ; and to add to many other formidable gradients, the engines have to face the terrific climb from Blair Atholl to Druimuachdar summit, 1,484 ft. above sea level, which includes 14 miles at 1 in 70-80, together with another climb from Aviemore to Slochd summit, 1,350 ft. above the sea, with 6 miles at 1 in 60-75. In the opposite direction, too, there is a fearsome start out of Inverness, including 12 miles almost continuously at 1 in 60 up to beyond Daviot.

In recent years the Highland workings have been greatly improved by the advent of the Stanier 6 ft. 4-6-0's of power class " 5," which usually hunt in couples, and in double-harness can handle loads up to about 500 tons. In the summer season the up night workings from the Highlands to Euston were very complicated, and no train was described officially as the " Royal Highlander " ; nor was there a winter train with this title coming south, though actually the counterpart of the down working was the 4.15 p.m. from Inverness, leaving Perth at 8.30 p.m., and due in Euston at 6.55 the following morning. The Aberdeen train, leaving the Granite City at 7.50 p.m., was 95 minutes later from Perth and due in London at 8 a.m.

During wartime this service was of such importance, for naval and military reasons, as to require two trains nightly, at 7.20 p.m. from Euston to Inverness and at 7.30 p.m. to Perth, though neither carried a name. The 7.20 p.m. resembled its peacetime counterpart, for it made stops at Crewe, Beattock (for the banker), and Motherwell (to drop the Glasgow vans), to Perth, reached at 5.26 a.m., or 40 minutes later than before the war. A wait of 49 minutes was enjoined at Perth, and at 6.15 a.m. the sleeper set out on a run of just over 4 hours to Inverness, arriving at 10.18 a.m. The heavy train formation from London, save for the Glasgow vans, was run through over the whole journey, and with various accretions at Perth, provided a considerable problem of haulage on the Highland line.

Between Euston and Crewe " Royal Scot " 4–6–0's have been largely used, and Pacifics have taken up the working between Crewe and Perth. The engines used on this duty fill in their day at Perth either by running to Glasgow and back, or to Aberdeen and back; if the latter, a Pacific is seen working the southbound " Postal " from Aberdeen to Perth.

On October 1st, 1945, this train had the distinction of being one of the first L.M.S.R. trains to have a post-war acceleration, and its time was cut to less than the pre-war allowance. For the first part of the " Royal Highlander," still leaving Euston at 7.20 p.m., was booked into Inverness 1¾ hours earlier, at 8.37 a.m. This was done in part by cutting the Perth stop from 49 to 19 minutes (4.46 to 5.5), a.m. but chiefly by paring the running times. But the timing proved too tight; the wait at Perth once again has been expanded to 45 minutes, and Inverness is not reached till 9.34 a.m. The train no longer carries a name.

64—The "Royal Scot"

West Coast rival to the East Coast " Flying Scotsman," the " Royal Scot " has had an even longer, though not unbroken, history; and it was not until 1927 that the title of " Royal Scot " was conferred. One break in the sequence of departures from Euston at the familiar hour of 10 a.m. occurred in the latter part of the First World War, when it was decided to concentrate the morning London to Glasgow traffic on the 8.50 a.m. train from St. Pancras, and the Edinburgh passengers on the corresponding train from King's Cross. For the sake of intermediate stations from Rugby onwards, a Perth portion was run on the 9.10 a.m. down Liverpool train, but no through travellers were supposed to use it from London to Glasgow or Edinburgh.

Up to 1914, the 10 a.m. from Euston, tied down by the East and West Coast agreement to a minimum journey time of 8¼ hours to Glasgow, was a train with through sections for Glasgow and Edinburgh, each with its own restaurant car, and a through portion on the rear for Aberdeen. As with a number of other London & North Western expresses, except in summer it continued to call at Willesden Junction to pick up passengers, and then at Rugby and Crewe, where it divided. From here the Glasgow and Edinburgh portions ran independently, both having acquired through coaches from Birmingham, and both non-stop to Carlisle. The only remaining stop of the Glasgow train was at Symington, and Glasgow Central was reached at 6.15 p.m. The Edinburgh train followed close behind, slipped a carriage at Lockerbie, dropped its Aberdeen portion at Symington, and was into Princes Street also by 6.15 p.m.

Coming south, the two trains, 10 a.m. from Glasgow and 10.5 a.m. from Edinburgh, in the same way ran independently of one another as far as Crewe ; the Glasgow train could be " flagged " to stop at Motherwell by anyone wanting to join it ; both called at Carlisle, and the Edinburgh train had an additional stop at Preston before Crewe was reached. At Crewe the through Birmingham coaches were detached, and the Glasgow and Edinburgh sections were joined for the run to London, calling only at Rugby and terminating at 6.20 p.m.

In the recovery period from 1919 onwards, the down and up trains reappeared in much their previous form, but from 1927 onwards developments began to take place. As the terms of the agreement forbade competition in time, a kind of race in non-stop running began instead. In the summer of 1927 the L.M.S.R. made the " Royal Scot " a train for through passengers between London, Edinburgh and Glasgow only. A " Claughton " 4–6–0, piloted by a " George the Fifth " 4–4–0, hauled the train non-stop to Carnforth, 236 miles from Euston ; here a stop was made at Carnforth No.2 box, south of the station, to examine the train, and a couple of 4–4–0 compounds took over for the run over Shap and Beattock summits to Symington, 130 miles distant, where the Edinburgh portion was detached before the final run into Glasgow.

That summer the L.N.E.R. tried non-stop running from London to Newcastle, 268·3 miles, so the L.M.S.R., now in possession of its new " Royal Scot " 4–6–0 engines, cut out the Carnforth stop, and on the northbound journey ran through over the 301 miles from Euston to Kingmoor, 2 miles north of Carlisle. When the L.N.E.R. decided to go a step further, in May, 1928, by making the entire journey of 392¾ miles from King's Cross to Edinburgh without a stop, the L.M.S.R. was no longer in a position to retaliate owing to the necessity of calling at Symington for the division of their train. But with sly humour, and entirely without warning, on the Friday before the " Flying Scotsman " started its daily world record run, the L.M.S.R. stole the L.N.E.R. thunder by dividing the down "Royal Scot," and running *both* sections without a stop from starting-point to destination. "Royal Scot" 4-6-0 No. 6113, *Cameronian*, took the Glasgow train on its non-stop break of 401·4 miles, and compound 4-4-0 No. 1054 handled the 6-coach Edinburgh portion. The latter's run of 399·7 miles was the longest without a stop ever made by a 4-4-0 locomotive in Great Britain, while the former was a British record for any type of locomotive.

All this time the 8¼-hour overall schedule still persisted, and it was not until 1932 that acceleration began. By 1939 the "Royal Scot" had become a far faster train. In summer it was booked to reach the Citadel station at Carlisle at one minute before 3, so covering the 299·1 miles from Euston in 299 minutes, at precisely 60 m.p.h. For the whole journey to Glasgow the time had come down to 7 hours, and with this load the work required of the locomotive was considerably harder than that of the "Coronation Scot" streamliner on its 6½-hour schedule.

On the winter schedule the allowance was eased by 20 minutes to allow for additional stops at Rugby and Crewe. The train was booked to run the 82·6 miles from Euston to Rugby in 80 minutes, and the 75·5 miles on to Crewe in 75 minutes—two runs in succession at over 60 m.p.h. Leaving the Aberdeen section at Crewe, to be attached to a following express from Birmingham to Glasgow, the "Royal Scot" then covered the 141 miles from Crewe to Carlisle in 154 minutes, and had a minute over 2 hours in which to complete the run of 102·3 miles to Glasgow, Symington stop included—a rather easier task than that required in summer.

On the up journey, the "Royal Scot" by 1939 was maintaining a non-stop run from Carlisle throughout the year. In summer, there were two up non-stops daily. The Glasgow train carried Glasgow to London passengers only, and stopped only at Carlisle No. 12 box, south of the station, to change the engine-crew. The Edinburgh portion stopped at Symington to attach a through section which had left Aberdeen at 6.50 a.m. and Perth at 8.55 a.m.; the next stop was Carlisle Citadel station, and then Euston.

Including the "Coronation Scot," therefore, there were five daily non-stop runs between London and various points at Carlisle from 297·9 to 299·1 miles away. In winter the Glasgow and Edinburgh sections were joined at Symington, and then made the non-stop run from Carlisle Citadel to Euston. While the summer "Royal Scot" reached Euston in 7 hours, the winter train, though with only one additional stop, required 7 hours, 25 minutes—5 minutes more than the down run, even though the down "Royal Scot" stopped also at Rugby and Crewe—from Glasgow.

The year after the accelerations began, the first Stanier Pacifics became available for the haulage of the train. The load was substantial; in summer the down train, from the engine backwards, usually comprised third brake, two compartment thirds, two open thirds, kitchen car, open first, corridor first, and brake for Glasgow;

and first brake, open first, kitchen car, open third, compartment third, and third brake for Edinburgh, total 15 vehicles of about 450 tons. In winter, from Euston, the train usually had about eight in the Glasgow portion, four for Edinburgh, and two for Aberdeen.

A wartime version of the " Royal Scot " ran in both directions throughout the Second World War. Load was generally limited to 17 bogies, including brake, first brake, two open firsts, open composite, and the remainder third class. It soon became necessary to split off the Perth section, and this ran as a second train at 10.5 a.m., the first portion of which, familiarly known as the " Jellicoe " from 1914—1918 war associations, was reserved for Service personnel travelling to the Highlands. The through journey of the latter to Thurso, 721½ miles in all, has been the longest regular through passenger run in Great Britain, and lasted until 7.20 on the following morning, 21¼ hours after leaving London.

On the down journey, the wartime 10 a.m. from Euston called at Rugby, Crewe, Carlisle and Symington, but had no through coaches for Edinburgh; latterly it was due in Glasgow at 6.55 p.m. Coming up, a feature of the working was the daily *queue* of passengers at Glasgow Central, often extending from the barrier out to the front of the station, and at times well round the corner and 100 yards or so down Union Street. For most of the war period, the non-stop run from Carlisle to Euston was maintained, and the arrival in Euston was scheduled at 6.56 p.m.

Restaurant cars were restored in both directions on October 1st, 1945. A fortnight later the trains ceased to call in Carlisle passenger station; the 10 a.m. from Euston stopped at Kingmoor for examination and change of engine-crew, and the 10 a.m. from Glasgow at Carlisle No. 12 box for the same purpose. From October 7th, 1946, the up express was accelerated to reach Euston at 6.15 p.m., 41 minutes earlier, but the down train required 8½ hours to reach Glasgow. With the introduction of the 1950–1951 winter service, the stops in both directions at Carlisle passenger station were reinstated; the time from Euston to Glasgow became 6 hours 35 minutes, and that from Glasgow to Euston 6 hours 13 minutes. During the early part of 1950, the up " Royal Scot " was frequently worked through by the twin diesel-electric units Nos. 10000 and 10001.

In the summer of 1952, a complete set of new standard stock displaced that previously in use on the " Royal Scot," and the times in both directions between Euston and Glasgow were reduced to 8 hours. The up 8-hour timing remained in the 1952–1953 winter timetables, but with the re-introduction of the usual winter stops on the down run, the Euston-Glasgow time became 8 hours, 10 minutes. In summer the train loads to 14 bogies each way; in winter the down train, with both Glasgow and Perth sections and restaurant cars in each, is frequently 16 bogies, whereas 12 bogies suffice on the up run.

65—The "Scarborough Flyer"

In the years before the First World War, the attractions of Scarborough and other resorts on the North East Coast were thought to appeal mainly to the citizens of the West Riding of Yorkshire and the Midlands ; facilities for travel to and from London were not of the best. But after the grouping of the railways, the London & North Eastern Railway lost no time in attempting to popularise Scarborough with Londoners also, who by now had learned not to fear long journeys in taking their holidays. In 1923, the first year of the grouping, a through summer express was put on from King's Cross at 11.50 a.m. to Scarborough, with a non-stop run in 3½ hours over the 188·2 miles between King's Cross and York, the longest regular break ever scheduled over Great Northern and North Eastern metals to that date. Scarborough was reached at 4.20 p.m., in 4½ hours from London ; and a corresponding up express left Scarborough at 3 p.m., running non-stop from York and reaching London at 7.30 p.m.

In 1933 the London-York allowance was brought down to 3¼ hours, and Scarborough was reached in 4 hours, 10 minutes from London ; then, in 1935, by a bold stroke the schedule over the 188·2 miles between King's Cross and York was cut to the even 3 hours, and the start to stop speed rose to 62·7 m.p.h., making the " Scarborough Flyer " one of the fastest trains on the L.N.E.R., apart from the streamliners subsequently introduced. The 42 miles between York and Scarborough were allowed 50 minutes, and with 5 minutes spent at York, the overall time between London and Scarborough had now come down to 3 hours, 55 minutes for a journey of 230·2 miles.

In its earlier days, the down " Scarborough Flyer " had been combined with a portion for Glasgow, and later for Newcastle, but this had now disappeared, and had been replaced by a through composite brake for Whitby, attached next to the engine going north. This was transferred to a train leaving York at 2.15 p.m., calling only at Pickering, Goathland and Grosmont, and reaching Whitby at 3.55 p.m. The normal formation of the " Scarborough Flyer," including the Whitby coach, and two restaurant cars, was about 11 bogies, 365 tons tare and 385 or 390 tons gross, though the make-up varied somewhat according to traffic demand.

On the up journey the " Scarborough Flyer " left Scarborough at 10.40 a.m., reached York at 11.30 and there picked up the Whitby coach (which had started at 9.40 a.m.) ; departing from York at 11.35 a.m., it was due in King's Cross at 2.35 p.m. according to the public timetables, though the working book allowed 2 minutes more. In both directions between King's Cross and York, Pacifics were used, often of the streamlined " A4 " type, and the North Eastern Area handled the train between York and Scarborough with " D49 " class " Shire " or " Hunt " 4-4-0's, or perhaps a " C7 " class Atlantic.

On Saturdays considerable expansion was needed to accommodate the traffic. During the height of the season, the " Scarborough Flyer," at 11 a.m., was preceded by a restaurant car train to Scarborough at 10.50 a.m., which called at York to change engines, though not publicly booked to do so; this was due in Scarborough at 3.7 p.m., and the " Scarborough Flyer " proper, with its timing to York eased to 3 hours, 20 minutes, at 3.15 p.m. To Whitby a special restaurant car train was run at 11.25 a.m., with two stops *en route*; it called first at Selby to detach a through portion for Bridlington, and then at York to change engines, though neither of these stops appeared in the public timetables; Whitby was reached at 4.39 p.m.

There were similar up Saturday arrangements, with trains from Scarborough at 10.20 and 10.40 a.m., due in King's Cross at 2.25 and 2.45 p.m., and, sandwiched between them, the 9.40 a.m. from Whitby, due in London at 2.35 p.m. All these trains, of course, had Pacific haulage on their non-stop runs between York and King's Cross.

The summer of 1950 saw a so-called " Scarborough Flyer " reinstated in the timetable, on Fridays, Saturdays and Sundays only in the down direction and Saturdays, Sundays and Mondays in the up, but with nothing in its speed to justify such a title as " Flyer." Leaving King's Cross at 11.5 a.m., and calling at Grantham, York and Malton (where a through section for Whitby was detached) the train was due in Scarborough at 3.52 p.m.; in the reverse direction the departure from Scarborough was at 11.30 a.m., and the arrival in King's Cross 4.16 p.m. By the summer of 1952 matters had greatly improved, though the running of the train was confined to Fridays and Saturdays down, and Saturdays and Sundays up. Leaving King's Cross at 11.20 a.m., and still calling at Grantham, the " Flyer " reached York at 2.50 p.m., and Scarborough at 3.48 p.m., in just under 4½ hours; the up journey was slower, with departure from Scarborough at 10.7 a.m., and arrival in London at 2.55 p.m. The through Whitby portion has been restored.

66—The "Sheffield Special"

After the Great Central Railway had opened its London Extension in 1899, many ambitious moves were made in the hope of attracting the travelling public to the new route from Marylebone to the Midlands and the North. But well-established travel habits are difficult to alter, and the G.C.R. was additionally hampered in that its new London terminus was not connected with any London underground line, though it did later acquire a station on the Bakerloo tube, when the latter was opened.

One Great Central slogan was " Every Express Vestibuled with Buffet Car Attached," and an attractive service of meals and light refreshments on all long-distance trains was a feature of the G.C.R. arrangements. Another feature was speed. Although the entry to London, over the Metropolitan line from Quainton Road to Harrow, with its difficult grades, was not conducive to speed, the new G.C.R. line between Quainton Road and Annesley, north of Nottingham, was laid out expressly to permit fast running, and only through Leicester and Nottingham were any service slacks in force.

In the year 1903, a new afternoon express for Sheffield appeared in the G.C.R. timetable. The starting time was fixed at 3.25 p.m., and with the help of the water-troughs at Charwelton and Killamarsh the train was booked to make the run of 164·7 miles non-stop in 3 hours 8 minutes. By 1904 this was cut to 2 hours 57 minutes, and in 1905 to the fast time of 2 hours 50 minutes. This was the fastest schedule ever in force between Marylebone and Sheffield, and equalled the best bookings introduced at any time over the competing Midland and Great Northern routes. The train became known as the " Sheffield Special," though this name did not appear in the timetables or official literature. There was an up non-stop also, at 8.50 a.m. from Sheffield to Marylebone.

At first a formation of three coaches, headed by a Robinson 4–4–0 locomotive, sufficed to carry the traffic. Later, when the Robinson Atlantics had come into use, the normal formation was four bogies, with an additional non-corridor coach which was slipped at Leicester, and worked from there through to Grimsby and Cleethorpes. In the course of time, the allowance to Sheffield was eased to 2 hours 57 minutes, at which it remained up to the First World War, and the Marylebone departure was altered to 3.15 p.m. The main train continued from Sheffield to Manchester, slipping at Penistone a portion for Bradford, which consisted of a composite slip brake, and a through coach from Bournemouth which had been brought to Sheffield immediately ahead on the Bournemouth-Newcastle through train. The only other stop was Guide Bridge, after which the " Sheffield Special " was worked round the southern outskirts of Manchester into the Central Station, where it was due at 7.25 p.m., in time to connect with the 7.30 p.m. to Liverpool. In earlier years it had a very tight timing of 50 minutes from Sheffield to Manchester London Road, a distance of 41¼ miles over Dunford summit, and including a Guide Bridge stop.

During the First World War the " Sheffield Special " continued to run, complete with its restaurant car, and at speeds but little inferior to those of peace (like most of the G.C.R. services), but with stops at Leicester and Penistone replacing the slip portions, and an additional stop at Nottingham. Sheffield was reached at 6.37 p.m. and Manchester at 8 p.m. After the war this arrangement continued, and the express, still without any official name, settled down to a departure from Marylebone at 3.20 p.m. The 103·1 miles to Leicester were run in 109 minutes ; in the compass of this run came the 6-mile climb at 1 in 105 from Rickmansworth up to Amersham, a gruelling task for the engine. After a two-minute stop at Leicester, from 5.9 to 5.11 p.m., the 23·4 miles on to Nottingham had to be run in the smart time of 25 minutes. The stop at Nottingham Victoria was from 5.36 to 5.38 p.m., and in view of the gradients between there and Sheffield, with 7 miles at 1 in 130 up to Kirkby South Junction, the continued rise on easier inclinations to Pilsley, and the not infrequent slowings for colliery subsidences, the allowance of 48 minutes for the 38·2 miles from Nottingham to Sheffield was by no means easy.

But the hardest task of all was reserved for the conclusion, in the tremendous pull from Sheffield up to the eastern portal of Woodhead tunnel, nearly 1,000 ft. above sea level, by grades which for 18½ miles continuously are at 1 in 120 to 1 in 132. In the middle of the ascent came the stop at Penistone, where a through coach for Bradford was detached ; leaving Sheffield at 6.30 p.m., the " Sheffield Special " ran the 12·9 miles to Penistone in 23 minutes ; the next 23·4 miles, over Dunford summit and down to Guide Bridge, took 32 minutes, and after a 2-minute stop there, the last stage of 11·1 miles into Manchester Central occupied 16 minutes. The arrival in Manchester was made at 7.45 p.m., and the 4 hours 10 minutes which the " Sheffield Special " was allowed in its heyday had thus expanded to 4 hours 25 minutes overall.

For many years the working of this express was entrusted to the highly efficient " Director " class 4-4-0's of Robinson's design, and it was on such workings that they were seen at their best. It is doubtful if any other 4-4-0 locomotives have been expected to handle so onerous a continuous locomotive working as this, nearly 4½ hours in length without respite, and including speeds up to and exceeding 80 m.p.h. on the well-laid-out line south of Nottingham, as well as the long and arduous gradients through most of the journey. It has been calculated that on this journey of 212 miles a locomotive requires to lift its train through an aggregate difference in level of no less than 2,900 ft. before Manchester is reached.

In L.N.E.R. years standard stock appeared on the train, and its normal formation was seven coaches, including the through L.M.S.R. Bradford composite brake on the rear. The rest of the train, from the engine backwards, was usually third-class brake, third corridor, third restaurant car, first-class restaurant and kitchen car, composite and third brake ; this made a tare weight of 243 tons, and a gross weight of about 260 tons. By now the " B17 " or " Sandringham " 3-cylinder 4-6-0's had replaced the " Directors." No up working ever ranked with the down train as the " Sheffield Special " ; the nearest approach was probably the 2.15 p.m. from Manchester London Road, making the same stops from Guide Bridge, and due in Marylebone at 6.38 p.m. Both trains were withdrawn on the outbreak of war in 1939.

There is once again a 2.10 p.m. express from Manchester to Marylebone, but it is only a pale shadow of its former self. With added stops at Rugby, Aylesbury and Harrow, it is not due in London till 7.20 p.m.—a journey slower by 57 minutes than in 1939.

67—The "Silver Jubilee"

History was made in Great Britain on September 27th, 1935, when, at 2.25 in the afternoon, the first British streamlined train with fully streamlined locomotive slipped out of King's Cross terminus in London for a test run to Grantham and back. It was 110 years, to the day, after George Stephenson had driven *Locomotion No. 1* over the Stockton & Darlington Railway at the opening of the first public railway to come into existence. The new " Silver Jubilee," so named in honour of the Silver Jubilee of the reign of King George V, which was celebrated in 1935, was a striking testimony to the tremendous advance in the luxury and speed of transport that had taken place in little over a century.

Few who participated in the " Silver Jubilee " trial are likely to forget the experience. For certain reasons it was desired to ascertain how much time the new " A4 " Pacific locomotive, No. 2509, *Silver Link*, might be expected to have in hand on the schedule to which the train was to run from the following Monday. From the start, therefore, the special began to gain time ; up the 1 in 200 ascent to Potter's Bar speed was increased steadily to 75 m.p.h. ; after the summit of the " Northern Heights " had been breasted near Knebworth, the 100 m.p.h. mark was crossed at milepost 25 ; and for the next 30 miles the speed was continuously above that figure, and might have remained so, but for the need of caution round the curves at Offord.

Twice in succession a maximum speed of 112½ m.p.h. was reached, the highest on record in Great Britain up to that time. For 43 miles continuously an average of 100 m.p.h. was maintained, and the 70 miles from Wood Green to Fletton Junction, where the driver began to reduce speed for the severe curve through Peterborough, were covered at an average speed of 91.8 m.p.h., notwithstanding the inclusion in this length of the long 1 in 200 climbs from Wood Green to Potter's Bar and from Hatfield to Woolmer Green. From King's Cross *Silver Link* passed Peterborough, 76·4 miles, in the unprecedented time of 55 minutes, 2 seconds, or 8½ minutes less than the time fixed for the train's regular running.

The " Silver Jubilee " went into service on September 30th, 1935. Its daily journey began at Newcastle Central at 10 a.m. ; the 36 miles to Darlington, with heavy gradients and the severe slack over Durham viaduct, were allowed 40 minutes, and from there, after a stop of 2 minutes, the 232·3 miles to King's Cross were run non-stop in 3 hours, 18 minutes, at a scheduled average of 70·4 m.p.h.

throughout, bringing the train into London at 2 p.m. Three and a half hours later, at 5.30 p.m., the return journey was begun, with exactly the same time allowance; Darlington was reached at 8.48 p.m., and left at 8.50 p.m., and the arrival in Newcastle was at 9.30 p.m.

From the first day the "Silver Jubilee" was highly popular—so much so, indeed, that intending passengers who had neglected the precaution of booking their seats well in advance stood the risk of being left behind. A supplement of 5s. first class and 3s. third class was charged for a seat, and it was rarely that the train ran with a single seat vacant. Despite the fact that the "Silver Jubilee" did not run on Saturdays or Sundays, in two years the supplementary fares alone accumulated to a sum sufficient to pay the entire cost of building the train. It had proved that the British public wanted speed, and was prepared to pay for it.

The schedule of the train was such as to demand speeds of 90 m.p.h. over considerable stretches of favourable track in order to maintain time. The fastest point-to-point timing was over the 27 miles from Hitchin to Huntingdon, in the northbound direction, allowed only 19 minutes; moreover, this booked average of 85·3 m.p.h. included a 70 m.p.h. slowing round the curves at Offord. Severe reductions of speed were necessary through Peterborough, Selby, and York in both directions. For the first time, also, in view of the high average speed of the train, it became necessary to impose limits of 70 to 80 m.p.h. at various points where speed restrictions had never operated previously.

In order to check the drivers' observance of these restrictions, the engines were fitted with self-recording speed indicators, which not only gave them a visible indication of their speeds, on a dial in the cab, but also recorded the speed automatically on a paper tape moved by clockwork, and so made it possible, at the end of each journey, for the speed throughout to be checked. Another precaution connected with the speed was that of keeping two block signalling sections clear ahead of the "Silver Jubilee" instead of the normal one.

The original formation of the train was three articulated sets of coaches, making seven vehicles in all, carried on ten bogies. At the north end was a "twin," consisting of brake third and third class, both compartment coaches. Next came the restaurant car "triplet," with open third-class car, kitchen and pantry car, and open first-class car. At the south end there was a second "twin," one vehicle of which was a first-class car, half open and the other half divided into three compartments, and a four-compartment first-class brake behind that. The demand for accommodation was such that at a later date an additional coach body was built into the leading "twin," making it into a "triplet," third class throughout. This addition increased the empty weight of the train from 220 to 248 tons, and the number of vehicles to eight.

In conformity with its name, the "Silver Jubilee" had an

exterior finish of silver-grey throughout, with stainless steel fittings, and the four locomotives specially built for the service—Nos. 2509, *Silver Link*, 2510, *Quicksilver*, 2511, *Silver King*, and 2512, *Silver Fox*—were painted in the same grey shade. Later, as more of the " A4 " streamlined Pacifics were built, and the Garter blue colour was adopted, Nos. 2509 to 2512 were painted blue also, and from that time onwards any of the " A4 " class engines might be rostered to work the train. In the four years up to the outbreak of war the " Silver Jubilee " train had run about 540,000 miles without mishap, and was reckoned to have earned for its owners a revenue of some 12s. 6d. a mile. The train was withdrawn on the outbreak of war ; since then, the restaurant car triplet has been in use between King's Cross and Newcastle, and the five passenger coaches on the " Fife Coast Express " between Glasgow and St. Andrews.

68—The "Strathearn Express"

Like its North British neighbour, the Caledonian Railway established several train services designed to induce businessmen in Glasgow (and Edinburgh) to spend their nights in more bracing air than that of the cities. The North British sought to attract to the East Coast ; the Caledonian to the Clyde and to the Highlands. Among the Highland temptations was the " Strathearn Express," which continued also into the L.M.S.R. era as a " titled train."

In the early years of the century there was an express that left Buchanan Street Station, Glasgow, for the Oban line at 4.50 (later 4.45) p.m. ; this distinguished itself by missing both Larbert and Stirling, and made its first stop at Dunblane, the junction for Oban. The train was followed into Dunblane by the 4.25 p.m. from Edinburgh to Perth, which gave a connection at Crieff Junction (later to become known as Gleneagles) for the Strathearn valley. But through passengers from Glasgow to Comrie had to leave on an earlier and slower train at 4.5 p.m.

From 1911 Strathearn got its own " Strathearn Express," leaving Buchanan Street at 4.55 p.m. ; and in the reverse direction a morning express from St. Fillans and Comrie after leaving Gleneagles called only at Larbert to divide into its Glasgow and Edinburgh sections. In 1912, however, the Strathearn coaches were attached to the 4.45 p.m. Oban train, and detached at Dunblane and run from there non-stop to Comrie, reached at 6 14 p.m. In 1913 a stop was included on the down run at Gleneagles.

The Edinburgh " Strathearn Express " ran independently throughout at 4.50 p.m. from Princes Street, except for joining the 5 p.m. " Granite City " express from Glasgow to Aberdeen between Dunblane and Gleneagles. On the inward journey, the

Right: Recovering from Skipton slack—rebuilt L.M.R. "Royal Scot" Class 4-6-0 No. 46108 *Seaforth Highlander* tackles the beginning of the long climb to Ais Gill with the northbound "Thames - Clyde Express"

[*C. Bendall*

Below: Southbound over the Waverley route—Class "A3" Pacific No. 60043 *Brown Jack* awaits the "right-away" at Edinburgh Waverley with the post-war equivalent of the "Thames-Forth Express"

[*E. R. Wethersett*

[C. R. L. Coles

Last lap—E.R. Class " A3 " Pacific No. 60062 *Minoru* hurries the up " Yorkshire Pullman "
out of Greenwood Tunnel, Hadley Wood

[H. Gordon Tidey

London-bound—The " Torbay Express " winds round the curve at Teignmouth behind
" County " Class 4–6–0 No. 1015 *County of Gloucester*

[*P. H. Wells*

The down " West Riding " in full cry past Essendine behind E.R. Class " A1 " 4–6–2 No. 60128 *Bongrace.* Next the engine are some of the streamline coaches from the pre-war " West Riding Limited "

[*E. Treacy*

Starting from Grantham—The up " White Rose " behind E.R. Class " A2/3 " Pacific No. 60513 *Dante*

Above: The down "Welshman" leaving Chester behind L.M.R. "Royal Scot" Class 4–6–0 No. 46144 *Honourable Artillery Company*

[*E. Treacy*

Left: On the 1 in 96 out of Aberdeen—Class "5" 4–6–0 No. 45168 with the Southbound "West Coast Postal"

[*J. B. C. McCann*

Below: Leaving Leeds with the up "Yorkshire Pullman"—E.R. Class "A1" Pacific No. 60118 *Archibald Sturrock*

[*K. Field*

" Strathearn " left St. Fillans at 7.40 a.m., called at Comrie, Crieff, Muthill and Gleneagles, and then only at Stirling to divide.   It was the only train of the day to run non-stop from Stirling to Edinburgh. Glasgow was reached at 9.45 and Edinburgh at 9.55 a.m.

But in later years the " Strathearn Express " did not succeed in retaining its title under L.M.S.R. auspices.   For a time it was restored between the two wars, but subsequently, up to the outbreak of the Second World War, the Strathearn passengers were being accommodated in through corridor coaches attached to the 5 p.m. Aberdeen express from Buchanan Street, Glasgow, with the advantage of the latter's restaurant car as far as Gleneagles, reached at 6.8 p.m.   Arrival at Crieff was at 6.36, and at St. Fillans at 7.3 p.m. The Edinburgh passengers, also in through coaches, were still being brought as far as Gleneagles by the 4.25 p.m. Aberdeen train from Princes Street.

In the morning, much as in earlier years, the through Strathearn coaches left St. Fillans at 7.45 a.m. and Crieff at 8.11 a.m.   After Gleneagles there were more stops than before, including Blackford, Dunblane, Bridge of Allan and Larbert, notwithstanding which the express reached Buchanan Street at 9.45 a.m.   But the Edinburgh section, detached at Stirling, was not into Princes Street until 10.5 a.m.

At different periods of Caledonian history, chiefly up to the First World War, there were other named trains between Glasgow and the Perthshire Highlands, such as the 5.30 p.m. " Stirling & Ben Ledi Express " from Buchanan Street to Callander, and the " C. & O. Hotel Express," which ran on Fridays at 3.55 p.m. from Glasgow to Oban, due at 7.30 p.m., and returned on Monday mornings at 7.30 a.m., getting back into Glasgow at 11 a.m.   But these trains had no more than a brief reign.

69—The "Sunny South Express"

It was in 1904 that the " Sunny South " idea first took shape. In the cities of the Midlands and the North there had been some agitation for the provision of through facilities which would make it unnecessary for those of their citizens desiring holidays on the South Coast to complicate their journeys by crossing London.   The first experiment was a service of through coaches between Manchester and Brighton in 1904 ; but the popularity of the service was so great that in the following year it had blossomed out into a complete restaurant car express, organised jointly by the London & North Western and London, Brighton & South Coast Railways, and formed of the former company's stock, between Liverpool and Manchester, Brighton and Eastbourne.

The idea was infectious, and before long the Kent Coast was sharing in the same facilities, while through coaches were being run from the Midland and Great Northern systems also, by way of the Metropolitan line through Snow Hill, Herne Hill and the Bickley junctions to Folkestone, Dover and Deal. One daily service, running in 1914, comprised coaching stock of the North Western, Midland and Great Northern Railways, marshalled at Herne Hill into one curious composite assemblage for its journey over the South Eastern & Chatham line to Ramsgate. For a short period one could travel through also from Paddington to Brighton.

A remarkable episode in the pre-1914 history of the " Sunny South Express " was the through working of locomotives between Brighton and Rugby arranged jointly by the London, Brighton & South Coast and London & North Western Companies in the latter part of 1909. The L.N.W.R. engine was one of the " Precursor " 4-4-0's, No. 7, *Titan*; but the L.B.S.C.R. placed reliance on one of the new 4-4-2 tanks of Earle Marsh's design, No. 23 of Class " I3." The round trip was one of 264 miles, which the tank locomotive used to complete on one heaped-up bunker full of coal, about 3¼ tons.

Most amazing of all was the fact that the Brighton engine, with a tank capacity no greater than 2,100 gallons, would daily run the 90 miles between East Croydon and Rugby without taking water, though this meant working a 7-coach 235-ton train non-stop over the 77·2 miles between Willesden and Rugby at 53 m.p.h. Consumption thus averaged 27 lb. of fuel and 22 gallons of water per mile. One essential factor of this success was that the Marsh tank had been fitted with a Schmidt superheater ; and this exchange with little doubt marked an important turning point in L.N.W.R. locomotive history, for it resulted in the building of the " George the Fifth " class, one of the most competent 4-4-0 designs in British annals.

After the First World War, during which these through services were suspended, the " Sunny South Express " duly reappeared. But, like many other through services to and from holiday resorts in pre-1914 days, eventually it became a week-end service only over a large part of the year. Through the summer season it reverted to a daily service once more, and at week-ends expanded to several independent trains.

In summer the main southbound train, with the restaurant cars attached, left Manchester London Road at 10.40 a.m., and was joined at Crewe by the 10.35 a.m. from Liverpool Lime Street. The combined train, leaving Crewe at 11.46 a.m., then called at Nuneaton, Rugby and Northampton to Willesden, which was reached at 3.11 p.m. At Rugby the express acquired some through coaches from Birmingham, which had left New Street at 12.30 p.m. At Willesden Junction the S.R. took over, and starting at 3.24 p.m., worked the " Sunny South Express " round the West London Line, skirting the Metropolis through Kensington, Addison Road, and

Clapham Junction to East Croydon. From Clapham Junction onwards the express had to be fitted into the dense electric service, and was due into Brighton at 4.55 p.m. This was 15 minutes slower from Liverpool to Brighton than in 1904. Away again at 5.4 p.m., with an engine on the opposite end of the train, a non-stop run was made to Eastbourne in 41 minutes, and here a second reversal took place. The final stage of the journey, completing a total of 278½ miles from Manchester, was to Bexhill, St. Leonards and Hastings, reached at 6.25 p.m., after a journey lasting 7¾ hours.

Going north, a start was made from Hastings at 11.10 a.m., Eastbourne at 11.49 a.m., and Brighton at 12.35 p.m., reaching East Croydon at 1.27 p.m., Kensington at 1.53 p.m., and Willesden at 2.2 p.m. Here the L.M.S.R. took charge, and the next stop was Northampton, where the Birmingham coaches were detached, instead of at Rugby. The " Sunny South Express " then made a non-stop run over the 94·6 miles to Crewe (where the Liverpool and Manchester sections separated), in 106 minutes, reaching Crewe at 5.15 p.m. By arrivals in Manchester at 6.19 p.m. and Liverpool at 6.24 p.m., the northbound " Sunny South " improved on its southbound times by 36 minutes.

On summer Saturdays the workings were very complicated. Additional through restaurant car trains ran in each direction between Birmingham and Hastings, by the " Sunny South " route, and also between Birmingham and the Kent Coast resorts. The latter were diverted beyond Addison Road through the Latchmere and Longhedge junctions on to the Eastern Division main line from Victoria, continuing to Chatham, Herne Bay, Margate and Ramsgate. Through coaches were run on the latter train from Liverpool and Manchester, and the Midland Division of the L.M.S.R. contributed a through section from Sheffield and Leicester to Hastings, which was attached at Northampton. The Second World War brought these " Sunny South " activities to an abrupt end, but they are now restored between Birmingham, Leicester, Brighton, Eastbourne and Hastings on Saturdays only during the summer. The name " Sunny South Express " is no longer in use.

A train from Manchester leaves on Friday nights at 11.40 p.m., a second starts from Birmingham at 11.40 a.m. on Saturday mornings, and a third from Leicester, via Market Harborough and Northampton, at 12.35 p.m. The L.M.R. locomotive is changed for one from the S.R. at Mitre Bridge Junction, just clear of Willesden on the West London line; from here the S.R. locomotive works through to Brighton, and other engines continue to Eastbourne and Hastings. There are similar workings in the reverse direction, all on Saturdays, from Hastings at 10.45 a.m. to Birmingham, 10.51 a.m. to Leicester, and 12.30 p.m. to Manchester.

70—The "Tees-Tyne Pullman"

Early in 1948, strong rumours began to go the rounds that the "Silver Jubilee" was to go into service once again, and the hopes of *ex*-L.N.E.R. enthusiasts began to rise accordingly, though it was obvious that nothing approaching the pre-war standard of speed was to be anticipated as yet. But when the new train materialised, on September 27th, 1948, it turned out to be another addition to the British Pullman fleet, with the name of "Tees-Tyne Pullman." It reproduced the "Silver Jubilee" to the extent of leaving London at 5.30 p.m., and having no publicly-booked stops over the the 232.3 miles between King's Cross and Darlington; but whereas the "Silver Bullet," as its regular patrons always called it, bridged this distance in 3 hours, 18 minutes, at 70.4 m.p.h., the new train was found to have been given no less than 4 hours, 27 minutes (52.2 m.p.h.), and the Pullman was to reach Newcastle at 10.50 p.m. as compared with the "Jubilee's" 9.30 p.m. The up journey was to be similar; leaving Newcastle one hour earlier than the "Jubilee," at 9 a.m., the "Tees-Tyne Pullman" would be into London at 2.16 p.m., 16 minutes later.

In May, 1949, however, the first welcome acceleration of the "Tees-Tyne" took place, bringing the London–Newcastle time in each direction down to the even five hours, and in September, 1949, a year after the train's inauguration, there was a second speed-up. In the winter of 1949–1950, therefore, the "Tees-Tyne Pullman" was reaching Newcastle in 4 hours, 55 minutes from King's Cross, and the southbound train was making the run in 4 hours, 52 minutes, a cut of 25 minutes northbound and 24 minutes southbound on its timings of a year earlier. The original timings included an unadvertised stop at Grantham to change engine-crews, but the men now work through between Newcastle and King's Cross. This change made possible a cut in the King's Cross-Darlington times to 251 minutes northbound and 247 minutes southbound, the latter requiring a respectable overall average speed of 56.5 m.p.h.

From May, 1949, the up "Tees-Tyne Pullman" has left Newcastle at 9.15 a.m. Also, from the same date, the down "Tees-Tyne" changed places with the "Yorkshire Pullman," and gained a much earlier departure from London, at 4.45 p.m., in order to make possible an arrival at Darlington (8.56 p.m.) and Newcastle (9.40 p.m.) not far removed from the pre-war "Silver Jubilee" times. Later adjustments in timing make the present arrivals of the down train 8.50 p.m. at Darlington and 9.37 p.m. at Newcastle, while the up "Tees-Tyne" is due in King's Cross at 2.8 p.m.; between Darlington and King's Cross the non-stop times are 248 minutes up and 245 minutes down. The train is very popular, especially with Tees-side and Tyneside business men, and runs well filled in both directions. But the supplementary fares (12s. first class and 6s. 6d. third class) are more than double the 5s. and 3s.

supplements of the " Jubilee."

The " Tees-Tyne Pullman " normally is made up to eight cars, three first class, and the remainder of the accommodation third class. Independent kitchens are provided at the two ends of the train, and passengers are served with their meals just where they sit, in the usual Pullman fashion. The total weight of the train is about 320 tons—a relatively light formation by normal East Coast standards. Locomotive power provided is usually one of the last batch of Peppercorn " A1 " Pacifics.

It is of interest that over the 30 miles of line between York and Northallerton the " Tees-Tyne " is the first regular Pullman working that has ever been seen. From Northallerton northwards the " Queen of Scots " has been a regular working, and from Doncaster southwards both the " Queen of Scots " and the " Yorkshire Pullman " ; during the short period from October, 1937, until the war, when the " West Riding Limited " streamliner had upset the up " Yorkshire Pullman " working, the Harrogate section of the latter used to travel *via* York, so that the York–Doncaster section saw a regular Pullman train also.

71—The "Thames-Clyde Express"

Among the titles bestowed by the L.M.S.R. on various trains in 1927, the morning services in each direction between St. Pancras and Glasgow, linking the Thames with the Clyde, received the appropriate name of " Thames-Clyde Express." Under L.M.S.R. auspices, after the 1932 accelerations, the trains which figure in this chapter had settled down to a 10 a.m. departure from St. Pancras and 9.30 a.m. from St. Enoch.

The Midland and Glasgow & South Western route is not merely longer than that of the one-time London & North Western and Caledonian Railways—424½ miles (or 426¼ miles *via* Sheffield) as compared with 401½ miles—but it is much more heavily graded, so that it could never compete effectively in time. It is, however, the scenic attraction of the former, especially through the Pennines from Hellifield and down the Eden Valley to Carlisle, that caused it to be preferred by many even as a route between London and Glasgow, apart from its value to the intermediate cities of Leicester, Nottingham, Sheffield and Leeds.

By 1939 the " Thames-Clyde Express " had participated in the general acceleration, and began its day by running the 72 miles from St. Pancras to Kettering, the first stop, in 71 minutes, notwithstanding the hard uphill start, to just beyond St. Albans, and such banks as the 3 miles at 1 in 119 to Sharnbrook summit.

Leicester, 99·1 miles, was reached at 11.44 a.m., in 32 minutes from Kettering. From Leicester the next stop was at Chesterfield, and the 47·2 miles from Leicester were allowed 57 minutes, with a fine level start to Trent, a very severe slack through that junction, and a moderate climb up the Erewash valley. After 3 minutes' wait at Chesterfield, the express avoided Sheffield and the stiff grind up to Bradway tunnel, by taking the old main line direct to Rotherham ; the Chesterfield-Leeds stretch of 49·7 miles was run in exactly one hour. At Leeds the engine which had worked through from London, almost invariably a " 5XP " 4-6-0, was left in the platform, where the usual reversal of the train took place.

In recent years there has been a through engine working on this train between Leeds and Glasgow, 228½ miles, and until the Second World War this was generally assigned to a " Patriot " 4-6-0 ; but during the war the rebuilt " Royal Scots " with taper boilers appeared on the scene, and did great execution with loads up to fourteen and even fifteen bogies without pilot assistance, though, of course, on a much slower schedule. The pre-war " Thames-Clyde," after making the 36-mile run from Leeds to Hellifield in 45 minutes, then had the sharp booking of 51 minutes for the 46 miles from Hellifield to Appleby, including the 15-mile climb from Settle Junction to Blea Moor tunnel, almost entirely at 1 in 100. The downhill 30·8 miles from Appleby to Carlisle had an easy 35 minutes, and the Border city was reached at 4.9 p.m.

Over the Glasgow & South Western line also there were latterly some very smart timings. Stops were made at Annan, Dumfries, Mauchline (to give a quick connection to Ayr), and Kilmarnock, but notwithstanding the long climb from Dumfries over the high ground near New Cumnock, 616 feet above sea level, with its 13 miles of almost continuous 1 in 200—150 grade to Drumlanrig tunnel, beyond Carronbridge, and the even steeper ascent out of Kilmarnock, at about 1 in 80 for 3 miles of its 4½ miles of length, the train was due in St. Enoch at 6.38 p.m., in 2 hours, 23 minutes from Carlisle and 8 hours, 38 minutes from London.

Coming south, the running to Carlisle was similar to that in the reverse direction, except that there was no stop at Mauchline ; the 115·5 miles required 2 hours, 20 minutes and Carlisle was reached at 11.50 a.m. Here passengers who wanted to make a fast run to London could change into the " Royal Scot " and save a clear hour. Five minutes only were allowed at Carlisle, and at 11.55 a.m. the " Thames-Clyde " was away on a non-stop run of 113 miles to Leeds, reached at 2.20 p.m.

From Leeds the stops were at Sheffield, Trent (where until 1937 a Nottingham coach was detached) and Leicester, and the journey concluded in St. Pancras, after a 60 m.p.h. run over the final 99·1 miles from Leicester in 99 minutes, at 6.25 p.m. Like the " Royal Scot," the " Thames-Clyde " was thus slower coming south than going north, needing 8 hours, 55 minutes—17 minutes more—

though with six intermediate stops as compared with eight. The diversion through Sheffield added 1¾ miles of distance and an entirely disproportionate amount of very hard work, for the start out of Sheffield to the south end of Bradway tunnel is for 5½ miles at 1 in 100.

Through much of the year a set of eight coaches sufficed for the through working—third-class brake, compartment third, open third, third restaurant, kitchen, composite restaurant, composite and first-class brake. An extra composite or third might be attached from St. Pancras to Leeds. At Carlisle the composite from Nottingham, which had been brought thus far by the down " Thames-Forth Express," was added. In the reverse direction, the head of the train included through composite brakes for Bristol, detached at Leeds, and for Nottingham, which ran through as far as Trent.

The Second World War had a remarkable effect on this train. Though still leaving St. Pancras at 10 a.m., it was not due in St. Enoch station, Glasgow, until all but 3 hours later than before, at 9.32 p.m. On the southbound journey it started 30 minutes later at 10 a.m., and was due to reach St. Pancras at 9.40 p.m., 3¼ hours later—a journey not far short of 12 hours, and often considerably more than that by reason of late running.

The northbound run was increased in length to 444 miles by reason of a circuitous course from Kettering to Chesterfield by way of Nottingham and Derby. Through some years of war this had the extraordinary result that both the 10 a.m. from St. Pancras to Glasgow, and the 10 a.m. from Glasgow to St. Pancras, stopped at the same platform at Trent, travelling in the same direction—the latter coming direct from Chesterfield to Leicester, and the northbound train momentarily running due south through Trent on its way from Nottingham to Derby. Another curious characteristic of the northbound run was that the 10 a.m. from St. Pancras has passed daily through more tunnels than any other train in Great Britain. There are nine, for example, between Kettering and Nottingham, and fourteen between Hellifield and Carlisle alone, helping to make up a total of 40 on the run. Of these no fewer than six—Belsize, Corby, Glaston, Clay Cross, Bradway and Blea Moor—are tunnels over a mile long ; the 40 tunnels total about 15 miles in length.

Heavy loads have been invariable on this run ; from London at least nine in the Glasgow portion and four through coaches for Edinburgh, with an additional coach always attached to go as far as Nottingham or Leeds, replaced at Leeds by an additional brake van, have composed the train. The motive power between St. Pancras and Leeds has been a " 5XP " 4-6-0, sometimes assisted by a 4-4-0 for all or part of the journey, and latterly, as previously mentioned, one of the highly efficient taper boiler " Royal Scots " between Leeds and Glasgow.

From 1st October, 1945, both trains regained their restaurant cars, and lost their through Edinburgh coaches. The southbound express was greatly accelerated, and calling after Carlisle only at Leeds, Sheffield, Nottingham and Kettering, was due in St. Pancras 80 minutes earlier, at 8.20 p.m. October, 1946, witnessed a complete timetable recasting, in which the 10 a.m. down, altered to start at 9.55 a.m., returned to the Leicester route, became non-stop from Leeds to Carlisle, and was into Glasgow St. Enoch by 7.23 p.m. Coming south, also *via* Leicester, the 9.50 a.m. from St. Enoch, as it then became, was due in St. Pancras at 7.24 p.m. Since then the " Thames–Clyde Express," which has recovered its name, has been slowed down lamentably, the deceleration being due is part to the reduced speed enforced over much of the route between Trent and Leeds because of pitfall subsidences in the mining area. In the 1952–1953 winter timetables the down train was leaving St. Pancras at 9.50 a.m., and taking no less than 10 hours, 5 minutes to Glasgow; the up train, starting from St. Enoch at 9.15 a.m., required 10 hours, 13 minutes to St. Pancras. The name of the train has been restored since the war.

72–The "Thames-Forth Express"

It is strange to recall that the first access of the one-time Midland Railway to Carlisle was over London & North Western metals, and, moreover, by a route 1¾ miles shorter than the independent route *via* Appleby which the Midland built later. Indeed, the L. & N.W.R., which the Midland reached at Low Gill Junction, in Westmorland, by way of Hellifield, the Yorkshire Clapham Junction, and Ingleton, was so inhospitable to the Midland trains, from Low Gill over its main line on to Carlisle, that the latter company was practically forced to build and open in 1875 its Settle and Carlisle Railway. With its many viaducts and tunnels, and rock blasting throughout its length to find a foothold for the track, this 72-mile line was a very costly project, and the cost of operation has been on a commensurate scale in view of the extremely long and severe gradients leading to Ais Gill summit. The summit level of 1,169 feet makes this the highest altitude reached by any main line in England.

Already the Midland had set about finding Scottish allies. To Glasgow, the Glasgow & South Western Railway, with no other affiliations, was the natural partner ; and this meant that the Midland trains, which had been to the east of the West Coast trains all the way to Carlisle, changed over, north of the Border, to the west side, when the L. & N.W.R. had handed over to its Scottish partner, the Caledonian. From Edinburgh the North British Railway had thrown out one isolated south-westerly tentacle to Carlisle ; and although the N.B.R. was one of the partners in the East Coast route, this connection between Carlisle and Edinburgh was a logical prolongation for the Midland, and a Midland and North British *entente* accordingly came about.

The result of these alliances was the building of jointly-owned stock, of Midland design, lettered " M. & G.S.W." (Midland and Glasgow & South Western), and " M. & N.B." (Midland & North British) for these joint services. When the joint stock workings were abandoned, after the grouping, the L.N.E.R. took over a proportion of the joint stock, which for years afterwards explained the appearance of typical Midland stock in L.N.E.R. colours, and, at the same time, the regular running of L.N.E.R. sleeping cars into St. Pancras, as well as L.N.E.R. coaches on the through day trains over the Midland main line.

In the heyday of the Midland Scottish services, some remarkable trains were run between St. Pancras and Edinburgh. Of special note was a summer night express to the Highlands, leaving St. Pancras at 7.10 or 7.15 in different years, and carrying through coaches and sleeping cars for Aberdeen, Perth, Inverness, and Fort William. In summer, too, what later became the " Thames-Forth Express " was booked to run non-stop from Leeds to St. Pancras, a distance of 196 miles, and for one or two summers the time for this run came down to 3 hours, 34 minutes—the fastest ever scheduled over Midland metals between Leeds and London.

Various departure times were tried by the Midland for the morning service from St. Pancras to Edinburgh, but in the L.M.S.R. era the start was fixed finally at 9.5 a.m. ; also the name " Thames-Forth Express " was conferred in 1927. In the last years before the outbreak of the Second World War it became a very fast train, which was necessary if connection was to be made at Edinburgh with the L.N.E.R. " Flying Scotsman " to Dundee and Aberdeen ; by 1938, however, this connection had been severed. Wherever possible, the L.M.S.R. had established a mile-a-minute standard over its main lines, and the down train therefore covered the 123·5 miles to Nottingham in 123 minutes, arriving at 11.8 a.m.

Curves, gradients, and service slacks over colliery workings beyond Nottingham lowered the speed on to Chesterfield and Sheffield, where stops were made, and Leeds—203½ miles from St. Pancras by the Nottingham and Sheffield loops—was reached at 1.5 p.m., in 4 hours from London. A through coach from St. Pancras to Halifax was left at Sheffield.

From Leeds to Carlisle the allowance of no more than 124 minutes was the fastest ever scheduled over the route, especially as it included a 2-minute stop at Skipton, a very severe slack through Shipley, and the tremendous climb from Settle Junction to Blea Moor. Actually the time allowed for the 86·8 miles from Skipton to Carlisle was 90 minutes, and required an average speed of 57·9 m.p.h.—an unparalleled requirement over such gradients. At the Border city of Carlisle the " Thames-Forth " was due at 3.14 p.m.

Over the " Waverley " route of the L.N.E.R., to which

company's care the train was now handed over, some more formidable climbing was needed, from not far above sea level at Carlisle to 880 feet at Whitrope, in the bleak Border hills, and again to 900 feet at Falahill, between Galashiels and Edinburgh. From Newcastleton through Riccarton Junction to the former summit the ascent is almost continuously at 1 in 75 for 9 miles. In the years before the war, however, Pacifics had been introduced to this route, and made light of such inclinations, though the timings were easy relatively to those between Leeds and Carlisle. Stops were made at Hawick, St. Boswell's, Melrose and Galashiels, and the Waverley station at Edinburgh was reached at 5.45 p.m., just under 2½ hours having been spent on the final 98¼ miles.

Coming south, the " Thames-Forth Express " was timed to leave Edinburgh at 10.3 a.m., and making the same stops to Carlisle, ran into the Citadel station there at 12.37 p.m. Appleby and Hellifield were added to the Skipton stop, and with considerably less energetic running than on the northbound run, the train reached Leeds at 3.8 p.m., and stood there 5 minutes. Calling as before at Sheffield and Chesterfield to Nottingham, the up " Thames-Forth " had one further stop—at Melton Mowbray—before setting out on a final mile-a-minute sprint to St. Pancras, allowed 103 minutes for the 105¼ miles. This brought the train into London at 7.20 p.m. The journey from Edinburgh to London had thus taken 9 hours, 17 minutes or 37 minutes more than that in the reverse direction. A Kettering stop was added in 1938, without change in the London arrival time, replacing the stop at Melton.

Through most of the year the main set of cars between St. Pancras and Edinburgh numbered five—third-class brake, composite, kitchen and restaurant first, open third, and third-class brake—with the Halifax composite also between St. Pancras and Sheffield, and another composite from St. Pancras to Leeds only. One or two " extras " were added by the L.N.E.R. from and to Carlisle, and on the southbound journey the train was made up to a more substantial formation from Leeds. Over L.M.S.R. metals " 5XP " 3-cylinder 4-6-0's were normally used, and over the L.N.E.R., as already mentioned, a Pacific.

From the outbreak of war, the only day service between St. Pancras and Edinburgh was by the 10 a.m. Glasgow train from St. Pancras, and the 10.5 a.m. from Edinburgh Waverley, by which the through times were spun out to 12¼ hours northbound and 11¾ hours southbound. In the down direction, for most of the war period, there was a 9.5 a.m. from St. Pancras, but only as far as Sheffield.

Through working of this train to Edinburgh was restored on October 1st, 1945, including a non-stop run over the 113 miles from Leeds to Carlisle, which was reached at 4.30 p.m. Arrival in Edinburgh was at 7.21 p.m., 96 minutes later than before the war. A much more drastic improvement came from October 7th, 1946, when the old non-stop run from St. Pancras to Nottingham was restored, though now with a start at 8.55 a.m. and a schedule of 142 minutes. Edinburgh was reached at 6.46 p.m. Since then the train has been badly slowed again ; the start from London is now at 8.50 a.m., and additional stops at Luton, Kettering, Skipton, Hellifield and Appleby have helped to extend the journey time to 10 hours, 32 minutes ; Edinburgh is not reached until 7.22 p.m. The corresponding southbound train left Edinburgh Waverley at 10.10 a.m., and until mid-September, 1952, took no less than 11 hours, 17 minutes to complete its weary journey to St. Pancras. But a welcome improvement took place in the 1952–1953 winter service, when the start was altered to 10.5 a.m., and all stops between Nottingham and London were cut out; St. Pancras is now reached at 8.45 p.m. Since the war, the name of the train has not been restored.

73—The " Tinto "

It was from Tinto Hill, a large rounded summit, 2,335 feet above sea level, which stands up prominently to the west of the L.M.S.R. London-Glasgow main line near Symington, that the " Tinto " took its name. This express was put on in Caledonian days chiefly for the sake of Glasgow businessmen who lived in what is known as the " Upper Ward " of Lanarkshire. Indeed, when after some preliminary running on Fridays only from Glasgow, and back to the city on Monday mornings, the train came into daily operation, it was known at first as the " Upper Ward Express," though soon afterwards the name was changed to the " Tinto."

The train was originally designed to run from both Glasgow and Edinburgh to Moffat, with the two sections joined at Symington, and a through section detached there for Peebles. Leaving Glasgow Central at 5 p.m., it ran non-stop to Thankerton, and called at all stations up the Clyde valley to Elvanfoot, after which it cleared Beattock summit, reversed in Beattock station, and finished at Moffat at 6.54 p.m. The Edinburgh connection left Princes Street at 4.45 p.m. In the morning the train was faster than it became in later years, for, leaving Moffat at 7.48 a.m. and Beattock at 7.55 a.m., it called only at Crawford, Symington, and Thankerton, and was into both Glasgow Central and Edinburgh Princes Street at 9.30 a.m. This was 12 minutes quicker to Glasgow and 27 minutes to Edinburgh than in the reverse direction.

By degrees the claims of passengers at other stations resulted in the morning " Tinto " also stopping at every station between Beattock and Thankerton inclusive, although only 6 minutes more was allowed, both for these three additional halts, and for a stop at Motherwell to set down passengers for that important steelworking area. The outward-bound " Tinto " was stopped similarly at

Motherwell to pick them up, without any increase of overall journey time. By 1914 the Edinburgh section of the train had ceased to run, except at week-ends.

In Caledonian days the fine 12-wheel non-corridor stock of that company was used for the " Tinto," and in 1914, when Pullman cars made their appearance on the Caledonian, a first-class buffet car was assigned to the train. But this was withdrawn during the First World War, and the limited patronage that it had received did not warrant its reintroduction when the war was over. In course of time, after the grouping of the railways, L.M.S.R. standard corridor stock replaced the Caledonian vehicles.

The spate of L.M.S.R. train naming which took place in the 1930's resulted in the " Tinto " having its name restored. For convenience, also, it was combined with a stopping train which previously had left Beattock for Carlisle about 20 minutes before its arrival at the former station, and from then onwards ran from Glasgow to Carlisle instead of to Moffat, arriving at Carlisle at 7.43 p.m. By now a Carstairs stop had been added. In the reverse direction, at the outbreak of the Second World War, the " Tinto " was starting its journey at Lockerbie, at 7.25 a.m., and was leaving Beattock at 7.44 a.m. ; despite the additional halts at Carstairs and Motherwell, it was booked into Glasgow Central at 9.22 a.m., 8 minutes earlier than in former years.

Though nameless and slower than in peacetime, the "Tinto" continued throughout the war. It now leaves Glasgow at 4.45 p.m., and once again terminates at Lockerbie at 7.1 p.m., having called at Motherwell, Carluke, Carstairs and all stations beyond, except Dinwoodie. In the reverse direction, leaving Lockerbie at 7.19 a.m. and with added stops at Carluke and Wishaw, it is into Glasgow Central at the old time of 9.30 a.m.

74—The " Torbay Express "

Little special distinction attaches to the " Torbay Express " of the G.W.R., other than that of being a fast and popular train. Before the First World War it left Paddington at 11.50 a.m., and followed the then prevailing G.W.R. fashion of slipping coaches by having a slip portion on the tail as far as Taunton, for Ilfracombe, in the course of its 3-hour non-stop run to Exeter. Just before the outbreak of war, the starting time was changed to 12 noon, and in the post-war recovery this became the permanent departure, though the Taunton " slip " did not reappear.

For a time, beginning in July, 1929, the " Torbay " had a rival in the " Torquay Pullman." This train was arranged to leave Paddington at 11 a.m., run non-stop over the 193·9 miles to

Newton Abbot in 205 minutes, and to be in Torquay by 2.40 p.m.
and Paignton by 2.50 p.m. Waiting here for just under 1¾ hours,
it began its return journey at 4.30 p.m., left Torquay at 4.40 p.m.,
and was into Paddington by 8.30 p.m. But the Pullman idea failed
to attract G.W.R. patrons, and this eight-car train had but a short
life, leaving the " Torbay Express " in possession of the field.

Before the outbreak of the Second World War, the " Torbay,"
leaving Paddington at 12 noon, was due into St. David's station at
Exeter at 2.49 p.m., having covered the 173·5 miles in 169 minutes,
at 61·6 m.p.h. A stop of 6 minutes was scheduled here, and the
26·1 miles on to Torquay required 35 minutes, making exactly
3½ hours from London. From Torquay the London engine, almost
invariably a " King " 4–6–0, continued with the train, calling at
Paignton, taking the train-staff for the single line at Goodrington
Sands, calling at Churston, and descending the steep incline to
Kingswear, to come to rest on the banks of the Dart opposite
Dartmouth at 4.5 p.m. The Goodrington-Kingswear stretch of
6 miles was probably the only piece of single track on the G.W.R.
used regularly by a " King."

On Saturdays in summer the traffic for Torbay was sufficient
to justify a non-stop run over 199·6 miles from Paddington to
Torquay, and the " Torbay Express " was allowed 3 hours, 28
minutes to do it. Times beyond Torquay, however, were unchanged.

In the reverse direction, the " King," after a level mile out of
Kingswear, had first to tackle the nasty climb to Churston, including
2 miles at 1 in 66 and 1 in 75. The start from Torquay is even
worse ; it begins at 1 in 55 for ¾-mile to Torre, and continues for
another ¾-mile at 1 in 73, so that banking assistance is often
needed. Leaving Torquay at 12 noon, the Torbay was due in
Exeter 35 minutes later, and after 6 minutes there, made the run of
173·5 miles to Paddington in 174 minutes, at an average of almost
exactly a mile-a-minute, arriving at 3.35 p.m. On summer
Saturdays a non-stop relief was run from Torquay at 11.50 a.m.,
taking 3¾ hours, and the main train was allowed an extra quarter
of an hour.

The Second World War at first saw the down " Torbay
Express " combined with the " Cornish Riviera Limited," but the
load of the combined train soon became too great for single engine
haulage, and the " Torbay " was split off and started separately at
10.40 a.m. With additional stops at Taunton, Dawlish, Teignmouth
and Torre, it was due in Torquay at 3.18 p.m. and Kingswear at
3.50 p.m.—only 15 minutes before its peacetime arrival, when the
start was 80 minutes later. Going up, the " Torbay " left Kingswear
at 11.25 a.m., as before the war, and Torquay 5 minutes earlier, at
11.55 a.m. ; at Newton Abbot it was linked up with a through
portion which had started from Penzance at 8 a.m., and the combined
train, calling at Exeter, Taunton and Reading, was due in Paddington
at 4.50 p.m. In the up direction, therefore, war added 1¼ hours to

the Torquay–London journey, but from October 1st, 1945, the arrival was accelerated to 4.35 p.m.

In the summer of 1946 the old 12 noon departure from Paddington was restored, and with a non-stop schedule of 183 minutes to Exeter, the down "Torbay" was accelerated to reach Torquay in 3¾ hours. The up "Torbay" has now come down to a run of 3 hours 50 minutes from Torquay to Paddington.

75—The "Ulster Express"

For long years the Midland Railway cast envious eyes on the North of Ireland, and hankered to obtain its own share of the traffic between Great Britain and Belfast. It had a half-share with the Furness Railway in the steamer service which was run between Belfast and the Ramsden Dock at Barrow-in-Furness, and ran through coaches to and from Barrow to connect with the boats ; also it had a share in the service between Stranraer and Larne, as well as in the Portpatrick and Wigtownshire Joint Railway, running from Castle Douglas to Stranraer, over which through coaches and a sleeping car were run nightly from St. Pancras. But finally the Midland ambitions were achieved by the completion in 1904 of the magnificent harbour and port installation at Heysham, near Morecambe ; and the plan was carried even more thoroughly into effect by the Midland acquisition of the Belfast and Northern Counties Railway, thereafter called the Northern Counties Committee, in the previous year.

To connect with the Belfast boat at Heysham Harbour a through express was run from St. Pancras at 6.0 p.m., by way of Trent (the first stop), Sheffield, Leeds, Hellifield and Lancaster ; for the distance of 267·7 miles, including stops, a time of 5 hours, 52 minutes was required. The train was booked to run non-stop from Leeds to Heysham, except for "conditional" stops at Skipton and Hellifield. In the reverse direction the boat train left Heysham at the uncomfortably early hour of 6.15 a.m. (at first an even earlier start was made, in the "small hours" at 4.55 a.m.), and was due in St. Pancras at 12.5 p.m. Competing with the Midland for the Belfast traffic was the service run jointly by the London & North-Western and Lancashire & Yorkshire Railways between Fleetwood and Belfast, which also had a connecting boat train from and to London (Euston) by the L.N.W.R. route.

After the formation of the London Midland and Scottish group, it was soon realised that services from both Fleetwood and Heysham were an unnecessary duplication of facilities, and that considerable economies might be effected if the whole of the traffic were concentrated on one port ; and as Heysham Harbour had more adequate space and more modern facilities, Heysham was chosen. But as the old L.N.W.R. main line offered much the more direct route from London than that of the Midland, it was arranged that the boat trains should run to and from Euston instead of St. Pancras ; the previous Midland connection from then on was run between Leeds and Heysham only, though with through coaches off the 5 p.m. express from St. Pancras, and the L. & Y. Leeds-Manchester-Fleetwood boat train was diverted to Heysham instead. Remodelling of certain connections at Morecambe made it possible for a train off the L.N.W.R. line to run to the Midland Promenade station instead of the L.N.W.R. Euston Road terminus, and to reverse in the former to reach Heysham Harbour. The distance from London was reduced from 267·7 to 239 miles.

The name of " Ulster Express " was conferred on the Belfast boat train in 1927, when it was still running from Euston to Fleetwood, and remained with it when the transfer to Heysham Harbour took place. From the railway operating point of view the alteration meant relatively little difference, for the route from Euston as far as Preston, 209 miles, remained the same. Consequently, the starting time of 6.10 p.m. at Euston kept on unchanged. From here the " Ulster Express," following the " Lancastrian " and the " Merseyside Express," ran non-stop to Crewe, 158·1 miles, in 167 minutes ; departure from Crewe was at 9.5 p.m., and the next stop at Preston, 51 miles further, was reached at 10.3 p.m. ; the last stage was from Preston, left at 10.8 p.m., to Morecambe Promenade, 25·2 miles in 30 minutes, and Heysham Harbour was reached at 10.52 p.m., exactly one hour earlier than the previous 6 p.m. from St. Pancras.

For several seasons before the outbreak of war, however, a more ambitious plan was brought into operation. The starting time of the " Ulster Express " was altered to 7 p.m., and the entire distance of 234·3 miles from Euston to Morecambe Promenade was run without any intermediate stop. Arrival at 11.12 p.m. made the journey time from London 4 hours, 12 minutes, and the average speed 55·8 m.p.h. ; a stop of 8 minutes was allowed for reversal, and Heysham was reached at 11.30 p.m. This non-stop run operated during the currency of the summer timetable only. In the up direction, the working of the " Ulster Express " settled down ultimately to a departure from Heysham Harbour at 7 a.m., and from Morecambe Promenade at 7.14 a.m. ; from here followed a non-stop run over the 76·2 miles to Crewe in 89 minutes, and then, after a 7-minute halt, another non-stop schedule of 165 minutes to Euston, bringing the express into London at 11.35 a.m. This was 75 minutes quicker than the old Midland run to St. Pancras.

Since the diversion of the " Ulster Express " to Heysham, both on the non-stop and the stopping schedule the run between Euston and Morecambe has been a through locomotive working, and a " Royal Scot " 4–6–0 has usually been employed. Loads varied considerably according to season, and in the down direction the

6.10 p.m. from Euston latterly carried a through coach for Rochdale, detached at Crewe. For some years the first-class end of the " Ulster Express " included one of the first-class lounge brakes—an open saloon furnished with leather-upholstered armchairs—built originally for the " Royal Scot " service.

The onset of the Second World War played havoc with the " Ulster Express " schedules. Both the train's name and, later, its restaurant cars were removed. At first it was altered to leave Euston at 4.50 p.m., and with stops at Rugby, Stafford, Crewe, Wigan, and Preston, to reach Morecambe at 10.17 p.m. ; but the delays at the time of the *blitz* were so severe that eventually the starting time was put forward to 3 p.m., and so remained until January 1st, 1946, when the start was altered to 3.35 p.m. In October, 1946, the start from Euston went back to 4.55 p.m., and with non-stop running to Crewe, Morecambe is reached at 10.0 and Heysham at 10.15 p.m. In the up direction the train was booked away from Heysham at 8.25 a.m., and from Morecambe at 8.50 a.m. ; stops to set down passengers were made at Preston, Crewe and Bletchley, and Euston was not reached until 2.50 p.m. But from the beginning of 1946 the start was altered to 6.25 a.m., and with stops at Morecambe and Crewe only the express was brought into Euston at 11.55 a.m. ; from October 7th, 1946, the Heysham start became 6.30 a.m., and the London arrival is now 11.35 a.m., as before the war. Restaurant cars in both directions returned on October 1st, 1945. On Saturdays the down " Ulster Express " leaves Euston at 6.30 instead of 4.55 p.m., and is not due at Heysham until 5 minutes before midnight.

76—The " Welsh Dragon "

Hardly as formidable as this intimidating title might suggest, the " Welsh Dragon " is a modest two-coach push-and-pull train, with 2-6-2 tank locomotive, that plies a busy trade with holiday-makers along the North Wales coast between Rhyl and Llandudno during the currency of the summer timetables, though it is not to be found either in the timetable books or on the station timesheets. The " Dragon " starts its day at Rhyl at 9.50 a.m., and finishes it at the same station at 11.3 p.m., having made a total of fourteen journeys, seven in each direction, between Rhyl and Llandudno in this period. Colwyn Bay is the only stop in each direction, and the fourteen runs, each of which takes 30 minutes, make up a total of 241½ miles each day. Some of the turn-around times at Llandudno are as short as ten minutes, but there are some longer halts at Rhyl, such as 12.30 to 1.45 p.m. and 4.30 to 5.20 p.m., when the needs of the locomotive can be attended to. The 2-6-2 tanks used on this service duly carry headboards with the inscription " Welsh Dragon."

77—The " Welshman "

In London & North-Western days, from 1909 onwards, the mid-morning summer express from London to the North Wales Coast resorts was of note as making the longest non-stop on that system, over the 209·1 miles between Euston and Rhyl. The time of 3 hours, 57 minutes allowed made the average speed over this distance almost exactly 53 m.p.h. At Colwyn Bay, the next stop, the train divided, the first section running on to Bangor, Criccieth and Pwllheli, and the rear section to Llandudno, reached in 4 hours, 42 minutes from Euston. Later on, the point of division was changed to Rhyl. The 11.15 a.m. down (later 11.10 a.m.) ran during the summer months only, up to the First World War; the corresponding up train was not so fast, and made various stops between Rhyl and London, arriving at 5.30 p.m.

It was not until the summer of 1923 that non-stop running was revived between Euston and the North Wales Coast, and the end of the run was no longer Rhyl, but Prestatyn, which had grown much in popularity in the interim, so reducing the length to 205·5 miles. Several years later the name " Welshman " was given to this service.

By the last summer before the Second World War, the " Welshman " was leaving Euston at the original departure hour of 11.15 a.m., and was due at Prestatyn at 3.4 p.m., so that the start-to-stop speed was now 53·8 m.p.h. Division of the train took place at Rhyl, and the Criccieth and Pwllheli sections, leaving at 3.17 p.m., ran non-stop over the 29·8 miles to Bangor in 37 minutes, but then waited in Bangor from 3.54 to 4.13 p.m. The last heavily-graded stretch through Caernarvon, and from there over the single line across the Lleyn peninsula, in charge, usually, of one or two tank engines, brought these coaches on to Great Western metals at Afon Wen. A final division here separated the Portmadoc and Pwllheli coaches; the former, travelling east, were in Portmadoc at 5.44 p.m., and their companions, going westwards, were in Pwllheli by 5.45 p.m. Meantime, the main section of the " Welshman," with the restaurant cars, had followed from Rhyl and arrived in Llandudno at 4.2 p.m.

In the reverse direction, the first portions of the " Welshman " to start left Portmadoc at 9.35 a.m. and both Criccieth and Pwllheli at 9.50 a.m., reaching Llandudno Junction at 11.44 a.m.; in nice time for lunch in the cars on the Llandudno portion, which had set out at 11.35 a.m. Departure from Llandudno Junction was at 11.55 a.m., and in this direction a stop at Chester was added to those at

Colwyn Bay, Rhyl and Prestatyn. But from Chester a non-stop run was made to London, 179·2 miles in 207 minutes, at 51·9 m.p.h., and Euston was reached at 4.20 p.m. The overall time was thus 4¾ hours in each direction between London and Llandudno, and 6½ hours each way between Euston and Pwllheli, a total distance of 271 miles.

In mid-week a load of eleven or twelve bogies sufficed for the traffic, usually hauled by a " 5XP " 4-6-0 or a " Royal Scot " between London and Bangor. On Saturdays, at the height of the season, however, three down trains were needed ; the 11 a.m. for Llandudno ran non-stop to Colwyn Bay, and the 11.5 a.m. for Portmadoc and Pwllheli was non-stop to Llandudno Junction, followed by the normal 11.15 a.m., non-stop to Prestatyn. Restaurant cars were run on all three trains, and there was a corresponding triplication in the up direction.

After a war interruption, the 11.15 a.m. down was reinstated, at first at week-ends in summer, but from October 7th, 1946, as a daily restaurant car train to Bangor, with a through Llandudno section. By 1950 the " Welshman," once again carrying a name, and with through coaches for Llandudno, Portmadoc and Pwllheli, was running daily through the summer only, with stops at Rugby, Crewe, Beeston Castle and Chester and at principal stations from Prestatyn onwards ; Llandudno was reached at 4.46 p.m. The Portmadoc and Pwllheli sections ran non-stop from Chester to Penmaenmawr, ahead of the Llandudno train, including the restaurant cars, which travelled as far as Bangor.

In the summer of 1952 the arrangement was similar, with division of the train at Chester ; Llandudno was reached at 4.46 p.m., Bangor at 4.29 p.m., Pwllheli at 6.10 p.m., and Portmadoc at 6.12 p.m. In the up direction, departures from Portmadoc and Pwllheli at 11 a.m. and for Llandudno at 1 p.m. made it possible to get the combined train—by now usually 15 bogies— away from Llandudno Junction at 1.24 p.m., and with the same stops as on the down journey, except that Stafford replaced Rugby, to be in Euston by 6.25 p.m.

78—The "West Coast Postal Express"

If a claim were to be made as to which was the busiest train in Great Britain—not from the standpoint of carrying passengers and freight but from that of the work actually done on board—the " West Coast Postal Express " in all probability would head the list. The staff carried on the train, almost exclusively postal officials, in normal times numbers all but 50, and throughout the entire journey there is little respite in the work that keeps them all busily engaged.

The peacetime formation of the Down " West Coast Postal, "

or "North Western Night T.P.O. Down," to give the train its official title, is 14 bogie vans, of which 7 are devoted to the sorting *en route* of letters and parcels. Of the latter at least five are special sorting tenders fitted with apparatus for picking up and delivery of mails at speed. The train is put into No. 2 platform at Euston at about 7 p.m., and from then until departure a constant procession of Post Office motor-vans from all parts of London brings its quota of mail matter for the North.

As punctuality, with a train of this description, is even more essential than high speed, the "West Coast Postal" has never been distinguished for exceptionally fast timing. From Euston to Rugby, the time allowed for the 82·6 miles was 94 minutes; and with departure from London at 8.30 p.m., Rugby was reached at 10.4 p.m. After a stop of 4 minutes, the "Postal" was booked to cover the 27·4 miles to Tamworth in 32 minutes; here a heavy consignment of mail arrived both from the West of England and from Lincoln, Nottingham and Derby, by the Midland Division line, and had been transferred from the High Level to the Low Level station in readiness for the "Postal's" arrival.

Leaving Tamworth at 10.47 p.m., the postal train ran the 48·1 miles to Crewe in 56 minutes, arriving at 11.43 p.m. On this important traffic centre connecting mail trains had converged from various directions, and the heavy interchange of mails required a stop of 16 minutes, releasing the "West Coast Postal" at a minute before midnight. Some of the staff left the train here, to return to London with the up "Postal." It may be added that this train regularly did a certain amount of sorting of Irish letters, to relieve the small staff of the "Irish Mail," which left Euston 15 minutes later; the sorted mails were transferred from one train to the other by the simple expedient of delivering them to the ground apparatus at five different points *en route*, from which the sorting vans on the "Irish Mail" picked them up at speed as it passed a short time after. That is to say, the mails were transferred from one train to the other without stopping either !

The next stop of the Down "Postal" was at Preston from 1.0 to 1.10 a.m.; then came the 90-mile run over Shap Summit to Carlisle in 99 minutes. At Carlisle, reached at 2.49 a.m., a good many more of the hard-worked postal staff left the train, and were replaced by Scottish staff for the remainder of the journey. Up to this point, the pick-up apparatus had been in use 14 times and the delivery apparatus 9 times; simultaneous picking up and delivery had taken place at Wembley, Watford, Bletchley, Blisworth, Nuneaton, Warrington, Lancaster, Carnforth and Penrith. The first division of the train was due to take place at Carlisle, as the Edinburgh vans were detached here; by running this section separately, there was no need to stop either portion at Beattock for assistance to Beattock Summit. The Edinburgh vans left at 3.7 a.m., and, calling only at Carstairs, reached the Scottish capital at 5.21 a.m.

Meantime the main portion of the "Postal," after 10 minutes at

Carlisle, had left for the north at a minute before 3 a.m., to run the 73·6 miles to Carstairs in 87 minutes. Here a second division took place. After 4 minutes, the Aberdeen section was the first to leave, at 4.30 a.m., followed by the Glasgow train at 4.35 a.m. Latterly it had been customary for the " Postal " to be one of the through Pacific locomotive workings between Euston and Glasgow, and the London engine therefore worked forward to Glasgow Central, stopping *en route* at Motherwell, and reaching the great industrial city at 5.15 a.m. Ahead were the Aberdeen vans, in charge, most probably, of a Class " 5XP " 3-cylinder 4–6–0, on a non-stop run to Stirling, which was reached at 5.20 a.m. From here onwards, with only two of the mailvans remaining, the " Postal " deigned to carry passengers. A passenger train, limited in weight to four bogie vehicles, had left Glasgow Central at 4.10 a.m., and had been worked into Stirling at 5.11 a.m. ; here the two were combined, and started away northwards as a 6-coach train at 5.24 a.m.

The weight restriction, which in Caledonian days, with 4–4–0 locomotives, had been even more severe, and permitted two passenger coaches only, was regarded as necessary in view of the tight timings of the Scottish run north of Stirling. Over Gleneagles summit, from Stirling to Perth, the 33 miles were allowed 38 minutes only, and the " Postal " was then worked forward over the 89·8 miles to Aberdeen, the only non-stop train of the day between these cities, in 99 minutes. This brought the last remnant of the " West Coast Postal " into Aberdeen at 7.52 a.m., having taken 11 hours, 22 minutes for the 540 miles from London.

In the reverse direction the first two vans of the " Postal " began their journey at Aberdeen at 3.30 p.m., also as part of a passenger train, which in this direction was permitted to be made up to a total weight of eight bogie vehicles. A stop was made at Forfar from 4.38 to 4.42 p.m., and Perth was reached at 5.17 p.m. At one time, in Caledonian days, the run of 32.5 miles from Forfar to Perth was allowed 32 minutes only. At Perth the passenger section was detached and the mailvans went forward alone at 5.24 p.m., calling at Stirling from 6.5 to 6.8 p.m., to the point where they reached the Glasgow to London main line at Law Junction, at 6.54 p.m. Here they stopped to await the main train, which with its Pacific at the head, working through to Euston, had left Glasgow Central at 6.35 p.m., and arrived at Law Junction at 7.3 p.m. For marshalling the train in right order, there was an allowance of 8 minutes, and departure for the south was at 7.11 p.m. In this direction, as the approach to Beattock summit is on easier gradients than from the south, the Edinburgh vans, which had left the Scottish capital at 6.38 p.m., were attached at Carstairs, for which 6 minutes were allowed, from 7.26 to 7.32 p.m. A swift run then followed, as the 73·6 miles over Beattock summit to Carlisle were covered in 81 minutes. This brought the " Postal " into Carlisle at 8.53 p.m.

More vans were attached here, and with the same considerable exchange of postal staff that had taken place on the northbound journey, a total of 12 minutes was spent at the Border town. Stops were made at Preston (11.0–11.10 p.m.) ; Warrington (11.44–11.49 p.m.) ; Crewe (12.19–12.31 a.m.) ; Tamworth (1.28–1.40 a.m.) ; and Rugby (2.14–2.22 a.m.) ; this brought the up "West Coast Postal" into Euston at 3.55 a.m., so that in the southbound direction the entire journey from Aberdeen had taken 12 hours, 25 minutes. On this trip the delivery and receiving apparatus were both in use simultaneously at Penrith, Carnforth, Lancaster, Stafford, Nuneaton, and Tring, and deliveries were made at five other stations also.

The onset of war did not bring to an end the carriage of mails, of course, but it did compel considerable alterations to the working of the postal train, cutting out the exchanging of mail matter at speed, and almost all the sorting *en route*, so that the wartime "Postal" consisted for the most part of ordinary vans. Additions of 71 minutes were made to the northbound and 76 to the southbound times. But from October 1st, 1945, the full postal working was restored, as well as the pre-war speed ; and apart from a minute or two of extra time over certain sections, the "West Coast Postal" was one of the first British expresses to return to full normal peace-time working, speed included, after the war.

On the down journey the 8.30 called at Rugby 10.3–10.7 p.m. ; Tamworth 10.39–10.46 p.m. ; Crewe 11.42–11.58 p.m. ; Preston 1.3–1.13 a.m. ; Carlisle 2.54–3.4 a.m. ; and reached Carstairs at 4.32 a.m. The Aberdeen portion was the first away from here, at 4.36 a.m., stopping at Stirling (5.30–5.34 a.m.) to collect the pass-enger portion which had left Glasgow Central at 4.20 a.m., and at Perth (6.14–6.25 a.m.). From Perth to Aberdeen the 89.9 miles were run in 95 minutes, 4 minutes quicker than before the war, and this 56.7 m.p.h. sprint for the time being was one of the fastest scheduled runs on the L.M.S.R. The Glasgow section of the down "Postal" reached Central at 5.20 a.m., and the Edinburgh portion was into Princes Street a minute later.

Coming up, with departures from Aberdeen at 3.30 p.m., Glasgow Central at 6.35 p.m., and Edinburgh at 6.38 p.m., the "Postal" made the same stops as in the northbound direction, and was due in London Euston at 4.0 a.m., 5 minutes later than the pre-war arrival.

At the beginning of June, 1948, in an attempt to cure the then unpunctual running of the "Postal," some considerable alterations were made in the working. The connecting 4.20 a.m. from Glasgow Central became an independent train throughout to Aberdeen, leaving Glasgow 15 minutes earlier, at 4.5 a.m., making brief calls at Forfar and Stonehaven in addition to previous stops, and getting into Aberdeen by 7.46 a.m., 16 minutes earlier. The timings of the London train were eased to bring it into Perth by 6.29 a.m., and starting away again at 6.40 a.m., and with 2 minutes added also to the Perth-Aberdeen allowance, the "Postal" now is due in Aber-deen at 8.15 a.m. In 1952 the practice of attaching the Glasgow passenger coaches at Stirling was resumed, but any passengers in them are involved in a 48-minute wait at Stirling before their journey is resumed.

While the departure of the southbound "Postal" from Aberdeen at 3.30 p.m. was not altered, the Glasgow start was put forward from 6.35 to 6.25 p.m., and with a departure from Carlisle 5 minutes earlier at 9 p.m., the "Postal" still is due in Euston at 4 a.m. The additions in both directions have been chiefly to the duration of the stops, for the "Postal" is booked to make some very smart runs in both directions, particularly the 35–minute allowance for the 32.5 miles from Forfar to Perth, and the 77 minutes for the 73.5 miles from Carstairs to Carlisle. Latterly the 3.30 p.m. from Aberdeen to Perth has been raised to the dignity of Pacific haulage, for the Crewe engine used to work the Inverness sleeper from Crewe to Perth and back often fills in the intervening day usefully by making a run from Perth to Aberdeen and back, the return being on the "Postal." A start to stop run over the 32.5 miles from Forfar to Perth in 32 minutes or even less is nothing unusual.

79–The "West Riding Limited"

Last of the three London & North Eastern streamliners to go into service, in October, 1937, was the "West Riding Limited," and it had been running a little less than two years when the war broke out. In Great Northern days the pride of the Leeds service was the 2 p.m. from Leeds Central to King's Cross, non-stop from Wakefield, and due into London at 5.25, or actually, according to the working timetable, at 5.27 p.m. It would have taken a bold man to prophesy a cut of three-quarters of an hour in this schedule ; but the cut was duly made when the "West Riding Limited" was inaugurated. Meantime, of course, the Pullman trains had been introduced, and the up "Queen of Scots" had brought the Leeds–London time down by degrees to 3 hours, 10 minutes.

Possibilities over this route had been demonstrated in November, 1934, when an experimental run was made from King's Cross to Leeds and back, with a four-coach train of 147 tons, headed by Pacific No. 4472. On this trip, for the first time in history, the 156 miles to Doncaster were covered in no more than 2 hours, 2½ minutes, and Leeds was reached in 2 hours, 32 minutes. The return journey was made in 2 hours, 37¼ minutes, and with 208 tons a speed of 100 m.p.h. was reached at Essendine—another L.N.E.R. record up to that date. It was thus proved that a greatly accelerated schedule would be practicable.

When the "West Riding Limited" made its appearance, however, it was a train almost double the weight of the test train of

1934. But experience had been gained with the " Silver Jubilee " and the " Coronation," and above all, the streamlined " A4 " Pacifics had now come into service, so that the allowance of 2 hours, 44 minutes from King's Cross to Leeds, and 2 hours, 43 minutes from Leeds to King's Cross, were both capable of punctual observance. The train was booked to run through to Bradford and for the London–Bradford journey the allowance was 3 hours, 5 minutes each way.

A set of cars identical with that in use on the " Coronation " was built for the service, consisting of four articulated " twins " with a tare weight of 278 tons. Also two " A4 " Pacifics, No. 4495, *Golden Fleece* and No. 4496, *Golden Shuttle*, were allocated to the " West Riding Limited," though a short time after its introduction other engines of the same class were taking their turns on the train.

Departure time for the down " West Riding Limited " from King's Cross was fixed at the comparatively late hour of 7.10 p.m. Doncaster, 156 miles, was passed at 9.19 p.m., in 129 minutes from London. The next difficult stretch, including the 1 in 150 ascent to beyond Hemsworth, the severe slowing through Wakefield followed by 4 miles at 1 in 100 and 122 up to Ardsley, and the extremely cautious approach necessary from Holbeck into Leeds Central, were allowed 34 minutes for the 29·8 miles, and Leeds was reached at 9.53 p.m.

Here reversal took place, and for the short run to Bradford two 0–6–2 tanks of the " N2 " type were backed on to the train—the only regularly rostered use on the L.N.E.R. of a pair of tank locomotives on an express train. The necessity arose from the extremely severe gradients out of Leeds Central in the Bradford direction, and in particular the 1¼ miles at 1 in 50 from Holbeck up to Armley, followed by 5 miles up mostly at 1 in 100. The 9·3 miles from Leeds to Bradford were allowed 18 minutes, and Bradford Exchange was reached at 10.15 p.m.

In the reverse direction the " West Riding Limited " left Bradford at 11.10 a.m., again with two 0–6–2 tanks at the head, and reached Leeds at 11.28 a.m. Here the streamlined Pacific backed on to the opposite end, and leaving at 11.33 a.m., joined the main line at Doncaster at 12.6 p.m., 17 minutes behind the " Silver Jubilee," after which the two flyers maintained a 15-minute space between them, the " West Riding " being due in King's Cross at 2.15 p.m. This arrangement enabled a business man in Leeds or Bradford to have a couple of hours at his office in the morning, and then to travel to London, spend all but five hours in the capital, and be back in his home city by or soon after 10 p.m.—a much appreciated facility. The " West Riding Limited " was withdrawn on the outbreak of war, and has never been reinstated.

80—The "White Rose" and the "West Riding"

In the days of the Great Northern Railway, and later of the London & North Eastern, there were two trains on the service between King's Cross, Leeds and Bradford that might be regarded as institutions. No matter how train services might be altered, or the tide of acceleration might swirl around them, nothing appeared to effect these " fixtures," and year after year, both before the First World War and between the two wars, they would carry on with schedules practically unchanged. Actually the two trains were one, a return working of the same set of stock ; they were the 10.10 a.m. from King's Cross and the 5.30 p.m. from Leeds. It is their successors which in the May, 1949, time-tables, first received the name of " White Rose."

In the earliest years of the present century, the principal morning express from King's Cross for the West Riding left at 9.45 a.m., ahead of the " Flying Scotsman," and made a non-stop run over the 156 miles to Doncaster in 169 minutes ; it reached Leeds in the smart time of 3 hours, 40 minutes. At that time there was a 10.20 a.m. from King's Cross to Sheffield, calling at Peterborough and Grantham, and continuing by way of Nottingham and the Great Central line. When, a few years later, the 10.20 a.m. was withdrawn, it was decided that the Leeds train must make the Peterborough and Grantham stops, and the starting time from London was therefore changed to 10.10 a.m. Leeds was now reached at 1.56 p.m., so no more than 6 minutes had been lost by introducing the additional stops.

In London & North Eastern days the 10.10 a.m. down still continued, practically unchanged in schedule, right up to 1939, with the trivial variation that the Leeds arrival had now become 2 p.m., 4 minutes later; also, to make room for the 10.5 a.m. " Junior Scotsman," as it was called, the 10.10 started at 10.15 a.m. during the summer months only. It had now grown into an extremely heavy train, with a through portion on the front for Hull, then the Leeds restaurant section, next a portion for Harrogate (worked between Leeds Central and Harrogate by the North Eastern Area), and finally the Bradford portion, detached on the outward journey at Wakefield.

Coming south, the timing of the train had remained equally static, if not more so. From Leeds Central 5.30 p.m. had been the absolutely unvarying departure time ; at first, King's Cross was reached in the even four hours, but the arrival time was soon brought back to 9.25 p.m. There it remained even after a Peterborough stop had been added to that at Grantham, previously the only halt between Doncaster and King's Cross. As the years passed, Great Northern Atlantics gave place to Gresley Pacifics in the working of these trains, and well they might, for on my last pre-war run with the 5.30 p.m. from Leeds, on leaving Doncaster with the normal load, we were made up to 16 vehicles of 474 of tons tare weight, or fully 500 tons loaded. I am not likely to forget that evening, as owing to a mishap we left Doncaster 18 minutes late, yet ran into King's Cross dead on time. The double chimney streamlined " A4 " Pacific *Osprey* had whirled us over the 76.4 miles from Peterborough start to the dead stop in the terminus in 73 minutes 44 seconds— a magnificent performance.

Included in the formation of these trains up to the war and on that run was a remarkable set of vehicles—quintuplet restaurant cars—designed and built at Doncaster in 1921 by Gresley specially for service on the 10.10 a.m. down and the 5.30 p.m. up. The articulated formation comprises a kitchen car in the centre (the first in the country to use electricity exclusively for cooking), flanked by open first and third class restaurant cars, and the first-class and third-class brakes at the outer ends ; a representation of roof-boards, lettered " King's Cross and Leeds " in red, is painted on the roof of each vehicle. Why the designer should have wasted space on the two completely useless brake compartments has always been a mystery to me ; it would have been far more valuable to have additional compartments, or, still better, to have built the end vehicles as centre-corridor or open stock, and thus to have provided supplementary restaurant accommodation when necessary. The quintuplet set is still at work, but not on this service.

When the name " White Rose " was decided on, the train selected was a relatively new express, the 9.18 a.m. down, which is, in effect, a logical successor to the 9.45 a.m. of long ago, for once again it is non-stop to Doncaster. The time allowed for the 156-mile run is 176 minutes, and Leeds is reached at 1.11 p.m., so that the present train is 13 minutes slower than the 9.45 a.m. of 1904. The " White Rose " is for Leeds and Bradford only, except that on Tuesdays and Saturdays during the winter it carries as far as Doncaster a through restaurant car portion for Norwegian passengers travelling to Tyne Commission Quay. This has to be worked specially through from Doncaster to Newcastle by the North Eastern Region.

For some time after the name " White Rose " had been conferred on the 9.18 a.m. down, the return working of the stock was on the counterpart of the pre-war 5.30 p.m. from Leeds, the present 5.15 p.m. up, making an extremely leisurely journey to London and taking 4½ hours to do it. Then the return stock working was transferred to the 3.15 p.m. up, an even more lethargic service calling at all principal stations on the way up, including even Hitchin, and not due until 7.56 p.m. It would be difficult to discover a train less deserving of a distinctive name than this.

And now for the " West Riding." For many years there has been a train out of King's Cross for Leeds and Bradford at about 4 p.m., calling at all principal stations, but the provision for the first time, in the summer time-table, of an express non-stop from London through to Wakefield, at 3.45 in the afternoon, was a novelty. This is the " West Riding," and the experiment has proved successful. As a special attraction, the front end of the train is composed in part of the beautiful cars used before the war on the streamlined " West Riding Limited." The 175¾ miles to Wakefield are run in 202 minutes, and Leeds Central is reached at 7.38 p.m., in 3 hours, 53 minutes from London.

The up " West Riding " is the 7.50 a.m. from Leeds to King's Cross, always a very well-patronised service. All stops have now been cut out between Doncaster and London, and the run of 156 miles is made non-stop in 182 minutes ; the arrival at King's Cross is at 11.49 a.m., in 3 hours, 59 minutes from Leeds. This is but a pale reflection in speed of the pre-war " Breakfast Flyer," which also left Leeds at 7.50 a.m., and made additional stops at Retford and Grantham, but was into King's Cross at 11.20 a.m., 29 minutes sooner. But that was at a time when it was possible to schedule an express to run the 105.5 miles from Grantham to King's Cross in 100 minutes, and to expect to see time kept day after day !

81—The "Windermere Club Train"

The success of the " Blackpool Club Train " was such as to encourage season-ticket holders in other resorts favoured by Manchester business men to seek similar facilities, and at a later date the London & North-Western Railway was prevailed on to provide club accommodation between Windermere and Manchester also. This service ran to and from Manchester Exchange, the L.N.W.R. station, partly terminal and partly through, which adjoined Victoria Station of the L. & Y.R., and in later years has been linked to the latter by a platform which, with its total length of 2,194 ft., has the distinction of being the longest in Great Britain.

For many years the Windermere train, leaving Manchester Exchange at 5.10 p.m., continued to use a route which, except in the height of the summer, had ceased to be followed by any other regular passenger train. Of this route another singular feature was that part of it belonged to the London & North Eastern Railway ; it was originally the Wigan branch of the Great Central Railway, and later became L.N.E.R. property.

From Exchange the 5.10 took the L.N.W.R. Liverpool main line to Eccles, and there branched northwards towards Wigan. But 2¼ miles short of Wigan it diverged again to the north, at Bickershaw Junction, in order to bypass Wigan on the east side. The L.N.E.R. Wigan branch was reached at Hindley & Platt Bridge station, and L.N.E.R. metals were followed for 50 chains to Amberswood East Junction, after which the Whelley line was taken, bringing the 5.10

up to join the L.N.W.R. London-Carlisle main line at Standish, 3¼ miles north of Wigan. The first stop was at Preston, and for this distance of 32·3 miles, 50 minutes were allowed.

After an L.M.S.R. interlude by way of Chorley, however, another curious route was devised for the down " Windermere Club Train." Leaving Exchange at 5.10 p.m., as before, it transferred immediately to the adjacent Lancashire & Yorkshire tracks, and ran over the L. & Y. Liverpool line as far as Hindley, near Wigan. Here it ran round a short spur to join the Whelley line, at a point which cut out the previous running over the L.N.E.R. From Manchester to Preston the time allowed was still 50 minutes. After Preston the express called at Lancaster and Carnforth, but was content to slow severely through Oxenholme, where it left the main line, instead of calling there. Kendal was the only remaining stop, and after the steep climb of Staveley bank, Windermere was reached at 7.20 p.m., 2 hours, 10 minutes in all from Manchester.

In the southbound direction, the " Windermere Club Train " was due out of that lakeside resort at 8.30 a.m., and stopped at Kendal and Lancaster (but not Carnforth) to Preston. South of Preston, the main line was taken as far as Wigan, and a stop was made there, before divergence eastwards through Tyldesley and Eccles into Manchester. This journey took exactly two hours, and Exchange was reached at 10.30 a.m.

A formation of about seven bogies sufficed for this service, including a single club saloon. For most of the years of the train's existence, non-corridor lavatory stock was provided for the ordinary passengers, but had given place to a corridor set before the outbreak of the Second World War. For locomotive power it was customary to use an ex-L.N.W.R. " Prince " 4-6-0 from Windermere to Manchester and a Midland compound in the reverse direction.

At present the train is still running, with corridor stock which includes an open vestibule first-class car as some substitute for the club saloon, but there are more stops and the running is slower. Still leaving Manchester Exchange at 5.10 p.m., the express calls at Preston, Lancaster, Carnforth, Oxenholme, Kendal, Burneside and Staveley, and reaches Windermere at 7.32 p.m. In the reverse direction the start is 20 minutes earlier, at 8.10 a.m.; the stops are as on the northbound journey, with the addition of Wigan and Eccles, and Manchester is reached at 10.30 a.m. There is a lively sprint over the 19.1 miles from Oxenholme to Lancaster in 20 minutes, which at 57.3 m.p.h. is one of the fastest post-war schedules from start to stop on the L.M.R. The locomotive used is generally a Class " 5 " 6 ft. 4-6-0.

A train of this description, of course, is by no means of use alone to Lakeside residents who wish to travel to and from Manchester. At Lancaster there is by far the largest influx, including passengers brought from both the Carlisle main line and the Furness line by connecting trains. Between Lancaster and Preston the "Windermere Club Train " usually is filled to capacity.

82—The "Yorkshireman"

It is a singular fact that although non-stop services have been tried by three different routes between London and Sheffield, none of them ever developed sufficient traffic to justify continuance, and either the trains have been taken off or additional stops have been introduced. One outbreak of non-stop running followed the opening of the Great Central Railway's London extension in 1899. By 1904 the G.C.R. was getting into its stride, and running some very fast trains. In summer the Midland, therefore, tried running its morning express to Glasgow non-stop to Sheffield, 158·3 miles, in 3 hours, 5 minutes, and the Great Northern followed suit in 1905 with a special express from King's Cross at 6.10 p.m., taking only 2 hours, 50 minutes for the 161·2 miles of the G.N. route. In the same year the Great Central, with the longest (164·7 miles) and hardest course of all three, brought the time of its afternoon " Sheffield Special " down to 2 hours 50 minutes also.

After a couple of years, however, the Great Northern train had intermediate stops introduced. The Great Central train continued to run non-stop up to the First World War, but had its time increased to 2 hours, 57 minutes. By 1906, the Midland had transferred its non-stop run to the 6 p.m. down Heysham boat express from St. Pancras, and in that year and 1907 was making the run in 3 hours, but by 1909 10 minutes had been added to this time, and the train was calling regularly at Trent. Then came the interruption of the First World War.

After the war, the G.C.R. never resumed its non-stop running between Marylebone and Sheffield. But when the L.N.E.R. had been formed, another attempt was made over the G.N. route, this time with the " Sheffield Pullman " which had been introduced in 1924, and had run *via* Nottingham. In April, 1925, this was altered to leave King's Cross at 6.5 p.m., and to run non-stop to Sheffield in 177 minutes, with a similar run in the reverse direction, reaching London at 2 p.m. But these runs disappeared in 1927, and were not seen again.

Meantime the L.M.S.R., in March, 1925, had put on the train which shortly after was to receive the title of the " Yorkshireman." It was an entirely new service between Bradford and St. Pancras, not serving Leeds but using the route *via* Thornhill which had been made available when, in 1909, the former Midland Railway opened the connecting spur from Royston, on its main line to Leeds, to Thornhill, on the then Lancashire & Yorkshire main line from Wakefield to Manchester. The original intention was to build a railway through Bradford which would enable Midland Anglo-Scottish services to pass through that city, but it was never carried into effect.

A new route was made possible, however, between St. Pancras, Sheffield and Bradford Exchange, and of this the 9.10 a.m. from Bradford to St. Pancras, and the 4.55 p.m. from St. Pancras to

Bradford, duly made use. A feature of the new service was that for the first time the L.M.S.R. made up a train composed entirely of open vestibuled stock—third brake, third, first, kitchen car, two thirds, and third brake, seven vehicles in all. Later first and third class brakes with compartments replaced the previous two end vehicles. The time allowed in each direction was 3 hours, 10 minutes between St. Pancras and Sheffield, with an intermediate stop at Leicester, and 4¼ hours between London and Bradford.

No further changes of note were made until the radical acceleration of the Midland services which took place in October, 1937. Once again Sheffield was provided with a non-stop service to and from London, and the down " Yorkshireman " was one of the two trains selected for the experiment. The old G.C. and G.N. times were nearly reproduced with an allowance of 2 hours 52 minutes for the run; the starting time was altered to 5.10 p.m. from St. Pancras, and Sheffield was reached at 8.2 p.m. Bradford was reached at 9.11 p.m., in a minute over 4 hours from London.

Once again, however, it did not last. By 1939, the down " Yorkshireman " was back to its old departure time, leaving St. Pancras at 4.55 p.m., taking 106 minutes to a stop at Leicester, 3 hours, 5 minutes to Sheffield, and as much as 4 hours, 20 minutes to Bradford. In the up direction it was leaving Bradford at 9.5 a.m. and Sheffield at 10.13 a.m., making an additional call at Chesterfield, and running from there to London by way of Nottingham, with a mile-a-minute run in 123 minutes over the final 123·5 miles to St. Pancras, reached at 1.21 p.m. Despite a journey of 205·5 miles as compared with 198·8 miles in the down direction and an extra stop, the up train therefore had the advantage of the down by 4 minutes. The service was withdrawn on the outbreak of war.

83—The " Yorkshire Pullman "

Such was the success of the Harrogate all-Pullman train, when inaugurated in 1923, that the L.N.E.R. soon began to cast about for similar sources of revenue in other directions. Sheffield appeared to offer attractive possibilities, and in June, 1924, a five-car " Sheffield Pullman " was introduced, leaving King's Cross at 11.5 a.m., 10 minutes ahead of the " Harrogate Pullman." It was thought that the citizens of Nottingham might also be tempted by such luxurious facilities, and the train was therefore diverted from Grantham to Nottingham Victoria, running thence over the Great Central main line into Sheffield. The call at Nottingham was from 1.28 to 1.32 p.m., and Sheffield was reached at 2.20 p.m. ; after a wait just short of 2½ hours, the " Sheffield Pullman " set out on its southward journey at 4.45 p.m. and was back in London by 8 p.m.

The new service failed to attract, however, and a month later the times were completely altered. The Pullman was now based on Sheffield instead of London; it left the Yorkshire city at 10.30 a.m. and reached King's Cross at 1.45 p.m.; on the return journey it set out from London at 6.5 p.m.—a popular departure time for Sheffield before the 1914–1919 war—and was back in Sheffield at 9.20 p.m. But the people of Nottingham still showed no Pullman interest, and in April, 1925, it was decided to cut them out of the itinerary and to try Manchester instead. So the " Sheffield and Manchester Pullman " now was booked non-stop from King's Cross to Sheffield *via* Retford instead of *via* Nottingham—161·2 miles in 177 minutes, average 54·6 m.p.h.—and continued non-stop from Sheffield to Manchester Central, which was reached at 10.12 p.m., in 4 hours, 7 minutes from London. Returning at 9.50 a.m., the Pullman ran to Sheffield in 70 minutes, left there at 11.3 a.m., and was into King's Cross at 2 p.m.

Unfortunately neither Manchester nor Sheffield responded appropriately to these Pullman blandishments, and five months later both were deprived of their Pullman cars. For in September, 1925, as mentioned in the " Queen of Scots " chapter, the latter train began to run non-stop from King's Cross to Harrogate, and to serve Leeds and Bradford a new Pullman service was run 10 minutes ahead, at 11.10 a.m. For this the Sheffield and Manchester train was used. Leeds was reached non-stop at 2.35 p.m., and two cars continued to Bradford, arriving at 3 p.m. The Leeds cars were then worked empty to Harrogate to return at 11.15 a.m. to London *via* Leeds, where the Bradford cars, starting at 11.20 a.m., were picked up; leaving Leeds at 11.50 a.m., this service reached London at 3.15 p.m. Harrogate now had one daily Pullman train from London, but two in the reverse direction; also two complete trains were needed for the Leeds and Bradford service, as well as the two Edinburgh trains.

The arrangement was again altered entirely, however, in May, 1928. When the " Queen of Scots " was diverted once again to serve Leeds, the down working of the " West Riding Pullman," as it now became, was changed from 11.10 a.m. to 4.45 p.m. from London, giving Leeds, Bradford, Harrogate, and Newcastle the much appreciated convenience of two fast Pullman connections with London twice daily each way. From September, 1926, the " West Riding Pullman " had been calling at Wakefield to detach the Bradford Pullmans, which from there had been worked direct through Batley to Bradford; from Bradford they proceeded through Queensbury tunnel into Halifax, giving the last-mentioned city a service in just under 4¼ hours to and from London. This arrangement was continued with the 4.45 p.m. down. One set of cars now sufficed for the return journey.

In 1935 it was decided to extend the Pullman facilities to Hull, which thus acquired, for the first time, not only Pullman cars, but also a 3½-hour service to and from London. To detach and attach the Hull section, the " West Riding Pullman " had to be stopped at

Doncaster, and this resulted in the appearance of two brilliant bookings in the time-table; the 4.45 p.m. down was scheduled to run the 156 miles from King's Cross to Doncaster in 156 minutes, at precisely 60 m.p.h., and the up train in one minute less. In view of the wider orbit of the train's operation, also, it now became the "Yorkshire Pullman"; but with the advent of the "Silver Jubilee" streamliner, the Harrogate section no longer worked through to Newcastle.

Two more changes only remain to be chronicled. In the autumn of 1937 the "West Riding Limited" streamliner came into service, and as this was given a mid-morning departure from Bradford and Leeds, there was no purpose in providing a Pullman service at much the same time. The Harrogate portion of the train, consisting of four cars and leaving at 11.15 a.m., was therefore diverted to run *via* York to Doncaster, where it joined the two Hull cars and the two cars which had come from Halifax *via* Bradford and Wakefield. Eight cars was the minimum formation of the "Yorkshire Pulman," but it has been known to grow at busy week-ends to as many as eleven or even twelve. Normally, Pacific loco-motives worked the train, but 2–6–2 engines of Class "V2" often handled it successfully, especially in the up direction.

On its final schedule, before the outbreak of the Second World War, the "Yorkshire Pullman" left King's Cross at 4.45 p.m., and made its first stop at Doncaster at 7.21 p.m.; its various constituents reached Hull at 8.15 p.m., Leeds at 8.13 p.m., Bradford at 8.30 p.m., and Halifax at 8.57 p.m. In the reverse direction the main train left Harrogate at 11.15 a.m. and York at 11.45 a.m., and the Hull cars at 11.30 a.m.; in order not to compete with the "West Riding Limited," the Halifax cars were worked quietly down to Doncaster as a non-passenger service. The combined train then left Doncaster at 12.25 p.m. and made its way into King's Cross at 3 p.m.

During the war, the "Yorkshire Pullman" was withdrawn, but it came into service again on November 4th, 1946, on a schedule allowing 4½ hours each way between King's Cross and Harrogate. Departure from London was at 3.50 p.m., and from Harrogate at 10.20 a.m. In September, 1948, the start from King's Cross was altered to 4.45 p.m., and a year later the "Yorkshire Pullman" changed places with the new "Tees-Tyne Pullman," to the start at 5.30 p.m. An eleven-car train is now needed regularly, Hull portion, which reaches that city at 9.30 p.m., requiring four cars; the arrival time at Leeds is 9.16 p.m. and at Harrogate 9.56 p.m., and the restored through Bradford section is due in that city at 9.42 p.m. The 156-mile run to Doncaster is allowed 172 minutes. Coming south, the departures are at 10.7 a.m. from Harrogate, 10.15 a.m. from Bradford, 10.45 a.m. from Leeds, 10.30 a.m. from Hull and 11.50 a.m. from Doncaster, from which a run of 178 minutes brings the "Yorkshire Pullman" into King's Cross at 2.38 p.m.